I0882311

The Whilton Dispute, 1264-1380

THE WHILTON DISPUTE, 1264-1380

A Social-Legal Study of Dispute Settlement in Medieval England

Robert C. Palmer

PRINCETON UNIVERSITY PRESS

Princeton, New Jersey

Published by Princeton University Press, 41 William Street,
Princeton, New Jersey 08540
In the United Kingdom: Princeton University Press,
Guildford, Surrey

Library of Congress Cataloging in Publication Data will be
found on the last printed page of this book
ISBN 0-691-05404-5

Publication of this book has been aided by a grant from
The Whitney Darrow Fund
This book has been composed in Linotron Bembo type

Clothbound editions of Princeton University Press books
are printed on acid-free paper, and binding materials are chosen
for strength and durability. Paperbacks, although satisfactory for
personal collections, are not usually suitable for library rebinding

Printed in the United States of America by Princeton
University Press, Princeton, New Jersey

TO MY WIFE

Patricia Rochford Palmer

Contents

Table of Documents

Preface

THIS BOOK is designed to serve as a teaching tool, as a researcher's guide, and as a scholarly investigation. The latter two purposes need little explanation. The book takes the form of a case study that puts litigation into a familial, social, and societal context. The material on which it is based is perhaps uniquely suited for such a task in this area. As a guide, the book will enable researchers to hypothesize better the kind of material that might be found to supplement nonlegal material or to fill out an isolated entry in a plea roll, as well as to piece together the kind of social reality that lies behind the often seemingly sterile record of a single lawsuit.

The book's intended use as a teaching tool, however, has shaped the format. There is little written in legal history that is accessible to nonspecialists, and nothing that discusses the law of property in a properly social instead of a doctrinal framework. The discussion here thus begins at a very basic level. Moreover, numerous documents have been provided in translation, many incorporated into the text and others in the appendixes. The placement of documents in the text is the result of my belief that familiarity with the documents themselves is necessary for an understanding of the subject. The text provides a general overview, but it also assumes that the reader will undertake a close analysis of the documents, for each one raises fundamental legal issues that will demand and repay close consideration and discussion. Furthermore, enough statutory material has been provided in Appendix 2 both to support problems raised in the text and to illustrate the difficulties of statutory interpretation. Notes have been kept to an absolute minimum and have not been used for bibliographic purposes. For such purposes recourse may be had to S.F.C. Milsom, *Historical Foundations of the Common Law*, 2nd ed. (London, 1981), and John Baker, *An Introduction to English Legal History*, 2nd ed. (London, 1979).

Certain aids have been incorporated into this book for students. The extensive chronology of the dispute should help the reader to retain an overall view of events. There is likewise a simplified genealogical chart and a glossary of legal terms. The few notes are of two varieties. Those without asterisks are simply references. Those with asterisks are references further to documents in the appendixes. It should be noted that some of those documents are very interesting and were excluded from the text merely because they would have been somewhat tangential to the material.

I have been working on this book for several years in combination with other projects. The American Bar Foundation supported part of my time in London in 1976-1977. I am also indebted to the Izaak Walton Killam Scholarship Fund for a postdoctoral fellowship at the University of Alberta, where I began writing up this material in 1978-1979, and to the Michigan Society of Fellows and the University of Michigan Law School for the postdoctoral fellowship during which I completed work on this project from 1979 to 1981. I am further indebted to Dr. Paul A. Brand of University College, Dublin, for transcipts of two documents I had overlooked while in England.

Abbreviations

MANUSCRIPT SOURCES

C 133	Public Record Office, London, England, Inquisitions *Post Mortem*
CP 40	Public Record Office, London, England, Plea Rolls of the Court of Common Pleas
E 13	Public Record Office, London, England, Plea Rolls of the Exchequer
JUST 1	Public Record Office, London, England, Plea Rolls of the Justices Itinerant
KB 26	Public Record Office, London, England, *Curia Regis Rolls*

PRINTED SOURCES

CCR	*Calendar of Close Rolls*, prepared under the superintendence of the Deputy Keeper of the Records (London)
CFR	*Calendar of Fine Rolls*, prepared under the superintendence of the Deputy Keeper of the Records (London)
CIPM	*Calendar of Inquisitions Post Mortem*, prepared under the superintendence of the Deputy Keeper of the Records (London)
CPR	*Calendar of Patent Rolls*, prepared under the superintendence of the Deputy Keeper of the Records (London)
CR	*Close Rolls: Henry III*, prepared under the superintendence of the Deputy Keeper of the Records (London)

A Simplified Whelton Genealogy

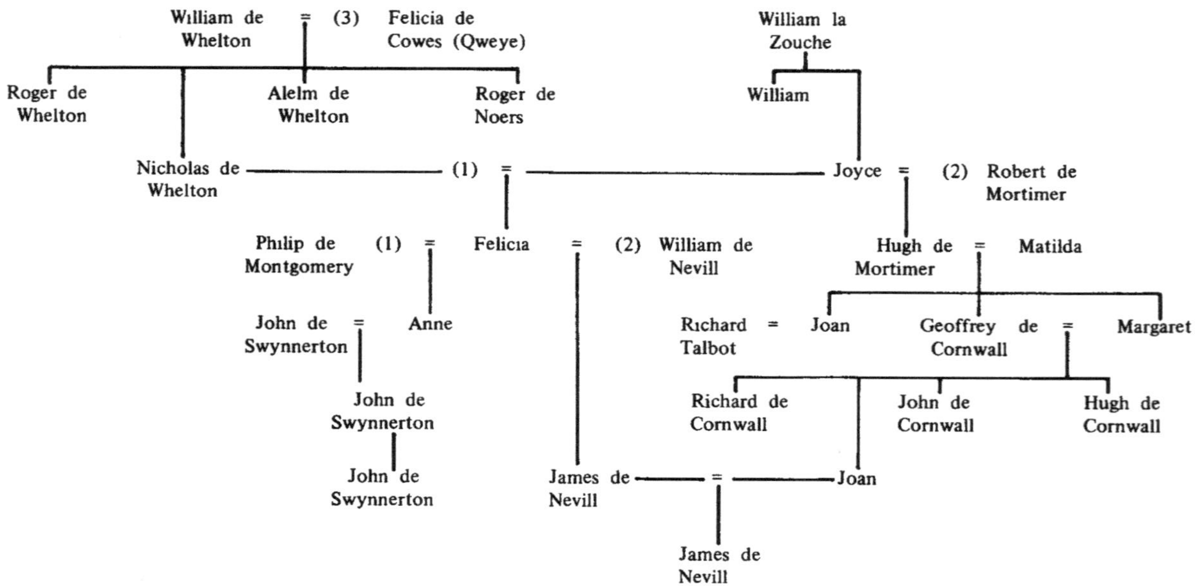

A Whilton Dispute Chronology

THE REIGN OF KING HENRY III

1264	?	Grant and regrant between William de Whelton and Nicholas de Whelton
	5 April	The Battle of Northampton
1266	25 February	William de Whelton receives a safe conduct
	?	Death of Nicholas de Whelton
	?	Birth of Felicia de Whelton, daughter of Nicholas
	31 October	Dictum of Kenilworth
1267	?	Death of William de Whelton
	4 March	The Zouche–Roger de Whelton compromise
	18 November	The Statute of Marlborough
1268	January	The Whelton claims for redemption
	May-June	Certification to King's Bench
	24 August	Columbers surrenders Wymington to Roger de Noers
	October	Vouching to warranty: *Savage* v *Whelton* in plea of dower *Qweye* v *Savage* for Wymington
	October	*Whelton* v *Noers & Qweye* for Wymington
1269	?	Jury on the feoffment and quitclaim
	?	The determination of William de Whelton's guilt
1270	20 October	A final concord: *Zouche* v *Whelton*
1271	June-July	Noers and Qweye win in *Whelton* v *Noers & Qweye* for Wymington
1272	16 November	The death of King Henry III

THE REIGN OF KING EDWARD I

1273	?	Joyce marries Robert de Mortimer
	?	William la Zouche dies

A Whilton Dispute Chronology

	?	Felicia's possession of Whilton by guardian; ejection by the Mortimers
	?	First assize of novel disseisin: *Whelton* v *Mortimer*
1274	8 January	Death of Gilbert de Preston, justice in *Whelton* v *Mortimer*
	October	The assize *Whelton* v *Mortimer* summoned into the Court of King's Bench; the Mortimers sent without day by Ralph de Hengham
	?	Hugh de Mortimer is born
	25 December	Robert de Mortimer inherits from his father
1275	3 February	Second assize of novel disseisin: *Whelton* v *Mortimer*
	9 April	Statute of Westminster I
	22 April	Continuation of the second assize
	25 June	Felicia wins in the assize *Whelton* v *Mortimer*
	7 October	The attaint *Mortimer* v *Whelton*
	mid-October	The Mortimers win in *Mortimer* v *Whelton*
1276	April	Death of Joan de Stuteville
1277	21 January	First action of entry: *Whelton* v *Mortimer*
1280	?	Felicia attains majority
	June	Process in execution of attaint judgment
1285	25 March	Statute of Westminster II (c. 1: *De Donis*)
	6 October	Second action of entry: *Whelton* v *Mortimer*
	15 November	Felicia wins the second action of entry
	?	Marriage of Felicia to Philip de Montgomery
1286	February	*Certiorari* in *Whelton* v *Mortimer*
	June	Action of entry: *Montgomery* v *Mortimer*
1287	January	Montgomerys win in *Montgomery* v *Mortimer*
	January	Action of besaiele: *Montgomery* v *Tywe*
	February-March	Death of Robert de Mortimer
	July-October	Philip de Montgomery fighting in Wales
	October	Joyce regains Norton
	November	Montgomery withdraws from prosecution in *Montgomery* v *Tywe*

	12 November	Joyce receives part of her dower
1288	January	Joyce receives further dower
1289	April-May	Philip de Montgomery fighting in Gascony
	25 June	Philip de Montgomery makes debt recognition of £20 to Robert Burnel
1290	?	Thomas son of Philip de Montgomery killed
	13 March	Joyce dies
	17 April	Vouching to warranty: *Lee* v *Mortimer* in *Montgomery* v *Lee*
	5 June	A final concord: *Burnel* v *Montgomery*
	8 July	Statute *Quia Emptores*
1291	?	Anne de Montgomery is born
	?	Felicia de Qweye surrenders her life estate to Felicia
	24 November	Joan, daughter of Hugh de Mortimer, is born
1292	June	Philip de Montgomery distrains the prior of Daventry
	October	Robert Burnel dies
1293	October-November	Action of replevin: *Prior of Daventry* v *Montgomery*
1294	?	An assize of novel disseisin: *Lee* v *Montgomery*
	?	Margaret, second daughter of Hugh de Mortimer, is born
1295	May	Philip de Montgomery dies
	June	Action of entry by intrusion: *Mortimer* v *Montgomery*
	September	Hugh de Mortimer purchases writ of right *precipe* against Felicia
	December	Hugh de Mortimer comes of age
1296	?	Felicia de Qweye dies
	12 November	Pleading in actions of right and entry: *Mortimer* v *Montgomery*
1298	?	Felicia marries William de Nevill
1299	11 May	Actions of right and entry *Mortimer* v *Montgomery* stayed by royal intervention
	?	Action of debt: *Montgomery* v *Nevill et al.*

A Whilton Dispute Chronology

1300		Hugh de Mortimer participates in the seige of Caerlaverock
1301	January	William de Nevill makes a debt recognition to his lawyer, Adam de Harwedon
1302	1 May	Sale of marriage of Anne de Montgomery to John de Haldenby *Scire Facias* in *Harwedon* v *Nevill*
1303	June	Action of neifty: *Nevill* v *Richard*
1304	5 August	Hugh de Mortimer dies of poisoning by Matilda, his wife
	16 September	Matilda pardoned of Hugh de Mortimer's death
	?	Guardians of Anne summoned to give dower to Alice, wife of William Passelawe
1305	20 October	Anne de Montgomery attains majority
1306	June-July	Anne married to John de Swynnerton; stewardship of Cannock Forest delivered to Swynnerton; the Nevills sue for dower
1307	7 July	Death of King Edward I

THE REIGN OF KING EDWARD II

1308	?	Matilda, widow of Hugh de Mortimer, dies
1309	?	Margaret de Mortimer marries Geoffrey de Cornwall
	?	John de Swynnerton, son of Anne, is born
1310	25 May	John de Swynnerton pardoned for the rape and detention of Joan, late wife of Peter de Greseleye
1311	?	Felicia, wife of William de Nevill, dies
1312	January	Action of trespass: *Nevill* v *Nevill & Whelton*
	January	Actions of debt and detinue: *Nevill* v *Nevill & Whelton*
1314	?	William de Nevill marries Constance Action of debt: *Nevill* v *Nevill*
1315		Death of Edward Burnel

A Whilton Dispute Chronology

1318	May-November	William de Nevill acting as sheriff of Warwickshire and Leicestershire
1319		A levy of money: *Ernefast* v *Nevill*
	December	William de Nevill appointed sheriff of Warwickshire and Leicestershire (term ended October 1321)
1321	28 January	An action of entry: *Talbot & Cornwall* v *Nevill*
1322	11 July	John de Swynnerton makes fine to save life and lands
1327	20 January	Death of King Edward II

THE REIGN OF KING EDWARD III

1330	February-March	An action of aiele: *Spenser* v *Neville*
	12 March	An action of entry by intrusion: *Talbot* v *Nevill*
	27 April	Geoffrey de Cornwall makes debt recognizance to Hunte
	10 May	William de Nevill dies
	?	James de Nevill marries Joan de Cornwall
	23 May	A final concord: *Nevill* v *Cornwall*
	15 June	Cornwall and Nevill make joint debt recognizance to Staunforde
?		James de Nevill, son of James and Joan, is born
1340		John de Swynnerton, husband of Anne, dies
After 1347		Anne dies
1362	28 June	Commission of *oyer* and *terminer* in *Syer* v *Nevill*
?		James de Nevill, son of James and Joan, dies
1375	?	James de Nevill dies
		Joan, widow of James, sells Whilton to John Holt and John parson of Whilton
1376		An action of formedon: *Swynnerton* v *Latymer et al.*
1377	21 June	Death of King Edward III

A Whilton Dispute Chronology

THE REIGN OF KING RICHARD II

1379		John de Swynnerton (II) dies
1380	April-May	An action of formedon: *Swynnerton* v *Latymer et al.*
	May?	John de Swynnerton (III) grants Whilton to Holt
1383		John Holt appointed justice of the Court of Common Pleas
1388		Holt condemned by Merciless Parliament and exiled; Whilton forfeited for his life

The Whilton Dispute, 1264-1380

CHAPTER I

Introduction

THIS BOOK is concerned with the social history of the English state, particularly with English law in the thirteenth and fourteenth centuries. A few words are therefore necessary to explain the nature of the social history of the state and the particular relation of legal history to social history.

Social historians will not immediately consider the state to be within their proper purview. There is no precise determination of the nature of social history, but the standard areas of demography, wealth distribution, family structures, and social mores will seem quite distant from the traditional investigation of the growth of the state. That task has generally fallen to those who regard themselves as constitutional, institutional, or intellectual historians and who claim as their territory the analysis of the distribution of power and the protection of rights, the elaboration of governmental institutions, and the conceptualizations of state power, authority, and devotion. If it were possible thus to shear off an organization as important as the state from the study of society and constrict historical inquiry into set channels, the sometimes passionately maintained boundaries between social history and other kinds of history would make any attempt to contribute a social history of the state futile from the beginning.

The growth of the state, however, was not primarily a constitutional, administrative, or intellectual phenomenon: it was a social development. In one direction, this assertion coincides with the well-worn maxim that one should not reify the state, should avoid thinking of the state as an organism that acts monolithically, that has thoughts, that in some personal sense wages war—that it is a thing. That maxim is true enough. Any state is only composed of individuals: battlefield dead are dead individuals, not merely an injured part of a continuing whole. The concern here is not with that maxim but with the similarly obvious fact that it can so easily obscure: individuals do act as if the state were a thing. The state, after all, is highly coordinated power that can be brought to bear with crushing effect on innumerable aspects of an individual's life. Whether or not one is at any given moment the subject of such attention, the awareness of the presence of that power remains. People take it into account in their everyday lives: it conditions actions and expectations so continuously that some reflection is necessary to realize its subtle influence. In our own society, one need only consider the pervasive awareness of the state activities of revenue collection, policing, and adjudication of disputes to note also the consequent modifications of behavior either to conform to requirements or to avoid certain unwanted consequences. Although the impact of the state on the individual is incalculably greater today, of course, than it was in the thirteenth and fourteenth centuries, the investigation of such behaviors, thus modified by the awareness of state institutions, cannot but be properly within the scope of social historical studies.

From this perspective, legal history is of paramount importance to the early history of the growth of the state. In the most simple form, it speaks of the ways in which and the degree to which people made use of a certain set of state institutions to settle disputes. For England, it also speaks of an inflexible set of legal remedies and rules of law that set limits to what could be protected or remedied without recourse to violence. Thus these rules set obstacles in the way of the desired actions of a multitude of individuals, obstacles that invited circumvention. Furthermore, the interplay between, on the one hand, legal remedies and rules of law and, on the other hand, the ingenuity exercised in circumventing the law and using it for untoward purposes is extremely complex. The nature of that interplay changed gradually and repeatedly from the twelfth to the sixteenth century, but always in the direction of a law whose substance was more internally unified and less directly related to commonly held ideas of what was morally just. This is not at all to say that common morality (moralities?) did not affect the law. It did. And it did so just as much as the law affected common morality, so that neither the law nor common morality can be a stable reference point: the workings of each presuppose the other. But their interplay became characteristically more convoluted, less predictable, and with roots less easily recognized. This is a theme quite fertile for the historical understanding of society, but one, I hope, more easily understood at the conclusion of this work than in the introduction. Some detailed examples in this matter are truly worth much more than reams of theory.

The method of this book is precisely that: example. It examines an archetypical dispute to illustrate the ways in which some individuals used the law. The Wheltons, the Mortimers, and their descendants, though far from insignificant, were not the individuals who were shaping the destiny of England in the thirteenth and fourteenth centuries. Were this book really about them, it would merit only specialist interest. It happens, however, that the ways in which they acted show patterns of activity and of expectation that were broadly typical of those members of English society who had access to the king's court and the common law. From those patterns we shall eventually derive a comparison to show how the world in which the English lived changed drastically from 1160 to 1264, from 1264 to 1378, and from 1378 to 1540. The dates are not of particular importance; the changes are.

The degree to which a discussion of patterns of litigation will illuminate the social structures of medieval England depends of course on the degree to which the law was used. An accurate assessment of court utilization is not yet available. We do know, however, that in the two-year period 1327-1328 there were 13,031 cases brought in the Court of Common Pleas, the busiest branch of the king's court. Not all of these cases were determined by judgment, but that fact is irrelevant here. The initiation of litigation will force the opponent to examine one's claim more thoughtfully and to examine his own chances in relation, among other things, to the law. That examination, even in our society, usually results in some kind of settlement. And such a settlement demonstrates the potency of the law. Thus the number of cases initiated is satisfactory for our purposes, and a figure of 6,500 cases a year is impressive. But even that figure is certainly low, perhaps a result of political uncertainty in 1327-1328 while Roger Mortimer and Isabella were still controlling Edward III. The court records for 1327 at least are unusually short. As a counterweight, I have catalogued the litigation from only two counties in the king's court between 1331 and 1334. Those figures would argue a caseload 34 or 40 percent higher than in 1327-1328. A conservative estimate of a normal caseload only 33 percent greater than in 1327-1328 results in more than 8,500 cases a year in the Court of Common Pleas. No cases came from London, Cheshire, or Durham, of course. Thus, for the thirty-seven counties with regular access to the court, one must think of an average of 230 cases a year from each county, but with enormous variations between large, populous, or wealthy counties and small, sparsely populated, or poor counties. The actual and projected figures are presented in Table 1.

The number of people involved is more important than the number of cases. Some individuals, as is well known, were very litigious. In 1331-1334, counting all the litigation from the two counties of Bedfordshire and Cornwall in the two main branches of the king's court (the Court of Common Pleas and the Court of King's Bench), there was a total of 1,266 cases. The 636 cases from Cornwall involved 1,273 different persons as plaintiffs or defendants; of those litigants, only 10 percent were involved in more than two cases over the four years. The 630 cases from Bedfordshire involved 1,379 different individuals; once again, only 10 percent were multiple litigants. (In this calculation, for legal reasons, women appearing with their husbands were not counted as separate

TABLE I
Litigation in the Court of Common Pleas in the Fourteenth Century

	1327-1328			*1331-1334*	
County	*No. of Cases*	*% of Total*	*Per Year*	*Actual No. of Cases Per Year*	*Projected No. of Cases Per Year*
Norfolk	1,539	11.8%	768		1,024
Yorkshire	1,510	11.6	755		1,007
Lincolnshire	1,215	9.3	608		811
Suffolk	725	5.6	362		583
Essex	531	4.0	266		355
Northamptonshire	497	3.8	249		332
Kent	402	3.0	201		268
Devon	391	2.9	196		261
Hampshire	391	2.9	196		261
Somerset	378	2.9	189		252
Cambridgeshire	342	2.6	171		228
Warwickshire	326	2.5	163		217
Nottinghamshire	294	2.2	147		196
Middlesex	291	2.2	146		196
Sussex	284	2.2	142		189
Leicestershire	276	2.1	138		184
Wiltshire	271	2.1	136		181
Staffordshire	229	1.8	115		153
Surrey	226	1.7	113		151
Oxfordshire	224	1.7	112		149
Gloucestershire	214	1.6	107		143
Buckinghamshire	211	1.6	106		141
Hertfordshire	210	1.6	105		140
Cornwall	201	1.5	101	141	(135)
Derbyshire	200	1.5	100		133
Berkshire	198	1.5	99		132
Dorset	193	1.5	97		129
Bedfordshire	168	1.3	84	114	(112)
Shropshire	163	1.2	82		109
Lancashire	161	1.2	81		108
Worcestershire	150	1.2	75		100
Huntingdonshire	122	.9	61		81
Herefordshire	117	.9	59		79
Northumberland	116	.9	58		77
Cumberland	65	.5	33		44
Rutland	54	.4	27		36

TABLE I (*cont.*)

County	1327-1328 No. of Cases	% of Total	Per Year	1331-1334 Actual No. of Cases Per Year	Projected No. of Cases Per Year
Westmorland	41	.3	22		29
Divers and uncertain county designations	105	.8	56		75
All Counties	13,031	100.0%	6,516		8,688

NOTE: Figures for 1327-1328 are taken from Public Record Office, *Index of Placita de Banco, A.D. 1327-1328* (Dublin, 1909), pp. 1-837. The figures for Cornwall and Bedfordshire in 1331-1334 are taken from CP 40/284–CP 40/300. My impression is that these figures would not be terribly misleading for the early fourteenth century; they would be much too high if applied before 1300. I can likewise make no estimate yet of the effect of the Black Death after mid-century.

individuals.) These figures allow us to ignore the discounting process necessary to accommodate the very litigious and the multiplication required to allow for multiple plaintiffs or defendants in the individual case. The two factors balance each other out, and one can calculate the total number of persons involved as twice the number of cases brought. Some further allowance must be made for people who brought suits from more than one county. My best estimate here is nothing better than a prudent guess: 10 percent. The end result of these calculations and hypotheses is that nearly 15,300 different persons can be considered as caught up in the processes of the Court of Common Pleas as litigants each year. I hope someday to produce better figures, but for now we must be satisfied with concluding that something in the neighborhood of 0.5 percent of the total population of England were litigants in the Court of Common Pleas every year. Since the figures were based on a catalogue of individuals over a four-year period, expanding that figure to 2 percent of the population every four years would be justified. That is an extraordinarily high level of court involvement with the country.[1]

Such a percentage, of course, underestimates the actual importance of the court, since it compares litigants with total population. Several corrections should be made to arrive at a better estimate. Married women should be excluded from the population figures because they were not able to sue on their own in the king's court. In the same way and for the same reason, monks and other members of religious houses—except for the abbot, prior, master, or other head of the house—should be excluded. Minors had only very limited access to the Court of Common Pleas and the Court of King's Bench; they should also be almost totally excluded from the population figures. Finally, some allowance should be made for London, the more important boroughs, Cheshire, Durham, and other great liberties that by and large precluded their inhabitants from litigating in the king's court concerning matters within their precincts. Our figures, however, are merely meant to fortify our assertions. The uncertainties involved in calculations to correct figures that are only guidelines boggle the imagination, and little would be gained for our present purposes. Yet it is clear the ratio of actual to total potential litigants was substantially higher than 0.5 percent annually or 2 percent over four years.

Even with such a hypothetical figure, many times corrected, one could not rest secure. Litigation affected many persons other than the litigants and their immediate families or houses. Neighbors and friends of litigants would have had some knowledge of the course of events and the problems encountered in the litigation. Likewise, the jurors from the county would have been directly involved in the trial and would gain firsthand knowledge of the law. Persons who felt wronged could themselves consult one of the band of saddle-sore attorneys who frequently traveled the roads between a county base and the courts at Westminster, even if, in the end, they decided not to sue. However one might arrive at a multiplier to yield an accurate assessment of the familiarity of Englishmen with the king's court and the degree to which it could and did affect their lives, there can be no real doubt about the final conclusion. A discussion of the common law is not confined to abstruse matters irrelevant to all but a handful of the wealthy. Rather, such a discussion can yield valid conclusions about normal social structure and behavior.

The primary considerations that could disallow such an undertaking concerning the common law would be the degree to which jurors were regularly bribed to perjure themselves and the degree to which violence was used as an auxiliary to lawsuits to bring one's opponents to forced submission. Both practices, if frequent, would nullify the law and legal rules as significant social features, and exaggerated statements have been made about both. It will not do, of course, to maintain that England was a quiescent country filled with staunchly virtuous and incorruptible landholders and altruistic aristocrats. But neither was England filled with a completely immoral population living in quasi-anarchy.

Bribery of and perjury by jurors was indeed a problem. There are cases alleging perjury on the part of jurors, but it should be emphasized that, in relation to the volume of litigation, these represent just a trickle. Moreover, many of these cases did not involve perjury at all; rather, they were mistakes made by jurors who were supposed to be self-informing about a factual situation sometimes long past and who were subjected to a trial in which the evidence presented was scanty and not governed by systematic rules about admissible evidence. The case we shall study offers an example of this kind of situation. This trickle of cases can be augmented by looking at the activity of the chancellor, who late in the fourteenth century began handling cases in which individuals maintained that their opponent was so feared in their county that they could not hope for a fair trial. This was a longstanding grievance. Yet the undeniable fact that bribery and perjury were problems does not mean that they were normal, and a handful of anecdotes and some literary satire will not replace quantification here—a quantification that is impossible. A measured estimate of the situation would take into account the great value placed on one's honesty and on one's oath. It would have been extremely strange if most juries were easily bought. Likewise, a self-informing juror seeking out the facts would almost certainly be the recipient of favors from both sides, but that does not mean automatically that he would sell his voice on the jury any more than he would unthinkingly sell his soul. Jurors were undoubtedly influenced by those who were influential, and a great deal of deference was due to authority. But the wealthy did not always win, and those in possession could be and were turned out by process of law. Finally, if the problem with perjury and bribery was as severe as some would have us think, it is hard to see why, among such an immoral population, people brought so many suits to the king's court instead of resorting to the more straightforward course of covert homicide. Bribery was a problem, but not one so rampant that it undermined the whole working of the law or even brought the law into severe disrepute. The rules of the law did bear a substantial relationship to the way in which cases were settled and to the way in which society worked.

Violence used as an auxiliary to litigation undermines our project as little as do perjury and bribery. Once again, it must be admitted that the problem existed. Anyone who has been involved in litigation can attest to the ferocious animosity that normal civil litigation can generate. It would be abnormal if occasionally that animosity were not converted into actual violence. There are examples enough in this period, and fortuitously one of the people involved in the litigation we shall investigate was a perpetrator of one of the incidents most often cited, although that incident had nothing to do with the litigation here examined. Men of the thirteenth and fourteenth centuries were accustomed to a certain amount of violence, but the vital question is whether the violence was systematic, so that it would undermine the legal system. Once more, colorful anecdotes, a few cases, and literary references will not suffice.

Violence used as an auxiliary to litigation was not frequent. We shall work on two assumptions: that serious nonfelonious violence (assault) would be more frequent in such matters than felonious violence (arson or homicide), and that land litigation would be a major source of such incidents. On these assumptions I examined the catalogue of Bedfordshire cases. Of those cases in the Court of Common Pleas and the Court of King's Bench from Bedfordshire, 28 percent went to the Court of King's Bench in the years 1331-1334. For Cornwall in the same years the figure was only 12 percent. Since King's Bench was more particularly concerned with trespasses and thus with violent activities, land litigation from Bedfordshire at this time would seem an excellent source for discovering auxiliary violence, if such was really rampant.

The Bedfordshire cases, however, reveal little violence related to land litigation. In these years 163 Bedfordshire cases directly concerned real property in the Court of Common Pleas, bringing persons into litigation 411 times. Only fourteen times did any of these participants complain of a trespass in the months preceding the litigation or in the years following the initiation of the suit (as far as the chronological limitations of my catalogue permit such a determination). These fourteen instances fall into two categories: those in which the alleged wrongdoer was the same as the plaintiff's opponent in the land litigation, and those in which he was different. Two of the fourteen are in the former class; we shall immediately class them as related to the land action. Of the twelve instances in which the alleged wrongdoer had no relation to the land action, five involved no violence or are clearly unrelated to the land action. Of the remaining seven, three contain allegations of violence and four never specify the nature of the complaint. Making the (completely unwarranted) assumption that all seven of those cases involved hired thugs and were directly related to the land litigation, there are still only nine instances from a possible pool of 411—something like 2 percent—and that figure is generously inflated.

Many reasons might involve a person in a case of trespass, reasons that have nothing at all to do with pending litigation, so that the figure of 2 percent in that respect is too high. But it is too low in another respect. Violence would occasionally have deterred people not only from pursuing the original cases but also from complaining of the violence. If the violence was really intimidation, however, it would have been suspected prior to bringing the initial suit; we can thus expect a fairly high rate of complaint about the consequent violence. The 2 percent figure can thus be stretched imaginatively no further than 4 percent, and even that is based on generous assumptions that all the violence was premeditated intimidation and not tempers running temporarily out of control. The more serious cases of intimidation might have been expected to have been handled by commissions of *oyer* and *terminer*, special commissions of justices sent out to hear and determine a particular case. Of the five commissions of *oyer* and *terminer* concerning Bedfordshire from 1331 to April 1334, none was related to land litigation in the Court of Common Pleas; none could be interpreted as revealing violence used as an auxiliary to any plea in the courts. There is thus no justification for describing England as a country dominated by mafia-style hoodlums who systematically cowed the populace by cold-blooded violence.[2]

I shall repeat here to be clear. Medieval England was no paradise. There were problems with both improper influence on jurors and with the intimidation of litigants, but these problems must be kept in perspective. Many persons used the courts. Masses of individuals did not resort to homicide after despairing of justice. The courts retained a fair degree of prestige. No one who has spent even a couple months reading the court records or who has examined the rigor with which legal argument in the courts was pursued can believe that only violence and wealth, not law, determined relations in that society. It was normal for litigation to be allowed to run its course, and this book is concerned not with investigating deviations but with discovering normal conduct. Legal remedies and rules thus constitute an important element in evaluating the normal workings of English society in the thirteenth and fourteenth centuries.

Even at the beginning of this period that part of the law with which we shall be concerned—the law of real property—was fairly mature. Litigation in general, and the course of the Whilton dispute in particular, was determined by royal writs. It is importnt not to take them lightly. Writs were, simply, written royal orders. Document I is an example of one important kind of writ: the writ of right patent. This hypothetical writ has been framed in the form that would have been required had it been used in the Whilton dispute.

DOCUMENT I
A Hypothetical Writ of Right Patent

Edward, by the grace of God king of England, lord of Ireland, and duke of Aquitaine to Baldwin Wake, greetings. We command you to hold full right without delay to Felicia de Whelton in respect of the manor of Whilton with appurtenances in Whilton, which she claims as her free tenement which she holds of you by the free service of one knight's fee for all service, which manor Robert de Mortimer and Joyce his wife withhold from her. And if you do not do so, the sheriff of Northamptonshire will, that we may hear no further complaint for default of right thereon. Witness, myself at Woodstock on the twentieth day of May in the third year of our reign.

*

Document I is an example of a "writ of course," a standardized writ; it was not framed particularly and specially to handle this case. Felicia had only to supply the details to the clerk who was drawing up the writ. He would merely copy from the appropriate form and fill in, as it were, the appropriate blanks—the names, the places, the service specified, the amount of land. However, any attempt to duplicate the work of such a clerk makes it immediately obvious that this is something of an oversimplification; the blanks sometimes became devilishly hard. Nevertheless, it remained essentially a task of filling in blanks.

Composed in the form of a simple command, this writ would have started a lawsuit between Felicia and the Mortimers. Other writs were addressed to the sheriff—the king's principal local officer in charge of a county—and were designed to initiate a plea in the king's own court. Document 1, however, would have initiated a case in Baldwin Wake's feudal court. It is immediately obvious that this writ involved only a few people. In itself, it would have had very little impact on society. Considered individually, then, writs are of only limited historical interest.

The existence of such standardized writs, however, is of great social importance. They embodied an institutionalized decision by the king to make his authority, his officials, and his courts available to provide a legal remedy for all those whose problems could be fitted into the circumstances prescribed in the form. Almost all the cases in the king's court were initiated by standardized writs, so that literally thousands of them were drawn up every year. Although not everyone would actually use standardized writs, their existence altered the lives and expectations of society at large. The sure knowledge that a remedy was available set limits to the ways in which people could order their relationships and provided greater security in their rights even for those who suspected no imminent danger. Standardized writs thus served to secure people's rights to land, the major source of wealth in medieval England. In addition, then, to providing, at the very least, a certain settling quality, standardized writs helped to define society by setting limits to social relationships.

On the other hand, standardized legal remedies, while defining certain relationships, do not stop social and economic change. Moreover, the provision of the remedy itself alters the situation. The setting in which the remedy was originally conceived was one in which this solution was not readily accessible. Once in place, the remedy in some degree alters expectations and actions. In a sense, then, a standardized writ, even at the very beginning, would be out of step with society. That might not be terribly important, except that standardized remedies in medieval England did not easily change form. Increasingly, therefore, the ideas embodied and frozen in the form of the writs and the actual situations in society diverged. Standardized writs thus, on the one hand, perpetuated archaic formulations of situations or rights that were no longer realistic and, on the other hand, encouraged artificiality, because people in new situations had to find some way to fit their problem into the old formulation or to evade the seemingly inevitable but now perverse effect of the rules enforced by that remedy. Both of these effects can be summarized by saying that the law began to have a life of its own partially independent of societal reality.

In England this divergence of law from its social origins began during the reign of Henry II (1154-1189), probably sometime right around 1176. Prior to that time, writs concerning similar situations could be similar and even contain some identical clauses; they were nevertheless composed for the individual situation. Afterward, there was a small but growing body of completely standardized writs: writs of the same type would be identical but for the peculiarities of the individual cases. These first standardized writs would become the classical writs concerning real property—among them, the writ of right patent, Document 1 above. The importance of these standardized writs is clear: they constitute the beginnings of the common law, and they provided a much-valued protection for landholders. Moreover, the end result of this involvement by the king's court was that feudal courts were replaced by the king's court in the adjudication of disputes concerning land held freely. Finally, those standardized remedies, the process they demanded, and the bureaucratic courts that their use called into being were sufficiently popular that one of the main themes of Magna Carta in 1215 was not that the courts be abolished but that they be made to work more effectively and within the proper bounds and that the king abide by the same standards in his treatment of his tenants-in-chief as his law had been making the barons use in treating their own men. The legal procedures had already worked their way so far into society and into men's minds that no one suggested abolishing the whole structure. And it was this acceptance of the law and of legal forms that was to be the core around which the English state formed, not loyalty to and love of the king.

The historical argument concerning the beginnings of the common law has to do with what Henry II and his officials meant to do when they formulated those all-important writs and remedies. The classical view, propounded by F. W. Maitland and cogently restated by Donald Sutherland, is that Henry II intended to protect property rights already in existence and to do so by remedies consciously ranked as proprietary and possessory. Proprietary remedies, characteristically slow, would determine who had ultimate property right. Possessory remedies, characteristically rapid, would allow quick preliminary decisions, such as reinstating someone who had been thrown out of his tenement unjustly and without any judgment. This view is thus marked by the conviction that property rights were somehow already present in and recognized by society before the writs, that the writs accomplished merely a transfer of jurisdiction over those property rights from feudal to king's court, and that the proprietary/possessory division of remedies was intentional. The normal concomitant of this view is that Henry II was consciously trying to centralize governmental authority to acquire the finances (through judicial profits) to carry out his designs on the Continent and to undermine baronial opposition to him in England.

Two alternate views have recently been proposed. S.F.C. Milsom argues that there was much less conscious intention in what Henry II did. For Milsom, property rights cannot simply subsist in society, as in the ideas of "yours" and "mine." What modern historians have viewed as pleas concerning property rights actually involved personal relationships and obligations, the focus of which was land. So long as landholding depended on the maintenance of a personal relationship, there survived discretion and feudal dependence, both of which are inimical to the nature of property rights. Thus the standardized writs were not provided to protect property rights because none existed. There were only obligations to be enforced or claimed against people, not abstract rights to a piece of ground good against the whole world. The difference may seem slight, but it is the difference between feudal England and the English state. What became the possessory level of litigation began for the most part as an attempt to supervise the feudal courts, to make them operate more consistently according to their own standards. Milsom's view is thus marked by a very precise conception of the nature of property rights and by a denial of the Machiavellian depiction of Henry II. He argues that the division of remedies was not the original intention but only the almost immediate result of Henry II's attempts at regulation. The end result of any project, after all, does not have to be the same as the original intention.

The third view is my own. In effect, I take the middle ground, although my argument is strictly derivative of Milsom's in the conception of the nature of property rights and the untoward nature of legal change. The vital event, I propose, was the compromise in 1153 by which the future Henry II made peace with King Stephen by allowing Stephen to remain king for life in return for Henry's succession after Stephen's death. That compromise was intended to be a model for those who had been disinherited during the war, and both Stephen and Henry agreed to enforce that kind of settlement in England. What became the possessory remedies thus originally maintained the relationship between current tenants—those figuratively in King Stephen's position—and their lords until they died (or the enforcement of the lord's undertaking toward the heir until a better claimant appeared). Proprietary remedies originally enforced, after the current tenant's death, the claims of those who had been disinherited. Possessory and proprietary were the two correlative sides of treaty enforcement. After 1176 they were rapidly hammered into standardized remedies, grew distinct from their origins, and, as administered by a bureaucratic court, became different levels of litigation.[3]

Scholarly consensus about the shape of the law by 1250, then, is not matched by a similar consensus about the essential process involved in its origins. By 1250, however, there had been a great proliferation of standardized writs available to begin cases in the king's court and in the county courts. Litigants took for granted the possessory/proprietary distinction for remedies concerning disputes over real property. There had even grown up, prior to Magna Carta, an intermediate level. The result was a bewildering maze of individual remedies arranged in a three-tiered hierarchy. A hard-headed litigant could thus start at the possessory level and pursue his remedies successively, since a loss at one level did not injure his chances at a higher level. It is the way in which this system worked and was used, not its origin, that is the concern of this book.

In this kind of investigation, the Whilton dispute is archetypical. By no means, however, should one conclude that all litigation would follow its same tortuous paths. Thus far, it is the only dispute known to have taken such a course. It came to my attention only because a fourteenth-century lawyer collected some of the early documents and transcribed them into a book of legal material, which I was reading for quite another reason. With luck and diligence, however, a modest number of similar cases could undoubtedly be found.[4] Most disputes would admittedly be settled by a single case in court. The Whilton dispute is archetypical in the sense that it allows so thorough an exploration of the possibilities inherent in the system and of the way in which people maneuvered around the system. Moreover, the substantive issues in the dispute track central concerns of the law relating to real property over 120 years. There is no better example to demonstrate the nature of the common law and the attitude of the English people both toward the law and toward the state.

In addition to writs and attitudes, we shall be concerned also with the courts of medieval England. To the beginner, it will inevitably seem that medieval England was afflicted with an immense variety of courts. Most of those courts, however, can rest here with but a cursory description of the legal geography of 1300. To begin, there was an already well-developed system of ecclesiastical courts. These derived from the judicial/pastoral authority of the bishops of England and were subject ultimately to appeal to the papal court in Rome. In theory, the English ecclesiastical courts were restricted to pleas concerning the church, marriages, wills, and breaches of oaths. In practice, they strayed into many other areas, but seldom into land litigation.

Alongside the ecclesiastical courts was a system of secular courts, some of which were public, some of which were feudal. The feudal courts had a jurisdiction that was defined by a network of personal relationships, and by 1300 they were largely defunct. The public courts were public because, roughly, they were courts to which the individuals in a given territory could resort and were in some way related to the central government. The county courts were such public courts. They were presided over by the sheriff of the county and constituted the primary jurisdictional/governmental units of medieval England. In 1300 there were forty county courts. Territorial subdivisions of the county also had their own courts. These were, primarily, the hundred courts but also included the courts of boroughs, which formed enclaves in the hundreds. At an even lower level—a level that defies any easy classification into feudal or public categories—was the manorial court: the court held by the lord of a manor for his free and unfree tenants. Of these public courts, the county and hundred courts in 1300 were progressively being restricted to pleas concerning minor wrongs and small debts, while the borough courts and the manorial courts retained their traditional concerns with property.

In 1300 the most important court in England was the king's court, and this is the court with which we shall be most concerned. The king's court comprised those courts—for there was more than one—in which the king was theoretically present. Three branches of the king's court were central courts, national in nature, with regular terms of session: the Court of King's Bench, the Court of Common Pleas, and the Exchequer of Pleas. The Court of King's Bench was the highest branch of the king's court. Its jurisdiction was particularly related to major (felonious) and minor breaches of the king's peace and to the supervision of the other branches of the king's court. The Court of Common Pleas was by far the busiest branch of the king's court: it handled a wide range of litigation concerning property, obligations, and wrongs. The Exchequer of Pleas, that branch of the king's court particularly associated with the Exchequer, the accounting agency of the royal government, handled matters pertaining to debts owed to the king and those involving charges against officials, such as the sheriffs, who were appointed in and accountable to the Exchequer. In 1300 the Chancery was still primarily the king's secretarial office and issued the writs that originated suits in the king's court; it was not yet the great Court of Chancery that it would be becoming by the end of our story. These, then, were the branches of the king's court that had the longest future before them, and they are the focus for most of English legal history after 1300.

Other instances—they can hardly be called branches—of the king's court were temporary in nature. The eyre was the king's court specially convened in one county. It took over all the cases from that county pertaining to the king's court while it also checked vigorously into royal finances and official misconduct in the county. Eyres were not regularly scheduled; the last ones were held in 1329–1331, by which time they had become so cumbersome that they had lost their original flexibility and utility. There was also a great variety of limited special commissions, ranging from a commission to hear a specific case (a commission of *oyer* and *terminer*), to a commission to try all those held in specific gaols (a commission of gaol delivery), to a commission to hear and determine all cases of a specific nature on circuit (a commission of assize). All of these were instances of the king's court, because the court was not only a royal court in that it was owned and controlled by the king, but it was also a court that exercised the king's own power, because theoretically the king was present.

There was a close relationship between the standardized writs and the king's court, particularly the Court of Common Pleas. That court, although the busiest of the branches of the king's court, was a court of specifically delegated jurisdiction: it could hear only those cases the king ordered it to hear. That jurisdiction was conferred by writ. Ordinarily the writ was standardized, and it was normally described as both original and returnable. A writ was original if it "originated" a case, as contrasted with judicial writs, which were merely concerned with continuing a case already begun. In either case, of course, the writ should be seen primarily as the only means of communication possible, not as some magic device. In the same way, a writ was returnable if it had to be physically returned. It not only commanded an action but also demanded a report, which was written on the back of the writ and then returned to the court that had been given jurisdiction. Only returnable writs originated cases in the Court of Common Pleas. The combination of order and report provided the necessary contact between the court and the local officers who had to pressure the defendant into appearing in court and who were responsible for executing the court's judgments.

If writs were thus the life's blood of the king's court, real property was its flesh and bones. The king's court had grown into a regularly functioning institution by handling real property litigation. In 1300 the Court of Common Pleas still concerned itself primarily with land litigation, even though, since around 1275, its jurisdiction in personal actions—debt, trespass, and covenant—had markedly increased.

The Whilton dispute was a dispute about land—in particular, a dispute about a manor. The manor of Whilton was located in the Midlands of England in the county of Northamptonshire. From that base grew the present-day town of Whilton. Like any other manor, Whilton was an organized agricultural estate and also a complex of rights to real property and of rights over people. The manor centered on an imposing manor house, the residence of the lord of the manor, to whom those various rights pertained. For much of the time with which we shall be concerned, the lord of Whilton actually resided at Whilton; he was not an absentee landlord. The estate itself comprised something like eight hundred acres of cultivated lands, woods, meadows, and ponds. A calculation of the population of Whilton can only be made by assuming that it was typical in the distribution of the size of its holdings. There is absolutely no assurance that such an assumption is correct, but it does not do violence to the evidence and does give believable figures, so long as one realizes that they are hypothetical. We can picture a village of perhaps twenty-nine households, of which thirteen made their living from lands held freely and sixteen from lands held unfreely. Of these households, one would hold upwards of thirty acres, eleven would hold thirty-acre virgates, eleven would each hold half a virgate, one would hold a quarter-virgate; and five would hold only a few acres each. Those who held at least half a virgate could probably survive by working their lands; the rest would have had auxiliary occupations as servants, brewers and sellers of ale, minor craftsmen, and the like. There is, of course, no assurance that this picture of Whilton is even close to accurate. Twenty-nine households—perhaps a hundred people—may be much too low. The manor may have been much more heavily populated and worse off.[5]

Over those inhabitants of Whilton who were personally free, the lord of the manor had very limited control. From the point of view of the common law, the free inhabitants were completely insulated from the discretionary or arbitrary exercise of the lord's authority. Physical punishment, imprisonment, and the taking of a free inhabitant's goods could all be remedied in the king's court. For a well-off inhabitant who was free, the protection meant that he was indeed insulated from the exercise of the lord's power. Most free inhabitants, however, could not be so cavalier. The lord would naturally be a more influential person with greater resources; prudence would dictate deference. Moreover, free inhabitants were not isolated from their unfree neighbors. Regular intercourse with those neighbors, common agricultural habits and routines, and mere convenience dictated that free inhabitants also use the lord's manor court for settling disputes of all kinds. If not subjected to the lord, the free inhabitants of Whilton were nevertheless not quite independent.

The villeins of Whilton had no access to the common law against the lord, except in matters of life and limb. In the manor court, probably presided over by the lord's official, the lord exercised a general supervision of their lives, regulating moral and marital matters, resolving disputes, and supervising the agricultural routine. It was likewise completely within his authority to imprison a villein without court process, inflict corporal punishment on him, or take his goods. The lord's exercise of this authority, however, should not be conceptualized as absolutely arbitrary. The few limitations were not stringent, but they were adequate to prevent the worst kinds of oppression. The lord normally worked through a court and in an atmosphere that encouraged set penalties. The inhabitants, on the other hand, really did form something of a community and were stubborn enough to resist wholesale oppression. On the whole, the lord did not extract everything from the inhabitants that he could have in theory. But morality and group resistance—inevitably an infrequent and unreliable phenomenon—were not substitutes for external controls on the lord. The lord's scope of action may not have been completely arbitrary, but his position entailed a capacity for enormous and unsupervised discretion, which could be very burdensome to the tenants if, as was the case with the lords of Whilton, the lord was resident. Villeins were, in any case, severely dependent on their lord.

The rights of the lord of the manor of Whilton over Whilton's inhabitants were also determined by the way in which they held their lands. In 1300 it was generally true that free men held their land freely and villeins held in villeinage, but there are sufficient examples of free men holding in villeinage to require a sharp distinction between personal status and tenure. Those who held their tenements freely (who had free tenements) from the lord of Whilton were very secure in their rights. Their rents and obligations to the lord were fixed in nature, and the common law provided remedies for the lord to exact those rents and for the tenant to prevent ejection or increased rents. Though reciprocal obligations still existed, those obligations no longer were part of a vital personal relationship with the flexibility and dependence that such a relationship would have implied in the twelfth century. Most such tenants were probably tenants in socage anyway, so that they were obliged to render only relatively unburdensome rents. Both free status and free tenure involved isolation from the exercise of discretionary power by the lord.

By the same token, unfree tenure—tenure in villeinage—implied subjection to the lord of the manor. Tenure in villeinage was characterized in part by relatively burdensome services, either in money or in labor, and in part by lack of protection by the common law both for the possession of the land itself and for the amount of services exacted by the lord. As with villein status, however, the moral strength of common expectations and common resistance to unusual exactions prevented tenure in villeinage from being as insecure and burdensome as it might have been. At least on the large estates composed of many manors and many tenants, the administration of the tenements worked impersonally and with great regularity. Tenements were bought and sold routinely with the lord's license; lands passed regularly from one generation of a family to the next. An obstreperous tenant was more likely to be disciplined by levying a fine on him in court than by relieving him of his tenement. In a situation such as that at Whilton, however, one might expect more careful supervision of villeinage tenure and the occasional exercise of the full extent of the lord's power. It is unlikely, though, that those who held in villeinage at Whilton expected to be ejected the next day or doubted that the lord would allow their heirs to hold the family land. But it is also unlikely that they were unaware of the lack of external controls on the lord's treatment of villeinage tenures. It would be an imprudent tenant in villeinage who would openly oppose his lord without substantial community support.[6]

In addition to those who held free tenements and those who held in villeinage, there were the cottars. Their holdings were distinguished mainly by their diminutive size: they consisted of a cottage with a portion of land far less than that sufficient to support a family. Cottars made their living by farming their small plots and by wage labor, working either for the lord or for their more prosperous neighbors. They paid rent to the lord. Cottars could be either free or villein and could hold either freely or in villeinage. Their economic position made such distinctions of little importance. Such questions would arise for them only if, by marriage or succession to a relative or friend, they were about to come into a better holding. Until that happened, they would have lacked the resources necessary to make use of the king's court against the lord. For that matter, the lord, until that time, would probably have had little interest in clarifying their status. The cottars were the people for whom one can conclude that, for the time they remained cottars, legal distinctions concerning status and tenure were not meaningful. They had enough to do merely to survive.

The parish priest of Whilton was a different kind of tenant, although he would normally also be dependent on the lord. The priest was personally free, and he was protected by both secular and ecclesiastical courts. But the lord of Whilton had the right of advowson: that is, when the position fell vacant, the lord was entitled to nominate to the bishop the qualified person who would then assuredly be appointed as parish priest. The priest, after he was appointed, usually held some land

and received tithes from his parishioners. In Whilton the worth of the position was calculated at a little less than £7 a year.[7] Nevertheless, the priest was hardly a completely free agent. The lord inevitably chose a person of his own liking, often a relative. For a farsighted lord, prudence might dictate the use of perfectly legal methods to ensure the priest's continued dependence, providing as the alternative financial ruin. If the lord neglected such a safeguard, he could easily make the priest's position sufficiently difficult to bring him to heel eventually. Admission to the manor house was a matter of some importance. Such a situation will crop up in the Whilton dispute, although not entirely clearly. A docile priest in the manor church must usually have added to the lord's moral status in the village community.

More immediately important to the lord than his moral status in the countryside was his financial status. From all the secular tenures he received rents, which amounted to over half of the regular income from this manor. But not all of Whilton was occupied by tenants. The lord retained about half of the arable land of Whilton in his own demesne. He was responsible for its cultivation, and the crops were his to dispose of immediately. Those crops yielded about one-quarter of the revenue of the manor (the income, virgate for virgate, seems lower here than that from the tenants' holdings). The total annual income from Whilton was reported as £25 8s.[8] Some comparison is valuable to appreciate this income. The virgate was reckoned to be a sufficient holding to support a household comfortably, even after all exactions. The rent for a virgate in villeinage at Whilton was £1 yearly. An agricultural estate that yielded a yearly income of £25 was important, and litigation over the rights to such an estate would be pursued with intensity. The lord of Whilton, whoever he might be, was assured of both a living and a position of influence in the countryside.

CHAPTER 2

The Origins of the Dispute

✻

FOR THE FIRST decades of the Whilton dispute, argument focused on a transaction between William de Whelton and his second son, Nicholas de Whelton. At that time—the early 1260s—William was undisputedly the lord of Whilton. His father had held Whilton as early as 1235[1] and had been properly active in the affairs of the county, serving as one of the coroners of Northamptonshire, an elective office.[2] By 1257, however, he was dead. William, as his son and heir, had then inherited Whilton together with other manors, apparently without any problem. At his father's death, William was already married, and at least two of his four sons had been born. In 1264 Roger and Nicholas de Whelton were already old enough to function as adults in time of war.

More retiring than his father, William undertook as one of his first actions the purchase of a life exemption from being forced to serve on any assize, jury, or recognition and from being forced to become sheriff, coroner, escheator, or any other kind of royal official.[3] Such an exemption was not unusual, and William used it in 1261 to prevent the sheriff of Bedfordshire, in which county William also held lands, from forcing him into such an office.[4] He could not, however, evade all responsibilities. In the eyre of Northamptonshire in 1261 he served as one of the four knights who were made to assemble to choose the twelve men who would form the panel of a grand assize and to give their verdict concerning the right to parcels of land in three different cases.[5] The only other fact we know about William prior to 1264 is that, in that same eyre, he was one of the defendants in a case brought by some of his irate tenants concerning pasture rights. The case was settled in his favor.[6]

When William decided in 1264 to assure the future of all his sons, he was acting quite normally. Primogeniture was a legal rule, not an overwhelming moral imperative. Yet, like many other fathers, William wanted his lands to be divided—one manor to each son. Nicholas, the second son, was apparently preferred to Roger, because he was to receive Whilton, the chief manor. This division, however, could not be accomplished by will after William died. In the 1260s and until the sixteenth century, wills could only dispose of goods and chattles, not land. Except for tenements in boroughs, the inheritance of land was determined solely by strict rules. Land held by knight service—as William held his land—descended strictly by primogeniture. Thus, if William waited until he died, Roger, as the eldest son, would inherit all four manors, leaving Nicholas and any other sons totally dependent on Roger's generosity. On the other hand, if William gave land to Nicholas while he was still alive, Nicholas would be secure, but William himself would have fewer resources. Worse still, he would lose control over his son. William would have to face and avoid these legal problems and personal considerations if he were to respond not only to his affection for Nicholas and the others but also to his reluctance to yield control.

Natural affection was here reinforced by a practical situation. Roger, as the firstborn son, might well be able to marry without being secure in a landed estate, so long as there was still a substantial estate that he would inherit. Indeed, Roger would, as it will appear, have a reversionary interest in at least some of his younger brothers' lands. But those younger brothers would find suitable marriages hard to come by without a secure estate in property. Nicholas was apparently about to marry at this time, and an irrevocable right to a landed income—at least in the future if not in the present—would have been a prerequisite for the kind of marriage that would bring into the family a properly endowed young woman and enlarge not only the holdings but also the influence the Wheltons could wield as a family. A father had to choose between letting his land descend by primogeniture, thus assuring a marriage for one son that would forge a single very important alliance, or dividing up his holdings among all his sons, thus allowing marriages with more modest but more numerous alliances. The latter might well seem more advantageous for one whose ambitions were largely local; it would often also be the course that accorded more closely with paternal affections. William chose this latter course, and his dealings with Nicholas were probably at least partly related to Nicholas's marriage to Joyce, daughter of William la Zouche.

Motivations for any particular act, of course, can be extremely varied. It was indeed said that William wanted to promote and advance Nicholas. But he did so sometime around 1264, just as opposition to Henry III was coming to a head. On 5 April 1264 that opposition broke into open warfare at the Battle of Northampton. William could early have seen that he would have to be involved. Northamptonshire, the county in which Whilton was situated, was one of the regions offering most support to Simon de Montfort, earl of Leicester, brother-in-law of the king, and leader of those dissatisfied with the king. Moreover, three of William's four manors—Whilton and Norton in Northamptonshire and Totternhoe in Bedfordshire—were situated right alongside Watling Street, one of the main thoroughfares of medieval England. They were thus not only strategically located but also open to attack. Even simply possessing four manors made William too substantial a person to be ignored by either side. The problem here was that, if William fought against the king and lost, all his holdings would be forfeit. One way to avoid that drastic consequence would be to divest himself of at least part of his lands in favor of his sons. If that was the motive, however, Nicholas should have stayed well clear of the fighting. He did not. We may be nearer the mark to suppose that William wanted to advance Nicholas partly because of his fatherly affection for a younger son, partly because Nicholas was now acting as a knight, and partly because Nicholas was now marrying.

Whatever William's motivations, there was a well-known way out of his quandary. He could convey Whilton to Nicholas in fee—that is, heritably—on the strict understanding that Nicholas would then return the manor for the rest of William's life. Both would thus have a secure interest in the land. When William died, Nicholas would receive the manor not by inheritance but upon the termination of the term his father had held. William would thus not decrease his income but only alter the nature of his interest in Whilton. Moreover, Nicholas would remain fairly dependent on William, because the transaction, though it gave Nicholas the fee immediately, did not give him any further resources until his father died. Nicholas would not be able to obtain possession of the land, because his title was burdened with a life estate that gave William full possession for the remainder of his life. This transaction was a bit of legal sleight of hand to avoid the rigid rules of inheritance, in particular, the rule of primogeniture. It accomplished a gift made in one's own life, the beneficial consequences of which arose only at one's death. William could thus give without experiencing any loss.

Sleight of hand, however, depends on skillful execution. The execution of this transaction took place in four stages. First came the "livery of seisin": the delivery of lawful possession. William delivered seisin of Whilton to Nicholas at the manor house by putting Nicholas's hand to the door hasp in signification of his new possession of the chief dwelling of the manor and then by giving Nicholas a branch of the cherry tree, signifying Nicholas's new possession of the fruits of the land. William then left Whilton: he had delivered seisin to his son. The second stage was Nicholas's establishment of his seisin: his possession had to be actual and not merely symbolic. William thus stayed away completely for fifteen days. During that time Nicholas used the manor as his own by fishing, by burning wood, and by taking fealty (oaths of loyalty) from the tenants. The third stage was William's return to Whilton, with Nicholas granting him a life tenure, a much simpler matter. Finally—and this may have happened at the livery of seisin—Roger, the elder brother, consented to the grant to Nicholas by writing out a quitclaim—literally quieting his own claim by primogeniture to the land—having it read in county court, and then having it enrolled in the plea rolls of a royal justice.[7] William and Nicholas certainly must have thought that all the formalities for their bit of legal magic had been carried out, leaving Nicholas, at the end, with title to the land but no possession.

They were not justified in their certainty, however, for two shortcomings marred the transaction. In the first place, William did not make out a written document granting the land to Nicholas. To us, this might seem terribly serious, because today the making and registering of a deed causes title to pass from one person to another. In William's time, however, the written document had no such force: it was merely evidence and could be rebutted by proof that the land had not changed hands. The livery of seisin was the most important formality, but written evidence from William would have helped. The other defect was much more serious. When land passes by livery and actualization of seisin instead of by deed, when has the seisin been actualized? There was no set period of time, and the fifteen days Nicholas enjoyed before William's return were certainly sufficient simply as a matter of time. What he had done on the land, however, was insufficient. There was never any evidence that he had had the land plowed; on the contrary, there was such trouble in the countryside that he did not dare work the land. Nor, it seems, did he receive rent from the tenants, dismiss his father's bailiff (the estate manager) and replace him with his own man, or free any of the unfree tenants. All of these actions were customary ways of showing that one could now dispose of the property as one's own, that one had title. Nicholas would not have needed to perform all of them, but what he had done fell short of decisive use of the land. The actualization of his seisin was marginal and therefore questionable. If Nicholas had not done enough in law, William's return—no matter what either party said—would cause William's former seisin and title to spring back into existence in full vigor: the law would say that nothing had passed between William and Nicholas, despite their intentions and ceremonies. One had to be very careful to comply completely with the criteria accepted by the king's courts.

The problems inherent in such a flawed transaction were compounded by the concurrent dissatisfaction with King Henry III, who was neither an extremely prudent nor an extremely able king. His lack of prudence led him to display his religious devotion by cooperating too closely with the papacy. In part that cooperation took the form of increased papal taxation of English clergy. In part it took the form of an enormous debt undertaken in 1254 to make his younger son king of Sicily—a parallel on a much grander level of William's intention toward Nicholas. That plan was promoted by the papacy, which then threatened excommunication when Henry was unable to pay. It was likewise imprudent for Henry to have supported his foreign half-brothers and his foreign wife's foreign dependents. It seemed to many that Henry's court had itself become a French bastion. His lack of strength became apparent with his military failures in Poitou in 1230–1231 and 1242. His continuing demands for money for his futile foreign enterprises and his inattention to the work of governing England finally provoked baronial opposition headed by Simon de Montfort.

In July 1263 Simon de Montfort took over the machinery of government. As one of his first measures he appointed keepers of the peace in the counties, men who took over the functions (except some of the financial duties) that the sheriff had exercised—in particular, the leadership of the military contingents of the counties. The new keeper of the peace for Northamptonshire, William Marshal, in turn appointed constables in each hundred to aid him. William de Whelton had already shown an aversion to accepting any administrative position in the county, but a refusal to serve now would have been a declaration of opposition to Montfort. William thus became Marshal's constable of the Northamptonshire hundred of Nobottlegrove. Accordingly, he was ordered to raise money for Simon de Montfort's forces. He gave 10 marks to the earl himself at Kenilworth, and he also gave Peter de Montfort a war horse worth £15. It was, seemingly, in this increasingly tense atmosphere that William granted Whilton to Nicholas. Finally, after a compromise effort between King Henry and Simon de Montfort failed, Marshal in March 1264 ordered William to come to Northampton to defend it against an expected attack by the king. William went, together with his wife and his family. No matter how reluctantly, William had been caught up in the revolt.

The battle on 5 April 1264 was disastrous for all who had taken up arms against the king and attempted to defend Northampton. William cannot be shown actually to have participated in the battle. Indeed, since he was now probably at least in his forties, he may not have been in any shape to fight. Moreover, when it was his turn to stand watch on the wall, he sent Nicholas in his place. Nevertheless, after the town fell during the surprisingly short battle, William was one of the eighty or so knights and barons captured. He was found in his lodgings, where Nicholas's arms were discovered also. His lands, like those of the other captured lords, were held as forfeit to the king, as having escheated, and the king used them to reward his followers. Accordingly, he granted the manor of Whilton to Thomas de Turberville.[8] The Whelton claim to Whilton was jeopardized.

Precisely what happened immediately after the royal grant of Whilton to Turberville cannot be ascertained. Turberville may have attempted to take control of the manor immediately. But the triumphant royal victory at Northampton was completely reversed six weeks later at the Battle of Lewes, 14 May 1264. One would expect that William then regained possession of Whilton and continued his possession at least until August 1265, when the opposition to Henry III collapsed with the death of Simon de Montfort at the Battle of Evesham. Thereafter, Thomas de Turberville would have been expected to make effective King Henry's grant to him of the manor of Whilton. Some such thing was seemingly in the offing, since on 25 February 1266 William de Whelton obtained a safeguard, lasting until the week of 11 April, to come to the king's court to stand trial,[9] apparently in an attempt to regain his position. The war had thus, without any reference whatsoever to the transaction between William and Nicholas, threatened to ruin the Wheltons: they were effectively at the king's mercy.

Had the Wheltons been alone in their plight, their cause would have been hopeless. Instead, the sheer number and importance of the people who had been disinherited, not only at Northampton but also at succeeding battles, made necessary some sort of compromise. Otherwise, those whose lands had escheated would have formed a militarily skilled and permanently dissatisfied body at loose in the countryside. Nevertheless, rebellion against the king could not go unpunished. A compromise was embodied in the Dictum of Kenilworth.

DOCUMENT 2

The Dictum of Kenilworth

Source: Statutes of the Realm, 1:12-17 *Date*: 31 October 1266

In the name of the Holy and Indivisible Trinity, Amen. . . . We, Walter bishop of Exeter, Walter bishop of Bath and Wells [and further bishops, earls, and others] having from the abovesaid lord king and from the other barons, councillors of the kingdom, and the leading men of England . . . full power to provide for the state of the country, namely, on the matter of the disinherited . . . have provided those things which according to the paths of right and fairness we think convene toward God's gracious purpose and the peace of the kingdom.

[1] We declare and provide that the most serene prince the lord Henry illustrious king of England have, fully obtain, and freely exercise his lordship, authority, and royal power without impediment or contradiction from anybody whomsoever whereby contrary to the approved rights and laws and the

long-maintained customs of the realm the royal dignity might be offended. . . .

[5] We declare and provide that the aforementioned lord king wholly spare and remit to all and singular who, from the beginning of the present disturbance of the kingdom until the present time and by occasion of that disturbance, have done any injury or offense whatsoever to him or the royal crown and who have come to his peace within forty days after the proclamation of this our provision, such that he shall not in any way or for any reason or occasion exercise any revenge on those offenders for past injuries or offenses or inflict on them a penalty of life, limb, prison or exile or payment of money, excepting those matters contained below in our present provision. . . .

[12] On the status and matter of the disinherited, among other things we have ordained and established, we, wishing to walk according to God and the path of fairness, have thought it fit to provide . . . that there be not disinheritance, but rather redemption; namely, that those who began the war and have continued it until now, likewise those who violently and maliciously held Northampton against the king, likewise those who captured and overcame the king at Lewes . . . pay five times the yearly value of their land. And if they pay the redemption they shall have their lands back. . . .

[26] Let laymen who openly managed the affairs of the lord earl and his accomplices by attracting men with lies, by goading the side of the earl and his accomplices with falsehoods, and by disparaging the side of the lord king and his son be punished by twice the yearly value of their land. . . .

❋

The Dictum of Kenilworth thus provided the Wheltons a way to recoup their fortunes. It granted amnesty to those who relinquished their arms within forty days and settled the terms for the disinherited to regain their land. William and Nicholas, of course, would fall into that group which had participated in the Battle of Northampton; the amount of the redemption for Whilton would thus be about £125. It would have to be paid to the person to whom the king had granted the land: Thomas de Turberville. That was a heavy burden: but, since it was only half the market value of the manor, it was a decent compromise.

William took it upon himself to redeem the land but was unsuccessful. He paid part of the redemption and borrowed another £75 to complete the amount. Although William apparently received the money, his death early in 1267 prevented him from paying the full sum to Turberville.[10] As it happened, Nicholas, the younger son and intended successor to Whilton, had predeceased his father sometime in 1265 or 1266. William's death thus left the problems concerning the manor of Whilton to Roger, the elder brother, and to Nicholas's survivors: Joyce, his wife, and Felicia, their only child. Joyce and Felicia will become the long-term protagonists in the Whilton story.

The claims that either Felicia or Joyce could make to the manor of Whilton depended completely on Nicholas's rights at the time of his death. Roger de Whelton, of course, as the firstborn son, would in the normal course of things have inherited all the lands and tenements held in fee by William at his death to the complete exclusion of all other children, male or female. But if Nicholas had actually established his seisin of the manor—that is, if William had effectively granted him the manor in the same way he might have granted it to any stranger—Felicia would inherit the manor with no difficulty whatsoever, since a woman or an underage girl had the same kind of right to inherit as a man. If a tenant died leaving only daughters, for instance, the daughters inherited in equal portions to the exclusion of male cousins. Felicia clearly had more right to inherit any land that Nicholas had held than did Roger, the brother of her father. Likewise, Joyce, as widow, would have received a third of the manor of Whilton, but only for the remainder of her life. This third she would hold together with a third of all the other lands and tenements her husband held in demesne as of fee—that is, held immediately possessed of the land in a heritable manner—since their marriage began. Those lands were her dower and would serve to support her for the rest of her life and to make her a more attractive prospect for remarriage. She would, however, receive her dower from Whilton only if Nicholas had established his seisin during the fifteen days he held the manor. Felicia, therefore, was entitled to take immediately two-thirds of the manor, with the remaining one-third reverting to her at the death of her mother—but only if Nicholas had originally been entitled to hold the manor. The livelihood of both Felicia and Joyce thus depended on whether or not that confused transaction between William and Nicholas had been valid. That issue, for them, was even more pressing than the redemption of the manor according to the Dictum of Kenilworth.

The rules applied to Joyce and Felicia, which in part determined their relationship, depended on the tenure by which Whilton was held—that is, the way in which the lord of the manor held Whilton from his next higher lord. Whilton was held by military tenure, so that William de Whelton, lord of Whilton, was also the vassal of Joan de Stuteville. The service William owed her for the manor was the service of one knight. Such tenure was based on the theory that the land had been granted to the tenant as payment for the continuing service as a knight, both militarily in time of warfare and also generally in the exercise of power in time of peace. This theory, which would seem to make William's hold on the manor somewhat precarious and conditional on his loyalty to Joan, had corresponded to reality well enough in the 1180s. By the 1260s, however, it was divorced from reality. Although there was still something of a personal commitment between lord and vassal, their relationship was coming to be described more accurately as a set of legally enforceable rights and obligations.

These legal burdens, which form the framework for much of what happened during the litigation over Whilton, can readily be summarized. The lord was entitled to the military services and to what have come to be called the "feudal incidents"—occasional profitable rights resulting from his position as lord. The tenant in turn was entitled to rely on his lord to guarantee for him that the original title, as given by the lord, was indeed valid. The two feudal incidents most important at this point were wardship and marriage. Both were originally necessitated by the lord's need to inculcate and perpetuate the loyalty of the heir; by the 1260s, however, they were increasingly regarded merely as legal rights and even as saleable commodities. Joan de Stuteville accepted that William de Whelton had granted to Nicholas. Therefore, Felicia now stood in the same relationship to Joan as had first William and then Nicholas. Since Felicia was only one or two years old in 1267 and would be considered underage until she reached fourteen,[11] Joan was her guardian. Felicia was taken from her mother, and Joan assumed not only the care and upbringing of Felicia but also the maintenance of Felicia's rights, both against strangers and against Felicia's own relatives. There was a moral element to this undertaking: this was the lord's duty. But there was also a financial incentive, since the normal revenue of Felicia's inheritance would all go to her guardian while she was underage. Finally, when Felicia reached marriageable age—but before she reached the age of fourteen and majority—Joan would have the right to determine whom Felicia would marry, and Joan would expect a payment for this bestowal of the bride and her income on the fortunate man. In short, Joyce, after the death of Nicholas, had nothing more to do with Felicia, her daughter. The legal rules surrounding military tenure did little to foster the growth of a strong relationship between a widowed mother and her heiress daughter.

But if Joan had every reason to stand up for Felicia's right, William (before he died) and Roger would have had every reason to ignore the grant made to Nicholas. Apart from Roger's obvious self-interest, both William and Roger had intended to benefit Nicholas with that grant. Felicia was, perhaps, a relatively insignificant concern; she may never even have seen her father; and she was, after all, only a girl. Moreover, since she was still an infant, her land would long be controlled by Joan. Finally, if Felicia's right were acknowledged, Joyce would get her dower, and her new husband—

for she would almost certainly marry again—would be a complete stranger to the family and would control that third of Whilton for the remaining decades of Joyce's life. There was no benefit to the Wheltons here. Both William and Roger can be expected to have wanted to forget the grant and the quitclaim. Joyce herself was still almost a stranger; Felicia, merely a nuisance. And these were hard times for the Wheltons.

With Felicia's interests thus clearly opposed to Roger's, Joyce's father in 1267 acted in such a way as to put Felicia's interests in opposition to Joyce's as well. When Nicholas died, Joyce was probably not yet twenty years old. At the death of her father-in-law, or before, her care was naturally resumed, it seems, by her own father, William la Zouche. She could have no dower until Felicia's right was proven. Joyce, however, was Zouche's only surviving child. Furthermore, Zouche had not forfeited his lands by fighting against the king and was therefore not burdened with a heavy redemption. Nothing prevented him from securing his daughter's position. He did this by completely ignoring the transaction between William de Whelton and Nicholas and by bargaining instead with Roger. Zouche could well force Roger into a compromise. Roger was, after all, Joyce's brother-in-law, and he had quitclaimed to Nicholas. Moreover, Roger was having some trouble redeeming the land. Finally, Zouche was willing to give Roger substantial compensation. On 4 March 1267 they reached an agreement that was made and witnessed in the king's Chancery and enrolled in the Close Rolls, one of the series of official documents.

DOCUMENT 3
The Zouche–Roger de Whelton Compromise

Source: CR, 1264-1268, p. 368 *Date*: 4 March 1267

Memorandum: Roger de Whelton, son and heir of William, came into Chancery on the Friday after Ash Wednesday and acknowledged that he would observe firmly and faithfully in perpetuity everything contained in the writing below, to wit:

To all faithful Christians who will see or hear this writing, Roger de Whelton, son and heir of William de Whelton, knight, greetings in the lord. Know that I have granted and given, on my behalf and on behalf of my heirs and assigns, to William la Zouche and his heirs and assigns all right and claim which I had or am able to have in any way by right or by inheritance in all manors, lands, and tenements, advowsons, reliefs, services, wards, escheats, mill-sites, and dowers with all other appurtenances pertaining to the said manor or to the said lands which could come to me by the name of the abovesaid William de Whelton, my late father, or by the name of Fina, my late mother, in any way by right or by inheritance in whatsoever counties they shall be in England in the power of the lord king such that neither I, Roger, nor my heirs nor my assigns nor another in our name for us or through us can exact or sell anything of right or claim in the said manors, lands, tenements, advowsons, reliefs, services, wards, escheats, mill-sites, and all the other abovesaid appurtenances nor sell or alienate in any way to the damage of the abovesaid William la Zouche or to our advantage the abovesaid right without the consent and full will of the abovesaid lord William la Zouche. In testimony of which business I have placed my seal to this writing, these being witnesses: William de Valence, Master G. Gyfford the chancellor, Roger de Leyburn, R. Waleraund, R. Aguylon, W. de Saint Omer, Alan la Zouche, and others.

Memorandum also: on the same day in the same Chancery the same Roger appointed his attorneys, to wit, John le Kue and William de Blechington or either of them, to restore all the manors and lands of the abovesaid Roger before justices which can accrue to the same Roger by whatsoever right and, when they have been restored, to deliver the seisin of them to the same William la Zouche.

*

This agreement drove an irrevocable wedge between Joyce and Felicia, between mother and daughter. Roger had granted all his inherited rights to Zouche and so, ultimately, to Joyce. Joyce's self-interest was now identical with what Roger's had been. The difference this made for Joyce was that, whereas she would previously have been hoping for but one-third of Whilton for the remainder of her life, she could now expect all four of the Whelton manors heritably. For Felicia, it meant that, if the grant to Nicholas were in fact ignored, her right to Whilton would come from her mother and not from her father. This might seem beneficial to Felicia, because, if Joyce had no more children, Felicia would eventually possess much more than Whilton. But if Joyce remarried and had a son—and so she would—Felicia would receive absolutely nothing, owing to the working of primogeniture.

The stage was thus set for the Whilton dispute. Felicia would want to maintain the validity of the grant to Nicholas. If it could be maintained, she would inherit Whilton; if not, nothing. Her guardians would be anxious to enforce her rights, because they had both a moral obligation and a financial incentive. Zouche, Joyce, and Joyce's future husband would work, at first through Roger de Whelton's attorneys, to destroy that grant and to establish their right from the compromise made between Roger and Zouche. That conflict surfaced first in making the redemption for Whilton.

After the Dictum of Kenilworth the king sent out royal justices to determine disputes raised by the now awkward forfeitures and grants made during the war and by the compromise embodied in the Dictum. Such courts, then, were the king's court, but with a jurisdiction limited to the determination of whether and at what rate redemption should be made and certification of who should pay and who should be paid. Nicholas de Yatingdon was the royal justice in charge of the court held by this royal mandate at Northampton, and it was before him that the dispute over Whilton first came. Turberville, of course, would demand that he be paid the redemption, because the king had granted him Whilton after the Battle of Northampton. The difficulty would come in deciding who should pay the redemption. Only the right heir should redeem: Zouche (through Roger's attorneys) and Felicia (through her guardians) would both claim the privilege of redemption.

The case first came up when Yatingdon was hearing pleas in Northampton sometime around January 1268. The attorneys of Roger de Whelton, working for Zouche in accordance with the agreement preserved in Document 3, then presented letters patent from the king certifying that Roger was ready to fulfill the terms of the Dictum of Kenilworth.[12]* Both Turberville and Baldwin Wake—the son of Joan de Stuteville, Felicia's lord—objected to the redemption being made in Roger's name.

DOCUMENT 4
Claims to Redemption

Source: JUST 1/618, m. 3 *Date*: late December 1267–January 1268

The lord king by his charter had given Thomas de Turberville the lands and tenements of William de Whelton by reason of the wrongs which he was said to have done before his death against the lord king in the time of the disturbance etc. And the same William while alive presented himself to stand to the Dictum of Kenilworth etc., and Roger de Whelton, son and heir of the abovesaid William, as he says, brought here to the lord Nicholas de Yatingdon, justice assigned to this matter, the lord king's letter patent that he was prepared to stand to the same Dictum and to redeem the lands and tenements, if they ought to be redeemed, in the form of the beforenamed Dictum.

And the abovesaid Thomas de Turberville, to whom the lord king had granted the abovesaid lands and tenements, comes and says that, as to the succession of the said lands and tenements, the abovesaid Roger is not heir of the abovesaid William, because he withdrew himself completely by a quitclaim which he made to Nicholas his younger brother, so that he cannot sell or exact anything of hereditary right. And if the true heir should present himself to stand to the Dictum of Kenilworth, Thomas de Turberville is prepared to take the redemption according to the beforenamed Dictum or to object against the true heir that he ought not redeem those lands and tenements.

And Baldwin Wake comes and says that it does not pertain to the abovesaid Roger to redeem those lands and tenements, because, even though the said Roger might be son and heir of the said William in respect of blood, he is not, however, heir in respect of the succession to the said lands and tenements, because whatever right he had in the said lands and tenements he wholly quitclaimed in his majority to Nicholas de Whelton his younger brother and to his heirs etc. This certain Nicholas recently died, as it is said; and he had a certain daughter and heir, Felicia by name, whose wardship, the same Baldwin says, pertains to him as the chief lord of the fee, as does the redemption of the land in the form of the Dictum, if it ought to be redeemed. And thereupon the abovesaid Felicia came and brought a certain writ of the lord king to the justices here in these words:

> "Henry by the grace of God etc., to the justices [assigned to hear] pleas concerning lands given etc., greetings. Since Felicia, daughter of Nicholas de Whelton recently deceased, is ready to show in court that those lands and tenements in Whilton which we gave to our beloved and faithful Thomas de Turberville by reason of the wrongs which William de Whelton [did] shortly before his death are the right and inheritance of that Felicia because the same Nicholas was enfeoffed and seised thereof by the abovesaid William his father, whereupon Roger, firstborn and heir of the abovesaid William, remitted and quitclaimed all his right and claim to the abovesaid Nicholas, as it is said, and the same Felicia presented herself to stand to the Dictum of Kenilworth and to redeem

> those lands and those tenements, if they ought to be redeemed, according to the form of the beforenamed Dictum, we order you, having made a diligent inquisition concerning the foregoing, to cause to be done for the same Felicia in this respect what ought to be done, according to the form of the Dictum and of your office."

Therefore, let there be an inquisition thereof.

Twelve sworn knights say upon their oath that the abovesaid William de Whelton never enfeoffed the abovesaid Nicholas of any tenement in Whilton nor withdrew himself from any tenement in the same town to the use of the abovesaid Nicholas, but they say that the abovesaid Roger de Whelton remitted and quitclaimed to the abovesaid Nicholas his brother all his right and claim etc., and brought that deed in open county court and made to read it and made to enroll that quitclaim in the rolls of the lord Gilbert de Preston.

*

No judgment was recorded pursuant to the verdict, and for good reason. The writ presented in Felicia's name (she was only two or three years old at the time) had authorized Yatingdon to inquire about William's grant to Nicholas and Roger's quitclaim. The verdict, however, did not yield a clear course of action. The jury's finding that William had not enfeoffed Nicholas supported Roger's right. The finding that Roger had quitclaimed supported Felicia's right. Could a mere quitclaim bestow right when the land had not first been granted and when the recipient of the quitclaim was not in seisin? Yatingdon declined to decide the issue. His hesitancy was well founded. His jurisdiction properly concerned matters touching the Dictum of Kenilworth; this question was clearly a matter of inheritance and not intrinsically related to the dictum. Nevertheless, the lines of the litigious conflict had been drawn between those who claimed through Roger's rights of inheritance (William la Zouche and his heirs) and those who claimed through the grant to Nicholas (Nicholas's heirs).

Yatingdon thus had the case sent before the king for decision. There were no rigid barriers between the branches of the king's court to prevent such referrals, and in May 1268 the case was put before the king and his council—that is, before the highest forum possible. All the parties and even the previous jurors were supposed to be present. Roger—but more likely his attorneys—came and made his complaint that Baldwin Wake was delaying him from his right. He demanded to be shown why he should not succeed to Whilton as heir. Wake declined to answer on that point, merely objecting that the wardship of Felicia properly belonged to his mother, Joan Stuteville, and that he could not put his mother's rights of wardship into litigation. Roger was therefore advised to sue against Joan. Thomas de Turberville, in possession of the manor, did not appear in accordance with the summons, so that the sheriff was ordered to take the manor into the king's hand to hold until he did appear. Finally, the jurors did not appear.[13*] The king's council had made no headway with the matter, and the case was rescheduled for June.

The record of the case in June is somewhat more informative about why Yatingdon had declined to render judgment but not at all revealing about what was happening in the King's Bench. The King's Bench record is really only a transcription of Yatingdon's record.

DOCUMENT 5

Certification to King's Bench

Source: KB 26/185, m. 2d *Date*: circa 12 June 1268

Northamptonshire. The lord king commanded his beloved etc. Nicholas de Yatingdon and his companions assigned to hear and determine in Northamptonshire the pleas concerning lands given on the occasion of the disturbance had in the realm that [in] the process of the suit entertained before you between

Roger, son of William de Whelton, and Felicia, daughter of Nicholas de Whelton recently deceased, demandants, and Thomas de Turberville, to whom we recently gave the lands and tenements which belonged to William de Whelton on the occasion of wrongs imputed to the same William in the disturbance had in the king's realm, tenant, the lord king wants the fulfillment of justice to be accorded to the abovesaid parties according to the form of the Dictum of Kenilworth. [Wherefore,] let him make to come before the king on the octave of Holy Trinity wherever [he shall be then in England] the record and the whole process of the abovesaid suit and similarly the jury of inquisition recently taken in the king's court before the abovesaid justices at Northampton with all the corroborative evidences and attachments touching the declaration of the abovesaid suit to certify the king in certain articles appertaining to the same suit etc.

And the abovesaid Nicholas [de Yatingdon] sent the record and process of the abovesaid suit in such form: [There follows a complete transcription of Document 4, with the verdict that Nicholas had not been enfeoffed and that Roger had quitclaimed. The two records are identical except that this record includes the names of the jurors.[14]]

And because the justices for pleas concerning lands given did not want to proceed on an investigation of heirs, they put the suit before the lord king. And after the lord king should be certified concerning the true heir of the said William de Whelton, let the said heir be sent to them. And they will assign to him those things which ought to be done concerning the redemption according to what they had inquired concerning the enmity of the said William.

*

The eventual result of the case was an order to Yatingdon to proceed first on a specific investigation of the feoffment and quitclaim and then on the problem of the redemption. The argument in favor of the right of Roger de Whelton then made substantial headway. The jury found that Nicholas, despite any alleged feoffment by William, had never really been seised. Felicia's guardians, of course, could present no written evidence of William's grant to Nicholas, and they probably were then (as I am now) unable to find Roger's quitclaim in the justice's rolls. The jury in fact did not even bother to mention Roger's quitclaim. Their finding on the feoffment seemed to preclude the necessity for having to consider that point.

The irrelevancy of a quitclaim if Nicholas was never seised may seem peculiar, but it was based on solid reasoning. Today, of course, one would reason that a formal renunciation of one's claim to land should thereafter prevent one from claiming it. Medieval law, however, started from a different point. It was already firmly established that title to land did not pass by deed but by livery of seisin. If a mere quitclaim could act as a title-passing deed, there would be no need for livery of seisin. The recipient of the quitclaim thus had to be already in such a condition that the quitclaim would merely evidence or complete some title he could show: he had to be somehow in seisin already. Since Nicholas, according to the verdict, had not been enfeoffed, he was not seised in any way and thus could take no benefit from a quitclaim.

DOCUMENT 6

Jury on the Feoffment and Quitclaim

Source: JUST 1/618, m. 2d *Date*: 1268-1269 (?)

The lord king ordered the justices here that they should diligently make an inquisition as to whether Nicholas, son of William de Whelton, was enfeoffed by the abovesaid William his father of lands and tenements in Whilton and was seised thereof and as to whether Roger, the firstborn and heir of the abovesaid William, remitted and quitclaimed all his right and claim to the abovesaid Nicholas.

Twelve sworn knights [say] upon their oath that the abovesaid William de Whelton never seised the abovesaid Nicholas his son of any tenement in Whilton nor withdrew himself from any tenement in the abovesaid town to the use of the abovesaid Nicholas; and they say on their oath that the abovesaid Roger is the firstborn and heir of the abovesaid William.

This jury verdict was decisive for the problems relating to the redemption. Since it had now been determined that William had not seised Nicholas and that Roger was the heir, Roger was the person who would be allowed to redeem the land. It is unlikely that this determination was meant in any way to settle in a permanent fashion the problems between Roger and Felicia. The verdict was probably strictly related to the redemption problem and the whole context of the Dictum of Kenilworth, a determination that had to be made to decide which claimant would be put back into the land after the redemption. Thereafter litigation between the parties could continue in the normal fashion without being precluded by this jury's findings. All that remained now was the judicial decision that the land had been properly forfeited on account of actual wrongs by William de Whelton. The jury was therefore charged to return a verdict on the guilt or innocence of William de Whelton.

DOCUMENT 7
The Determination of William's Guilt

Source: JUST 1/618, m. 2 *Date*: 1268-1269 (?)

The lord king ordered his beloved and faithful Nicholas de Yatingdon that he diligently cause to be made an inquisition as to whether William de Whelton, whose lands and tenements he gave to Thomas de Turberville on the occasion of the wrongs which [William] was said to have done against the lord king in the time of the abovesaid disturbance before his death, stands guilty of the wrongs imputed to him.

And the abovesaid Thomas de Turberville says that William was the enemy of the lord king, because the abovesaid William de Whelton was the constable of the hundred of Nobottlegrove through William the Mareschal, then keeper of the peace through the earl of Leicester [Simon de Montfort], and made to levy moneys in the abovesaid hundred to sustain the enemies of the lord king and similarly gave to the lord Peter de Montfort a horse worth £15; and he was captured at Northampton armed against the lord king in the battle had there.

The twelve jurors, knights and others, say on their oath that the abovesaid William de Whelton was constable in the hundred of Nobottlegrove through William Mareschal, then keeper of the peace through the earl of Leicester, and levied moneys in the abovesaid hundred to sustain the enemies of the lord king. They say also that the lord Simon, earl of Leicester, ordered him to come to him with horses and arms in his aid; and the same William went to Kenilworth and gave the abovesaid earl 10 marks to have peace and gave the lord Peter de Montfort one horse worth £15. They say also that the abovesaid William the Mareschal ordered the same William to come to him at Northampton to defend the abovesaid town. The same William came to the abovesaid town with his wife and all his family; and, when his turn came to stand watch in the abovesaid town, he sent Nicholas his son to stand watch for him. And when the town of Northampton was taken, the abovesaid William was found armed. They say also that Nicholas his son was accused, and his arms were found in the home of the same William his father.

And because the abovesaid William was taken in a black padded tunic defending the town against the lord king in the manner abovesaid, it is considered that Roger de Whelton, son and heir of William de Whelton, redeem the abovesaid lands and tenements at five years [value].

*

Thus Thomas de Turberville had appeared and made his case that the land should be redeemed. The jury agreed with him and gave an explicit account of the events at the Battle of Northampton, the earliest account available of William de Whelton's reluctant participation in the Barons' War. The necessary conclusions were drawn: the lands had been properly forfeited because of William's—not Nicholas's—activities; the redemption should be made at the highest rate; Roger de Whelton was the person privileged to make the redemption. In any further litigation Roger and those claiming through his right would be in the desirable position of tenant, able to use the revenue from the land to support them during the course of the litigation.

The resolution embodied in the last document cleared the way for William la Zouche to obtain possession of the manor of Whilton. Zouche was certainly not content with the agreement he had made with Roger in 1267 (Document 3). Since neither Roger nor Zouche had then been in possession, that transaction had merely masqueraded as a grant; no title could have passed to Zouche at that point. Now that Roger's right had been confirmed, something more was necessary. Zouche chose the most formal and binding way possible to secure his title to Whilton: a final concord.

The final concord derived its power—and peculiarities—from the fact that it was part of the official record of the king's court and was formally the resolution of a dispute in that court. Those who wanted to use this device had first to come before the court like normal litigants. Roger and Zouche came before the court by beginning a case of warranty of charters. This action was particularly appropriate, because Zouche was thus formally asking Roger to warrant his charter, to stand to the agreement embodied in Document 3. The suit, however, was mere formality; no one expected the parties to be actually in contention. Once in court, they immediately compromised the action, and their compromise was embodied in a tripartite indenture supervised by the court. Each party received one part of the indenture. The third part, that part written across the foot of the membrane and therefore called the foot of the fine (in medieval English law, "fine" meant "final concord," not "monetary penalty") remained in the possession of the court. The feet of fines constitute a well-preserved record of formal land transactions from 1195 until the nineteenth century. The peculiar advantage of the final concord—beyond its excellent protection against forgeries and its verifiability (a virtue obviously lacking in the alleged grant between William de Whelton and Nicholas)—was that until 1360 and then again after 1483 final concords could bind not only the two parties to the fine but also third parties. There were only two limitations to this barring effect against outside claims. First, the grantee had to remain in possession of the land for a year and a day after the fine was levied. Any stranger who felt he had a right to the land would have to put in his claim during that time. That claim would be endorsed on the fine itself and preserve that claimant's right to sue. Second, no one who suffered from some disability, such as being underage or abroad, at the time the fine was levied could be barred by the fine. In making a final concord embodying the whole agreement between Roger de Whelton and himself, William la Zouche was hoping to establish his right to the lands against any further claims from outsiders.

The final concord between Zouche and Roger concerning Whilton specified all the relevant tenurial details. Roger first acknowledged that Whilton, with all its exhaustively listed appurtenances, was the right of Zouche; this was the grant. Zouche undertook to perform to Roger's lord all the services owed from Whilton and also to acknowledge Roger as his lord. Zouche's services to Roger himself were to be insignificant and brief: one penny to be paid one year only at Easter. Roger was therefore to be relieved of both the regular burdens and the regular benefits of these tenements; but, since he became Zouche's lord, he retained such occasional incidents of lordship as escheat, wardship, and marriage insofar as they would arise from that tenure. All the regular benefits and burdens would hereafter fall to Zouche. Then Roger specified that the estates held in Norton by Felicia, the widow of William de Whelton, and by Hugh de Tywe and Margery his wife were only estates of dower. After the death of Felicia and Margery, therefore, those two tenements would once again accrue to Roger. Since Roger was already in possession of the heritable interest that formed the basis for the life estates of dower, he could grant them away. He did so. So that there would be no confusion in the future, Felicia, Hugh, and Margery were present and acknowledged that their tenements were held only as dower. Their presence and acknowledgments had been obtained by a separate piece of litigation initiated by the writ *quo jure* ("by what right"), which required tenants to acknowledge formally to the new holder the way in which they claimed to be on the land.[15*] Thus Zouche had eliminated two difficulties that could have arisen in the future.

Finally, Roger promised to warrant those lands to William. The clause of warranty bound Roger to defend those lands for Zouche and his heirs to the extent that, if the lands were successfully claimed by someone else and Roger's original right to the land was disproved, Roger or his heirs would be obliged to grant Zouche lands equivalent in value to the ones lost. Since Roger apparently had no other lands, the clause seems to imply the manor of Rockbeare, which Zouche granted to Roger in the same fine, following the agreement they had made on 4 March 1267. The grant of Rockbeare to Roger, however, was narrower than that to William. Whereas William's lands would descend to any of his heirs whatsoever on his death, the manor of Rockbeare could only descend to heirs procreated of Roger's body, so that only children and not brothers, cousins, or nephews could inherit. If Roger had no descendants—and that was a very real possibility—Rockbeare would escheat to (fall back into the hands of) William or his heirs. The whole agreement is preserved in Document 8.

DOCUMENT 8

A Final Concord: *Zouche* v *Whelton*

Source: CP 25(1) 283/17, no. 478 *Date*: circa 20 October 1270

This is the final concord made in the court of the lord king at Westminster three weeks from the feast of St. Michael in the 54th year of the reign of King Henry son of King John before Martin de Littlebury and Master Roger de Seyton, justices, and others faithful to the lord king then present there between William la Zouche, plaintiff, and Roger de Whelton, impedient, concerning the manor of Whilton with appurtenances, whereof a plea of warranty of charters was summoned between them in the same court, to wit: that the abovesaid Roger recognizes the abovesaid manor with appurtenances as in lordships, homages, services of free men, villeins, knight's fees, advowson of the church of the same town, woods, meadows, pastures, waters, ponds, mills, fisheries, and all other things pertaining to that manor to be the right of the same William as that which the same William has from the gift of the abovesaid Roger to have and to hold to the same William and his heirs from the abovesaid Roger and his heirs in perpetuity by rendering thereof for one year a penny at Easter for every service, custom, and exaction pertaining to the abovesaid Roger and his heirs and by doing thereof for the abovesaid Roger and his heirs all other services which pertain to that manor to the chief lords of that fee. And particularly the same Roger for himself and his heirs grants that all the tenements with appurtenances which Felicia who was the wife of William de Whelton and Hugh de Tywe and Margery his wife held in dower in the abovesaid town in Norton from the inheritance of the same Roger on the day on which this concord was made, which tenements with appurtenances after the decease of the same Felicia and Margery ought to revert to the abovesaid Roger and his heirs, should remain after the decease of the same Felicia and Margery wholly to the same

William and his heirs to be held together with the abovesaid manor with appurtenances which remains to them by this fine as is said above from the abovesaid Roger and his heirs by the abovesaid services in perpetuity. And the abovesaid Roger and his heirs warrant to the same William and his heirs the abovesaid manor with appurtenances which remain to them by this fine and similarly the abovesaid tenements with appurtenances which will revert to them as is said above by the abovesaid services against all men in perpetuity. And for this recognition, grant, warranty, fine, and concord, the same William grants to the abovesaid Roger the manor of Rockbeare with appurtenances in the county of Devon together with the advowson of the church of the same town to have and to hold to the same Roger and his heirs procreated from his body from the abovesaid William and his heirs in perpetuity rendering thereof one farthing per year at Easter for every service, custom, and exaction. And the abovesaid William and his heirs will warrant, acquit, and defend for the same Roger and his abovesaid heirs the abovesaid manor of Rockbeare with appurtenances together with the advowson of the church of the same town by the abovesaid service against all men in perpetuity. And if it happen that the abovesaid Roger should die without heir procreated from his body then the abovesaid manor of Rockbeare with appurtenances together with the advowson of the church of the same town will revert wholly to the abovesaid William and his heirs quit of all heirs of the same Roger to hold of the chief lords of that fee by the services which pertain to that manor in perpetuity. And this concord was made with the abovesaid Felicia, Hugh, and Margery present and acknowledging themselves to claim no right in the abovesaid tenements which they hold as said above except by name of dower.

[The dorse is blank.]

*

The whole agreement, therefore, while providing some compensation for Roger, was to Zouche's benefit. He had been reasonably thorough: the dower estates, which descendants might have tried to claim as heritable property, were carefully defined, and the land could now be relied upon to return to the main estate and thus into Zouche's hands when the women died. Even with such care, though, Zouche could not dispose of Felicia's claim, because she was underage. Nevertheless, the king's court had set that claim aside for the time being. It was always possible that Felicia might simply die or even be persuaded to enter a convent. In 1270 William la Zouche probably felt reasonably confident about his hold on Whilton.

The fate of William de Whelton's other lands can be treated more briefly. Wymington, a Bedfordshire manor likewise forfeited after the Battle of Northampton, had been granted by the king to William de Columbers. On 24 August 1268, probably at about the same time that the similar determination was being made about Whilton, Columbers surrendered Wymington to Roger de Noers according to the Dictum of Kenilworth. Noers, listed as a son of William de Whelton, was the one to redeem the land by the dictum because his father had enfeoffed him.[16] Roger de Whelton, the oldest son—the confusion occasioned by brothers having the same first name burdened their own contemporaries—immediately sued both this Roger de Noers and Felicia, widow of William de Whelton, claiming that Roger and Felicia were deforcing him, that is, keeping him off the land. Felicia, however, claimed the land only as her dower.

DOCUMENT 9

Whelton v *Noers & Qweye*

Source: Placitorum in Domo Capitulari Westmonasteriensi Asservatorum Abbreviatio, Record Commission (London, 1811), p. 169

Date: early October 1268

Bedfordshire. The sheriff had been ordered that, whereas it has been provided by the lord king and his magnates [who are of his council that those who faithfully adhered to the abovesaid lord king in the time of the war recently waged in that realm should have such seisin of their lands and tenements which were occupied during the same time as they had thereof at the beginning of the same war] and Roger de Noers and Felicia de Qweye deforce Roger de Whelton, son and heir of William de Whelton, who adhered faithfully to the king in the abovesaid time, of certain lands and tenements in Wymington, and whereof, the abovesaid Roger complains that the abovesaid Felicia deforced him of a third part of the manor of Wymington to his damage of £40.

And Felicia comes and says that she holds the abovesaid third part of the abovesaid manor in dower from the gift of William de Whelton late her husband and that she made no other occupation of the abovesaid third part of the abovesaid manor on the abovesaid Roger nor did she deforce him of any part of the same manor.

And Roger says that William de Whelton his father, whose heir he is, was in seisin of the abovesaid third part of the abovesaid manor at the beginning of the war and that the abovesaid Felicia deforced him as his writ says etc.

Therefore the sheriff was ordered that he should make to come twelve [as well knights as other free and lawful men of the county of Bedfordshire] by whom [the truth of the matter can be best known and who are related neither to the abovesaid Roger nor the abovesaid Felicia in any affinity etc.].

Afterwards the abovesaid jury of recognitors did not come at that day, and the sheriff did nothing thereof nor sent the writ etc.

*

This case was probably resolved in favor of Felicia, even though no verdict was recorded. Process in this case can be found dragging on until June 1271; thereafter it simply disappeared.[17] A jury verdict, however, was recorded in the companion case against Noers. That case had been argued down to a factual disagreement as to whether or not William de Whelton had ratified his grant by receiving rent from Noers after peace had been publicly proclaimed. If he had, then the law concerning this point was clear: the grant from William to Noers would be considered valid. The jury in that case assembled finally in early July 1271 and returned its verdict in favor of Noers.[18] Zouche thus had no claim to Wymington, and neither did Felicia, the daughter of Nicholas de Whelton.

Roger de Whelton was undoubtedly feeling very pressed at this time. Of course, he may not have been involved at all; Zouche could have been directing Roger's attorneys. It is more likely, however, that Roger was personally involved in this suit. It seems that Felicia the widow was already in possession of most of the third part of Wymington, which was her dower. Of one virgate of that third, however, she was not possessed. The widow thus brought a suit to claim that virgate from Hugh le Savage, her late husband's grantee. That action was completely proper, because a widow had a prior right to the land as compared with a grantee. Nevertheless, Hugh did have some recourse. He vouched Roger de Whelton to warranty; that is, he called Roger into court as his father's heir to stand by the grant his father had made or else to compensate Hugh with other lands Roger had inherited from William. We can speculate that Roger thus sued Felicia and Roger de Noers in desperation to avoid having to deplete his own estates. Document 10 is only the process by which Hugh was trying to bring Roger into court to warrant the grant, but it shows nicely the tangle in which William de Whelton's lands had become enmeshed at his death.

DOCUMENT 10

Vouching to Warranty: *Savage* v *Whelton*

Source: KB 26/195, m. 11d *Date*: early October 1268

Northamptonshire. Hugh le Savage presented himself on the fourth day against Roger de Whelton in a plea that he warrant him a third part of one virgate of land with appurtenances in Wymington which Felicia who was the wife of William de

Whelton claims in dower against him, and whereof the same Hugh vouches the abovesaid Roger to warrant it. And he did not come and the sheriff had been ordered to summon him to be [here] on this day. And the sheriff did nothing thereof, but reported that the abovesaid Roger has nothing in his bailiwick where he can be summoned. And it is testified that he has lands and tenements sufficient where he can be summoned. Therefore as before the sheriff was ordered that he summon him that he be [here] on the morrow of St. Martin and whereof the sheriff etc. The same day is given the abovesaid Felicia by her attorney in the Bench etc.

*

Roger de Whelton's attempt to reclaim lands in Totternhoe, William de Whelton's other Bedfordshire estate, was also unsuccessful. On 13 January 1273 Roger released his claims to Totternhoe to Alelm, called Roger's brother, in return for £5. Alelm was at that time already in possession of Totternhoe, except for that part of the manor still held by a widow, seemingly William de Whelton's long-lived mother. Alelm claimed to have a right in the manor in the same way Nicholas had acquired his: another grant made by William de Whelton to one of his sons.[19] We can speculate that William la Zouche initiated this resolution of the right to Totternhoe in return for some unrecorded quitclaim on Alelm's part regarding any claims he might have to Whilton should Felicia the daughter of Nicholas die. The inability to break the claims of Roger de Noers and Alelm to Wymington and Totternhoe enables us to limit our consideration to Whilton and the dependents and descendents of Nicholas de Whelton.

The final concord of 20 October 1270 (Document 8) thus concludes that portion of the dispute immediately concerned with the problems arising from the Dictum of Kenilworth. William la Zouche had profited from the situation by redeeming the lands through the agency of Roger de Whelton. Joyce, Roger's sister-in-law and William la Zouche's daughter, would soon profit from this arrangement. Joyce's profit, however, would become Joyce's daughter's disinheritance, for Joyce would remarry and give birth to a son. Felicia, therefore, would try to establish the validity of her claim to Whilton through Nicholas her father. Thus, by 1270 the dispute had hardened into the course it would follow thereafter. The cases heard before Yatingdon at Northampton, of course, were of a special genre, heard by virtue of a special commission. After the redemption, litigation concerning Whilton had to follow the now longstanding and accepted forms of litigation.

CHAPTER 3

The Assize of Novel Disseisin and the Attaint

THE NORMAL forms of litigation in the king's court in late-thirteenth-century England will inevitably seem strange to a modern student. We think most readily of making one's complete case in the first piece of litigation presenting all the reasons and evidence that support one's claim. Ultimate right and possession are determined at the same time in the same action. Any further legal action will normally be by way of appeal on the same facts, merely alleging that they have been misconstrued or that the first case was somehow procedurally incorrect. It was otherwise in England in 1300. The facts of the case could not just be presented; they had to be forced into a shape that would fit one of the prescribed remedies available in the king's court. Those remedies were conceptualized as falling into groups ranging from merely possessory actions to actions that determined right in the land. The most possessory actions were the assizes; actions of entry form an intermediate class of litigation that considered a limited category of flaws in a tenant's title; and actions of right put the dispute in the broadest possible form to determine the questions between the parties.

By the 1270s the use of these different forms of litigation followed a regular pattern. Immediate use of a writ of right might seem sensible in that it would cover all questions and save immense legal fees. No one, however, attempted to untie the Gordian knot in that way. It was safer by far to regain one's land in a less serious action. If something went wrong or if new facts came out in the course of the case so that one lost, it was possible to resort to the next higher form of litigation. Litigants could and regularly did proceed from assize to writ of entry to writ of right—but only in that order. An action of right precluded any assize or action of entry between the parties thereafter, unless, of course, it was based on some transaction subsequent to the judgment. Thus, the typical pattern was to bring a piece of litigation in which discussion was centered on lawful possession (seisin) and then, if necessary, to resort to actions that would progressively dispute how the tenant came into his land and, finally, which of the parties had, overall, greater right to the land. In the long run, this is precisely the course the Whilton dispute took.

The position of Felicia, daughter of Nicholas de Whelton, deteriorated rapidly between about 1272 and 1274. It seems that no one was willing to advance her right while William la Zouche was still alive and in possession. Having secured himself in Whilton and Norton, Zouche had sufficiently established the position of Joyce, his daughter, so that he could obtain a good marriage for her. It was probably in 1272 or 1273 that Joyce was married to Robert de Mortimer of Richard's Castle, who was still underage, although not in wardship because his father was alive. Robert was his father's prospective heir, and he figured to be one of the barons of England. William la Zouche had indeed done well for his daughter, but he died soon thereafter. In 1274 or thereabouts Robert and Joyce had a son, whom they named Hugh. Hugh, the young Felicia's new half-brother, would take precedence to Felicia in any inheritance derived from Joyce. Finally, and also in 1274, Robert's father died, so that he came into his estate.[1] Felicia and her guardians would therefore have to contend with a formidable adversary, because Robert de Mortimer would not easily surrender the estates his wife had brought with her into the marriage.

Felicia's guardians, of course, had a vested interest in securing her inheritance for her. While she was underage, her income went completely to her guardians; but as matters stood, she was merely an added expense. Moreover, Joan de Stuteville and Baldwin Wake had committed themselves fairly heavily to Felicia's cause. It was alleged that Baldwin Wake, acting for his mother, had paid Thomas de Turberville 100 marks for the redemption of the inheritance.[2] That payment would have been prior to Roger de Whelton's recovery and redemption of the land and would explain why Turberville and Wake seemed to be acting in concert against Roger de Whelton and William la Zouche. Moreover, after Wake paid Turberville, Felicia seemingly was in possession for a short time, and Joan de Stuteville received Felicia's homage.[3] That attempt at simple redemption of the land, however, obviously failed. The next occasion came when William la Zouche died. Robert de Mortimer and Joyce may have been then in the last stages of her pregnancy. Felicia's guardians therefore simply moved in upon Zouche's death and established her claim to Whilton. They were able to maintain themselves in Whilton for about three months before Robert de Mortimer and Joyce evicted them. Precisely what constituted Felicia's occupation and her eviction is not known. It could have been actual occupation and forcible eviction; more likely it was occupation by an official and eviction ordered by one of Mortimer's officials and obeyed peacefully. The eviction would have been expected; it laid the groundwork for the first normal phase of litigation.

Felicia's guardians had devised a situation in which they could advance her claims. They would begin by purchasing an assize writ from the king's Chancery on her behalf. Of the four "petty" assizes, two were clearly irrelevant. The assize utrum was used to determine whether contested land was a lay fee or free alms, and the assize darrein presentment was a possessory remedy concerning advowsons. Felicia's case in no way concerned such ecclesiastical matters. Her guardians thus had to decide only between the writ of mort d'ancestor and the writ of novel disseisin. The choice is instructive in the way that one had to fit the facts to the form of a writ. As is shown in Document 11, had Felicia's facts been inserted into a writ of mort d'ancestor, she would surely have lost.

DOCUMENT II
A Model Writ of Mort d'Ancestor

Edward, by the grace of God King of England . . . to the sheriff of Northamptonshire, greetings. Summon by good summoners twelve free and lawful men of the neighborhood of Whilton to be before our justices at the first assize, when they come to those parts, ready to recognize on oath whether Nicholas de Whelton, the father of Felicia de Whelton, who is underage as it is said, was seised in his demesne as of fee of the manor of Whilton with appurtenances in Whilton on the day on which he died, and whether the said Felicia is his nearest heir. And in the meantime let them view that manor and cause their names to be recorded in writing; and summon by good summoners Robert de Mortimer and Joyce his wife who hold that manor to be there then to hear that recognition; and have there the summoners and this writ. Witness etc.

*

The writ of mort d'ancestor was obviously designed only to help the heir of a person who had died in actual possession of a heritable estate to gain his inheritance. Now, that was precisely the situation in which Joyce had been when Felicia's guardians had occupied Whilton at Zouche's death. She could have brought an assize of mort d'ancestor easily, but she and her husband chose instead simply to eject the occupiers. If one has the power, straightforward self-help always seems less onerous than litigation, particularly if grave violence is not needed. Felicia, on the other hand, could not use mort d'ancestor. The writ had to specify that her father (or mother, brother, sister, uncle, or aunt) had been "seised in demesne as of fee" on the day he died; it could not be issued in any other way. Felicia's father, however, according to her account, had been seised in fee but not in demesne. Nicholas had given William, his father, a life estate. Thus, Nicholas had remained seised of the fee, the heritable interest that could devolve on his descendants; but William had been the person seised in demesne on the day Nicholas had died. Since Felicia's guardians could not safely allege that Nicholas had been seised in demesne as of fee on the day he died, they could not and did not attempt to use the assize of mort d'ancestor.

Instead, Felicia's guardians chose to bring an assize of novel disseisin. They had planned this action carefully at Zouche's death. The assize of novel disseisin, unlike that of mort d'ancestor, was based not on someone else's lawful possession but on one's own seisin. Anyone who had been seised of land as of a free tenement—that is, claiming to hold the land either for life or heritably—could use this assize, provided that he had been seised in time of peace. It would restore such a person to possession after he had been ejected unjustly and without judgment. It served, obviously, to prevent and remedy unjust exercises of self-help. To use this assize, however, Felicia herself had to be seised. Thus, when Zouche died, her guardians took the land in her name, an action that gave her sufficient seisin to fit her claim into the form demanded by the assize. The expected ejection by the Mortimers could thus be called a disseisin. Felicia's guardians therefore purchased a writ of novel disseisin that must have looked very much like Document 12.

DOCUMENT 12

A Hypothetical Writ of Novel Disseisin: *Whelton* v *Mortimer*

Edward, by the grace of God, King of England . . . to the sheriff of Northamptonshire, greetings. Felicia de Whelton has complained to us that Robert de Mortimer and Joyce his wife unjustly and without a judgment disseised her of her free tenement in Whilton after the first crossing of the sea into Brittany of lord Henry, king, our father. And therefore we command you that, if the aforesaid Felicia shall have given you security to prosecute her claim, you then cause that tenement to be reseised of the chattels which were taken therein, and cause the said tenement with the chattels to be in peace until the first assize when our justices come into those parts. And in the meantime cause twelve free and lawful men of that neighborhood to view that tenement and cause their names to be recorded in writing. And summon them by good summoners that they be at the said assize before the said justices ready to make recognition thereof. And put by gage and safe pledges the aforesaid Robert and Felicia or their bailiffs if they shall not have been found, that they be there at that time to hear that recognition. And have there the summoners, the names of the pledges, and this writ. Witness etc.

Felicia's claim was to be for only two-thirds of the manor of Whilton, because one-third was still held in dower. Her guardians initiated the procedure of the assize in 1273. Although the assize of novel disseisin had originally been a very fast remedy, by Felicia's time and in Felicia's case the assize did not move in a particularly expeditious fashion. It was a peculiarity of the assizes of novel disseisin and mort d'ancestor, guaranteed by Magna Carta, that they would be heard, at least the first time, by justices touring the local area. Felicia's suit was brought before justice Gilbert de Preston at Rockingham, Northamptonshire, and he was able to proceed immediately to the examination of the sworn panel of men, who were called either the recognitors of the assize or, as a group, simply the assize. Since the defendants had not appeared, they forfeited the opportunity to make specific objections in law. But the assize was not thereby limited; it could still consider anything relevant to the issues presented in the original writ. And it was at this point that the complexity of the case became apparent.

Felicia was clearly not a long-term tenant who had been

suddenly evicted without cause and without proceedings in court. Discussion in that simple kind of case would concern merely matters of possession. In Felicia's case, on the other hand, it was the view taken of the transaction between William de Whelton and Nicholas that would determine whether Felicia's disseisin by the Mortimers was just or unjust. If that transaction was valid, Felicia had merely entered onto her inheritance and had been unjustly thrown off. Such a conception, of course, was itself a novel realm for the assize of novel disseisin in the 1270s. An heiress's entry onto the inheritance was now seen to occasion the springing up and renewal of her father's right and seisin in her, so that she could use immediately all the remedies that would have been available to him, including novel disseisin. Thus, Felicia could in this way use the assize to claim her inheritance. But if the transaction between William and Nicholas were invalid, Felicia was a mere interloper and could rightly be ejected. The assize thus dutifully related all the difficulties concerning the transaction.

The problem was complex. Preston decided to refer the matter to the full Court of Common Pleas at Westminster. Those justices reacted in the same way as had the justices of the King's Bench when they considered the case sent them by Yatingdon: they wanted more information. Preston was therefore ordered to assemble the men who had been on the assize and examine them on certain points. Unfortunately, Preston died on 8 January 1274 before he could complete the task, and his place was taken by justice Master Roger de Seyton. Seyton re-examined the assize as Preston had been ordered to do, but the case, instead of being settled then before Seyton or in the Court of Common Pleas, was summoned into the Court of King's Bench in October 1274. There the chief justice, Ralph de Hengham, examined the case and felt very strongly that judgment should be rendered in favor of the Mortimers. The assize had already taken over a year.

At this point Felicia's lawyers struck on a gambit to limit the damage that would result from the adverse judgment they knew was pending. English justices were reluctant to render judgment when the losing party was absent. A judgment given in a person's absence, in some vague way, was weaker than otherwise, and when the judgment concerned a minor, its force was even less clear. Felicia was therefore removed from court before judgment was actually rendered. This action, according to Hengham's own account of the situation, put him in a difficult position. There had recently been before him a case between two other parties in which this problem came up—apparently the problem of rendering judgment against an underage plaintiff in novel disseisin, but perhaps also the specific problems of law presented in the Whilton case—and judgment had been rendered. Hengham knew that the losing party in that previous case was going to challenge the judgment by a review procedure initiated by the writ of error, whereas *Whelton* v *Mortimer* had only been removed during process into the King's Bench. It therefore seemed to him that, if he proceeded then to judgment, he could be accused of settling the case of error—a more solemn case than an assize of novel disseisin—without a hearing. Hengham's timidity was to prove costly to the Mortimers. Instead of rendering judgment plainly, Hengham sent Mortimer's bailiff (who had been representing the defendants) without day—that is, sent him off with no further day given in court. That amounted to quashing the case, since there would be no more procedure taken against the Mortimers. Nonetheless, Hengham had not explicitly stated that Felicia would take nothing by her action. Nor had he put her in mercy, subjecting her to the discretionary monetary penalty (an amercement) that was the inevitable result of losing a suit. That was crucial. The case had not resulted in a final judgment concerning the points at issue, even though the justices were in no doubt as to the facts or the law.

Since the case technically had not really been determined, Felicia's lawyers decided to try again. A different set of recognitors might think differently about the facts. They purchased another writ of novel disseisin, which initiated an identical, but new, action. The Mortimer lawyers, of course, quickly pointed out that Felicia had already prosecuted them in an identical assize of novel disseisin. The justices, they thought, should not simply ignore the previous case. The Mortimers thus tried to bar the assize from proceeding to verdict by reference to the former assize. Normally, Felicia would have been made to answer specifically to such an allegation, but, as a minor, she was legally incapable of acknowledging anything to her own detriment. The burden of proof concerning what had happened therefore fell completely on the Mortimers, and they alleged precisely that final judgment had been rendered for them against Felicia. The proof they offered was the rolls of the Court of King's Bench. Ralph de Hengham replied to the ensuing justices' request for the record of the case by explaining the situation and his reasons for stopping short of final judgment. The Mortimers had obviously blundered: they had alleged precisely—and wrongly—that judgment had been rendered against Felicia. Geoffrey de Leukenore and John de Mettingham, the justices presiding over the new assize, decided to take the verdict of the new set of recognitors because the exception raised by the Mortimers had failed. It was now July 1275, and Felicia was to have the rare benefit of a second assize on the same facts.

The second assize was undoubtedly more favorable to Felicia. They told the story of William de Whelton's grant and Roger de Whelton's quitclaim to Nicholas. On being questioned specifically, they made it clear that they thought that when William returned to Whilton after the fifteen days of Nicholas's possession, he came only as a friend and guest. Furthermore, they made a strange interpretation of the Wheltons' involvement in the Battle of Northampton. They stated expressly that the king had given Whilton to Turberville because of Nicholas's actions at Northampton, whereas the earlier records state clearly that the forfeiture had been made because of William's actions. The difference was vital. Since they considered that Nicholas was the rightful holder of the land at that time, only his actions could involve the land in forfeiture; he who forfeited was the holder. It followed rigorously that Felicia would have had the right to redeem and to hold Whilton; Roger de Whelton—and thus William la Zouche and Joyce—had no right. The assize's view of the sequence of events placed title in Felicia, so that her short occupation of Whilton had constituted valid seisin. Therefore, they thought that the ejection by the Mortimers was an unjust disseisin. The justices, unworried about contradicting Hengham's expressed opinions about the case, rendered judgment and ordered Felicia to be reinstated to Whilton and to be compensated by a payment of 20 marks by the Mortimers, half of which went to pay various clerks involved in the paperwork of that dispute.

DOCUMENT 13

The Assize of Novel Disseisin: *Whelton* v *Mortimer*

Source: JUST 1/1223, m. 25 *Date*: 3 February 1275

The assize summoned before Geoffrey de Leukenore and John de Mettingham at Hargrave on the Sunday next after the feast of the Purification of the blessed Mary in the third year of the reign of the lord Edward, king [3 February 1275].

Northamptonshire. The assize comes to recognize whether Roger de Whelton, Robert de Mortimer and Joyce his wife, Henry Turberville, Thomas de Montgomery, and William de Mortimer unjustly and without judgment disseised Felicia, daughter of Nicholas de Whelton, of her free tenement in Whilton after the first [crossing of the sea into Brittany of lord Henry, king, our father] whereof she complains that they disseised her of two-thirds of the manor of Whilton with appurtenances. And Roger, Robert, Joyce, Henry, and Thomas do not come. And Roger de Whelton was attached by William Ireis, John de Feure; and Robert was attached by Adam le Wyte, Thomas le Botiler. Therefore [let them be] in mercy. And the abovesaid Henry and Thomas were not attached, because they were not found. Therefore let the assize proceed against them by default. But the abovesaid William de Mortimer comes and similarly a certain Thomas le Chamberleng, bailiff of the abovesaid Robert de Mortimer, and for the abovesaid Robert and all others he responds and says that the assize ought not to be taken now, because he says that formerly in the court of the lord king before Gilbert de Preston, assigned justice at the bridge of Rockingham, the same Felicia brought an assize of novel disseisin concerning this same tenement against Robert and the others, such that a certain assize was taken there against them by default. And the same Gilbert after the taking of that assize, because of some difficulties found in that assize, fixed a day for the same Felicia to hear her judgment at Westminster before him and his other companions, justices of the Bench. And he says that the same Gilbert by common assent of his companions, justices of the Bench, made that assize to come before him again at Northampton and examined it concerning certain articles. Afterwards, indeed, because the same Gilbert died [8 January 1274] before that business was concluded, Master Roger de Seyton, who succeeded the same Gilbert as justice in the Bench, made the abovesaid assize to come before him again at Northampton and diligently re-examined it, such that after that re-examination the lord king by his writ ordered his justices of the Bench that they should make the record and the process of that assize to come before him on the octaves of St. Michael next following [early October 1274] and that they should adjourn the parties before him at that time. And since the same Felicia came before the lord king at that day through her guardian and believed that the judgment on the principal matter would injure her had she waited, she absented herself maliciously, so that thus judgment upon the principal matter was delayed. Wherefore, inasmuch as by the abovesaid assize taken at the bridge of Rockingham before the aforementioned Gilbert, assigned justice, and also by the re-examinations of the same assize made repeatedly before the aforementioned Gilbert and Master Roger by turns as has been said before, whatever could at present be found has sufficiently been recognized and found by that assize, he asks judgment if this assize ought to proceed.

And Felicia through her guardian says that it seems to her that the taking of that assize ought not to remain by any response made her above, because she says she is underage and that in this case she knows how to say or plead nothing except only to seek the assize for injury and disseisin done her. Nevertheless, inasmuch as the abovesaid Robert does not show that she withdrew herself from any assize arraigned formerly concerning this tenement nor even that judgment had passed on the principal matter whereby she ought to be precluded from that assize, she asks judgment.

Day is given them to hear their judgment on the morrow of the close of Easter at Northampton [22 April 1275].

Afterwards at Northampton on the morrow of the close of Easter, the abovesaid Felicia comes and similarly the abovesaid Robert comes in his proper person. And the parties on either side were asked if they wanted to say anything else. And the abovesaid Robert says that that assize ought not to proceed thereof between them, because he says, as his bailiff said above, that the same Felicia formerly arraigned a certain assize of novel disseisin against the same persons concerning that same tenement before Gilbert de Preston, who took that assize and adjourned that Felicia into the Bench to hear her judgment thereof. And after that judgment had been delayed for some time before the justices of the Bench, by order of the king the record and process of that assize were placed before the lord king on the octaves of St. Michael next following. At which day the abovesaid Felicia by her guardian came to hear her judgment thereof. And, when she perceived that the judgment would be reputed to injure her, she willfully absented herself so that by this the judgment on the principal matter would be delayed. But nevertheless, the justices at the pleas of the lord king, having no regard for the absence of the same Felicia, proceeded to judgment according to the recognition of the aforementioned assize on the prinicipal matter, considering that that Felicia should take nothing by that assize but should rather remain in mercy for a false complaint. And concerning this he puts himself on the record of the justices and likewise of their rolls of the abovesaid term.

And Felicia well denies that judgment on the principal matter ever passed against her, and concerning this she puts herself on the record of the abovesaid rolls.

Day is given them on the morrow of St. John the Baptist here [25 June 1275]. And meanwhile let the rolls be searched.

[The following passage is then deleted: And therefore Ralph de Hengham and his companions, justices of the lord king at the pleas of the lord king, are asked that, their rolls of the abovesaid term having been examined, they send the justices here their record thereof on the morrow of St. John the Baptist.]

Afterwards, on the morrow of St. John the Baptist [25 June 1275] at Northampton, the lord Ralph de Hengham sent his record, which is as follows:

> "To his companions and friends Geoffrey de Leukenore and John de Mettingham, justices of the lord king, Ralph de Hengham sends greetings. So that we might make you more certain concerning that which happened before the lord king between Felicia de Whelton and Robert de Mortimer, I signify that, when the record of the assize of novel disseisin taken before lord Gilbert de Preston between Felicia de Whelton and the abovesaid Robert concerning tenements in Whilton came before the lord king by a writ concerning this directed to Master Roger de Seyton and after the parties had been adjourned before the lord king, the abovesaid record having been inspected, it seemed to me and my companion that the judgment was manifestly to be rendered for the abovesaid Robert. And when we were ready to render that judgment, the abovesaid Felicia absented herself. Wherefore, by judgment the bailiff of the abovesaid Robert was told that he should go without day, but it was not expressly

pronounced that the abovesaid Felicia take nothing by her assize. And the reason for this was that there was a certain similar judgment made in the Bench between Matilda Longespeye and John de Breuse. I understood and still understand that the abovesaid John is going to complain concerning this judgment. That suit was determined in part by my judgment, therefore judgment was thus not expressly pronounced [in the suit between Felicia and Robert] because, if it had been, it would have seemed to all that I had confirmed the judgment between the abovesaid John and Matilda beforehand, for which action I could possibly be rebuked. It was said, however, that there would be saved to the abovesaid Robert whatever ought to be saved by such a default of the abovesaid Felicia. Farewell."

And because the abovesaid Robert formerly said manifestly that the justices at the pleas of the lord king proceeded to judgment on the principal matter against the abovesaid Felicia and of this vouched the record of those rolls, through which certain record it was not found that that judgment passed on the principal matter between them such that it was considered that the abovesaid Felicia take nothing by her assize, it is considered that this assize should proceed.

And Thomas le Chaumberleng, bailiff of the abovesaid Robert, says that the abovesaid Felicia never had any free tenement in the abovesaid manor, because he says that that manor at one time belonged to William de Whelton, who held it in his demesne as of fee until he was taken at Northampton against the lord Henry, king. And the same king gave that manor as forfeit to a certain Thomas de Turberville, against whom Roger de Whelton, son and heir of the abovesaid William, recovered that manor according to the form of the Dictum of Kenilworth. And when the same Roger had seisin thereof, he enfeoffed thereof William la Zouche, father of the abovesaid Joyce whose heir she is, and placed him in full seisin. And the same William died seised. And after the death of the same William, the abovesaid Felicia came and intruded herself into the abovesaid manor and held it for some time, so that the abovesaid Robert, who married the abovesaid Joyce, by reason of the same Joyce seised that manor and removed the abovesaid Felicia, as he was well entitled to do.

And John de Roseles, one of the recognitors, does not come; therefore let him be in mercy.

The jurors say that the abovesaid manor at one time belonged to William de Whelton, who had two sons, to wit, Roger the firstborn and a certain Nicholas, born thereafter. The same William, wishing to advance Nicholas his son, gave him the abovesaid manor with appurtenances and put him in full seisin thereof. And after the same William had put the same Nicholas in seisin thereof, he immediately withdrew and went to Wymington, a certain manor of his, to stay there. And he was there continuously for fifteen days, and for all that time the abovesaid Nicholas was in peaceful and separate seisin. They also say that the abovesaid Roger de Whelton was present at the abovesaid feoffment and confirmed the gift and deed of the abovesaid William, his father. The jurors were asked whether the same William ever afterwards returned to the abovesaid manor, and they say the same William returned after a fortnight, but, however, not as lord, rather as a friend and guest at the home of another friend. And they say that the same Nicholas held that manor and did and disposed thereof at his will as lord. Some time afterwards, indeed, the abovesaid William, father of the same Nicholas, and the same Nicholas went to Northampton to visit there. And when the lord Henry, king, father of the present lord king, arrived with his army to take those who held that town against him, the abovesaid William and Nicholas were captured there. Because of that, the lord king gave his lands as lands of the disinherited. And he gave the manor of Whilton to a certain Thomas de Turberville. And the jurors were asked whether the lord king gave that manor by reason of the forfeit of the abovesaid William or of the abovesaid Nicholas, and they say expressly that it was for the forfeiture of the same Nicholas. They were also asked if the abovesaid Roger de Whelton recovered that manor against Thomas de Turberville according to the form of the Dictum of Kenilworth, and they say that after the same Thomas de Turberville had held that manor for some time by reason of the grant made him by the lord king, the earl of Warwick seised that manor into his hands, asserting that it was of his fee. And thereupon Joan de Stuteville, chief lady of that fee, sent to the abovesaid earl and made him to understand that the abovesaid manor was the right and inheritance of the abovesaid Felicia, whose wardship pertained to her by reason of Felicia's being underage and that it was of her fee and not of the fee of the same earl, wherefore the same earl immediately returned seisin thereof to her. And immediately thereafter Baldwin Wake, son of the abovesaid Joan, went to the abovesaid Thomas de Turberville and satisfied him by a fine of 100 marks and more for his right. And they say that as soon as the seisin of the abovesaid manor thus was gained to the use of the abovesaid Felicia, the abovesaid Joan de Stuteville received the homage of the same Felicia thereof. And the same Felicia was in such seisin of the two-thirds of the abovesaid manor, whereof it is now complained, for a quarter of one year and more. Wherefore they say on their oath that the abovesaid Robert de Mortimer and all the others except Roger de Whelton and Joyce wife of the same Robert unjustly disseised the same Felicia thereof etc., as the writ says. And therefore it is considered that the abovesaid Felicia should recover her seisin thereof by view of the recognitors; and let Robert, Henry, Thomas, and William be in mercy for disseisin; and Felicia similarly in mercy for a false accusation against the abovesaid Roger and Joyce. Damages: twenty marks.

Damages: twenty marks, whereof seven marks for the clerks of the justices and forty shillings to the sheriff's clerks.

[Added later:] Afterwards, before the king, notwithstanding the recognition of the aforementioned assize, it is considered that the abovesaid [Robert] recover his seisin etc.

The Mortimers had every right to seek redress of that judgment, and the last sentence of Document 13 shows that in the end they were successful. After all, the first assize and the justices of the Court of King's Bench had considered that they were in the right. Moreover, Hengham had told them that they would not be damaged by his decision not to render judgment specifically against Felicia, that their advantage would be saved for them. It seemed strange, to say the least, that another assize could thereafter result in seisin being awarded to Felicia.

There were two processes that were appellate in nature. The writ of error complained of the justices' decision concerning the law. Since justices were presumed, rightly or not, to be acting in good faith, error led only to correction of the judgment and not to punishment of the justices. The other process, attaint, contested the verdict returned by the assize recognitors. The writ of attaint set in motion a cumbersome process. It demanded a jury of twenty-four to consider the same situation that had been put to the original assize and to ascertain whether the twelve recognitors had perjured themselves by making a false oath. The punishment for convicted assize recognitors was severe: imprisonment, loss of chattels, incapacity thereafter to have one's oath accepted in law courts. In practice, however, when the contrary verdict of the assize was clearly a matter of legal technicality or interpretation and not the result of malice or corruption, the justices used their discretion and imposed only modest amercements. Whatever the punishment inflicted on the recognitors, the verdict of the attaint replaced the verdict of the assize. The problem for the Mortimers was that the assize had declared that Felicia had been disseised. It was that verdict, not any decision by the justices, that they wanted to attack. Attaint was therefore the remedy open to them to correct what would have seemed to them manifest injustice.

The Mortimers purchased their writ of attaint immediately and pursued their complaint against Felicia and the assize recognitors. The jury of attaint accordingly assembled at Northampton on 7 October 1275 before Ralph de Hengham, the chief justice, who was certainly predisposed to favor the Mortimers, if only because of his decision during the original assize. The Mortimers made their complaint that the assize verdict was false, because Felicia had never been seised such that she could be disseised, whereas Felicia maintained that the verdict was true. The twenty-four jurors related the story once more, giving a few more details about the handling of Whilton after Zouche's death and lengthening the period of Felicia's occupation to a year and a quarter. More important, they were questioned closely on the transaction between William de Whelton and Nicholas and on the manner in which Nicholas was said to have established his claim. They thought that he had not been sufficiently in command of the land to obtain good seisin. Finally, the jury specified that the grant to Turberville had been occasioned by William's, not Nicholas's, actions and that Roger had recovered his father's seisin by judgment of the king's court before Yatingdon. Their story, as far as can be told, was accurate and undoubtedly corresponded with the verdict of the first assize and contradicted the verdict of the second assize. This verdict, at least, was such as would restore Whilton to the Mortimers.

The facts of the case, together with the unusual series of assizes and the conflict of judicial opinions, made it somewhat special. Hengham, therefore, did not render the judgment at Northampton; rather, he adjourned the case into the Court of King's Bench for judgment. Thus, for the second time, this case reached the highest forum in the land, for at that time adjourning a case there for special consideration effectively put it before the king and his council. Judgment was rendered in favor of the Mortimers, and two reasons were specifically given. First, Roger de Whelton had been awarded the privilege of redemption, and thereafter Felicia had not continuously prosecuted her right. Also, Nicholas did not seem to have established any true seisin, so that Felicia's occupation of Whilton after William la Zouche's death gave her no true seisin. Therefore, the Mortimers were restored to

Whilton and regained the damages previously awarded to Felicia. Felicia herself was amerced. The convicted recognitors of the assize, however, were rightly treated leniently. The establishment of seisin was a technical matter with which, it seemed, they had indeed been insufficiently acquainted. Ten years later the Statute of Westminster II, c. 30, took cognizance of this difficulty and allowed the assize merely to tell the facts and leave it to the justices to decide whether or not there had been a disseisin. These recognitors thus were only amerced.

DOCUMENT 14

The Attaint: *Mortimer* v *Whelton*

Source: JUST 1/1217, m. 34 *Date*: 7 October 1275

The jury taken at Northampton on Sunday, to wit, on the octaves of St. Michael in the third year of the reign of King Edward, son of King Henry [7 October 1275], before Ralph de Hengham, justice assigned to this, and those associated to him.

Northamptonshire. The jury of twenty-four knights to convict the twelve—Robert Mauntel, Hugh de Messenden, William de Turvyle, John de Myntens, Nicholas de Wythemale, William de Insula, Robert de Nodariis, Richard de Culeworth, William de Faukenberg, Thomas le Blunt, Nicholas le Sauvage, Roger de Neubury, Hervy de Solegrave, William de Nononcurt, William de Bray, Simon de Cranesley, Eustace Golafre, William de St. German, Henry de St. Maur, William Taylehaste, Adam de Assheby, Thomas de Craunford, William Russhynol, and William Abbot—come to recognize whether Robert de Mortimer and Joyce his wife, William de Mortimer, Henry de Turberville, and Thomas de Montgomery unjustly [and without judgment] disseised Felicia de Whelton of her free tenement in Whilton after the first crossing of the sea into Brittany of lord Henry, king, our father. And whereof the same Robert and Joyce complain that the jurors of the assize of novel disseisin which was summoned thereof between them and was taken at Northampton before Geoffrey de Leukenore and John de Mettingham, justices assigned to this, made a false oath in this, to wit, that they said that the abovesaid Felicia was disseised of two-thirds of the manor of Whilton with appurtenances as of her free tenement whereas she had no free tenement in those tenements, nor was she able to have [any such tenement] by such an intrusion which she made in the same tenements by her guardians after the death of William la Zouche, father of the same Joyce whose heir she is, who died seised thereof in his demesne as of fee. And this he asks to be inquired by a jury of 24 etc.

And Felicia comes and says that the abovesaid jury of the aforementioned assize which [was taken] before Geoffrey de Leukenore etc. made a good and legal oath, because she says that the same Felicia before the death of the abovesaid William la Zouche and after his death was in good and peaceful seisin of the abovesaid tenements as of her free tenement by her guardians until the abovesaid Robert and others unjustly [and without judgment] disseised her thereof. And she asks that this be inquired by jury.

The jury say upon their oath that the abovesaid two-thirds of the abovesaid manor with appurtenances belonged to a certain William de Whelton, who had two sons, to wit, Roger the firstborn and Nicholas born thereafter. This certain William, wanting to advance Nicholas his younger son, enfeoffed the same Nicholas of the same tenements in this way, to wit, he handed over to the same Nicholas the door of the chief messuage of the abovesaid tenements by [putting his hand on] the hasp and took a branch of a cherry tree and handed it to him in token of the seisin of the abovesaid tenements. And afterwards, he withdrew from there, the servants, plows, and movables having been surrendered to the other. First, however, he had accepted security from the abovesaid Nicholas, to wit, by pledge and oath, that after the same Nicholas should have gained good seisin thereof he would regrant the abovesaid tenements to the abovesaid William to hold at the term of the life of the same William. After his withdrawal, the abovesaid Nicholas remained in the abovesaid messuage for fifteen days. He fished in the fishponds, took wood in the garden to burn, made to clean a certain fishpond outside the courtyard, and took the fealty of the men. [The justices] asked them if he took any recognition from the same men; they say no. Asked if the abovesaid Nicholas plowed or sowed or in any way worked the lands pertaining to the abovesaid manor, they say no; because, they say, at that time scarcely anyone dared to work his lands. And, asked if the abovesaid William removed his servants or oxen or his other movables in his withdrawal or afterwards so that by that removal it would seem that the estate of the abovesaid William changed, they say in no other way than has been said above. And they say that after the abovesaid following fifteen days, the abovesaid William came to Whilton and asked the abovesaid Nicholas his son to keep the agreement with him and to return to him the abovesaid tenements to hold at the term of his life only. That certain Nicholas granted him this, but without any deed. And afterwards, when the lord King Henry, father of the lord king now, came to Northampton with his army, he found the abovesaid William in the same town. Deeming him his enemy, [the king] gave the abovesaid tenements to a certain Thomas de Turberville because of the wrongs of the abovesaid William. Afterwards the same William died while by grace prosecuting the abovesaid lord king and the abovesaid Thomas to redeem his abovesaid lands. After his death, Joan de Stuteville, asserting that the abovesaid tenements were of her fee and demesne, kept with her the abovesaid Felicia as daughter and heir of the abovesaid Nicholas, who died before the death of his abovesaid father. And she, also asserting that the wardship of the abovesaid heir pertained only to herself, proceeded against the abovesaid Thomas for the redemption [of the abovesaid tenements], which the same Thomas returned to the abovesaid Joan as to the guardian of the abovesaid Felicia. And they say that nevertheless the abovesaid Roger, son and heir of the abovesaid William, always had prosecuted his right concerning the abovesaid tenements in the king's court before Nicholas de Yatingdon and his companions, justices [to hear and determine] the pleas of the disinherited etc., before whom he as heir recovered such a seisin of those lands in the king's court as the abovesaid William his father had thereof at first. And after he had been put in seisin thereof by the bailiff of the king, immediately he enfeoffed William la Zouche of the same tenements. By that feoffment [William la Zouche] was in good and peaceful seisin thereof for four years and more, and afterwards he died seised. After his death the earl of Warwick seised the abovesaid tenements into his hands as chief lord, asserting that those tenements were held in chief of him. Afterwards, when that same earl had learned that the abovesaid Felicia was supposed to have been in the wardship of the abovesaid Joan because the abovesaid tenements were of her fee, he returned those tenements to the same Joan in the name of the same Felicia. She held them for a year and a quarter. And thereafter came the abovesaid Robert and Joyce, daughter and heir of the abovesaid William la Zouche, and ejected the same Felicia from the abovesaid tenements.

Day was given them to hear their judgment at three weeks after Michaelmas before the king wherever etc. [mid-October 1275].

Afterwards at that day before the king and his council, because it was found by jury that the abovesaid Roger who enfeoffed the abovesaid William la Zouche of the abovesaid tenements recovered the same tenements to be redeemed according to the Dictum of Kenilworth as heir by a certain judgment of the king's court—which certain judgment was never annulled in the time of the abovesaid Roger and which was found in the rolls of Nicholas de Yatingdon—and also that in the time of the abovesaid William la Zouche who was in seisin of the same tenements for as long a time as was said above by the abovesaid feoffment the right of the abovesaid Felicia was never declared, and because the same William la Zouche died seised of the same tenements in his demesne as of fee, whose heir the same Joyce is without mesne, it seems to the court that the seisin which the abovesaid Felicia had by the abovesaid guardians by descent from her father—which for a certain cause should be regarded as null—gives her no more free tenement in the abovesaid tenements than if some stranger had entered into the same tenements. And therefore it is considered that the abovesaid Robert and Joyce should recover such seisin of the abovesaid tenements as they had before the assize was taken before the aforementioned Geoffrey and John, together with the damages which had been adjudicated the aforementioned Felicia by the aforementioned assize. And let Felicia be in mercy. And because the twelve jurors do not disagree very much in their account from the verdict of the twenty-four jurors but rather are almost concordant except inasmuch as they said that the abovesaid Felicia had a free tenement in the abovesaid tenements, whereof they could well have been deceived, it is granted from the "equity" of the court and from the special grace of the king that the aforementioned twelve jurors not lose their law nor be redeemed, but rather only be in mercy for what they said.

By this attaint the Mortimers succeeded in reversing the verdict of the second assize, and Ralph de Hengham corrected the injustice done by not having gone to judgment immediately on the verdict of the first assize. No one, of course, denied that the Mortimers had ejected Felicia without a judgment. Nor had there been any question that Felicia had been on the land for a substantial time with a claim to the land that was at least plausible. The justice or injustice of the eviction rested on whether Felicia had had a "free tenement" at the time of the ejection. "Free tenement" had nothing to do with what was on the land, such as horses and crops. It was a legal definition and was treated as an incorporeal entity that one either did or did not have. It was defined as that kind of legal interest in land which would be protected by the assize of novel disseisin, because the term "free tenement" became a legal "thing" by its use in the writ of novel disseisin. In this case, whether or not Felicia had a "free tenement" could be determined only by examining not her own possession but her ancestor's title. When her ancestor's title was debilitated and it was seen that she had not continuously pressed her claim to the land, it was decided that she had no "free tenement." Since the assize of novel disseisin protected only "free tenements," she had not been seised in such a way that she could be disseised; that is, the Mortimers were legally entitled to eject her without legal process. The argument, of course, is circular. What had really happened was that a remedy that had long protected possession was being redefined so as not to punish the actions of owners against those without title.

The Mortimers were thus to be put back into Whilton and to be returned the twenty marks they had lost in the second assize. Restoring them to the land was fairly straightforward; recovering the money, the less important part of the judgment, was not. Any normal order concerning legal process or execution of judgment was directed to the sheriff of the county. The particular sheriff to be addressed depended on various factors: where the subject matter of the dispute was located, where the defendant could be found, which county could produce a more knowledgeable jury for the particular dispute. In the Whilton case, the sheriff of Northamptonshire was the one to whom all the writs were addressed, as indicated by the clerk's margination of that county's name (here appearing at the beginning of each document). The sheriff was responsible for executing the order and would perform his duty by relaying the command to one of his bailiffs. For certain portions of most counties, however, the bailiff of the relevant hundred would be the bailiff of a liberty, appointed and responsible to a magnate and thus not completely controlled by the sheriff. When that magnate wanted to shield a litigant or when there was some dispute between the sheriff and the magnate, the execution of the orders of the king's court could be long delayed.[4] In this case the relevant bailiff was the bailiff of that complex of manors and hundreds known as the honor of Leicester, only part of which was within Northamptonshire. Edmund, the king's brother, owned this liberty, so there is no particular reason why the bailiff should have been partial to Felicia; in fact, there is no reason to doubt that there was simply not enough time allowed to execute the order. In any case, the sheriff did not succeed in levying the money, and still in June 1280 he was being ordered to disregard the liberty of the honor of Leicester and its officials, to have one of his own officials levy the money. Commanding is one thing; commanding effectively, as the king's court well knew, is another.

DOCUMENT 15
Execution of the Attaint Judgment

Source: KB 27/55, m. 13d *Date*: late June 1280

Northamptonshire. The sheriff had been ordered not to omit on account of the liberty of the honor of Leicester to levy from the lands and chattels of Felicia de Whelton in whosesoever wardship they are in his bailiwick twenty marks and to have them before us here at this day to return to Robert de Mortimer and Joyce his wife, which twenty marks had been adjudged to the same Felicia recently in the court of the king before his beloved and faithful Geoffrey de Leukenore and John de Mettingham at Northampton by reason of a certain disseisin which the same Robert and Joyce did to the same Felicia, as was said, concerning the tenements in Whilton and which afterwards in the king's court before him had been readjudicated to the same Robert and Joyce. And the sheriff did nothing thereof but replied that the writ came too late for him to execute it. Therefore as before the sheriff is ordered not to omit on account of the abovesaid liberty to levy from the lands [and chattels of the abovesaid Felicia etc.] the abovesaid money and have it before the king on the octaves of the Purification wherever [he shall be in England] and whereof the sheriff replies [to our justices etc. that the writ came too late for him to execute it].

*

The possessory level of litigation thus terminated with seisin of Whilton being adjudged to Robert de Mortimer and Joyce his wife, daughter of William la Zouche, to whom Roger de Whelton had granted Whilton by final concord. It was possessory litigation, at least in theory, because the issue concerned the justice or injustice of an ejection; ostensibly the suit was to restore the evicted person to possession so that the claimant would be forced to make his claim peacefully in the courts and not by self-help. In these cases, however, some matters of title had entered into discussion. For the time being, Felicia had been deprived of her inheritance. Her wardship had in the end been only a burden to Joan de Stuteville, who died in April 1276.[5] Only those who believed that there had been a valid transaction between William de Whelton and Nicholas, his younger son, would see any profit in being her guardian or spouse. That profit would be completely in the future and wholly dependent on the success of further litigation.

CHAPTER 4

The Writ of Entry and the Writ Certiorari

❋

THE NEXT step in the attempt to regain Felicia's inheritance was the purchase of a writ of entry. During the litigation in the form of the assize of novel disseisin the recognitors had related the whole story about the Wheltons and the title to their lands. All that discussion was needed merely to discover whether Felicia's occupation of Whilton was such that it gave her seisin. The assize was not precisely concerned with matters of right and title. Writs of entry, on the other hand, put into issue a very specific point of title to land, how the defendant or his ancestor had "entered" the land. The verdict and judgment would be precisely on the derivation of title and not on seisin. Writs of entry thus went more deeply into right and title than did possessory assizes, and they could thus reopen a dispute that had been adjudicated by an assize.

A writ of entry could allege any one of a number of specific points of title to be faulty; it was up to the claimant's lawyer to decide which point the writ would actually specify. One could use a writ of entry to regain lands after the expiration of a lease or when the grant had been made while the grantor was underage or of unsound mind. It worked also against those who intruded themselves into the land after the death of a tenant who had held only for the term of his life and against those whose title originated in a disseisin. Women whose lands had been alienated by their husbands could reclaim them by a writ of entry after the husband's death, as could anyone whose lands had been granted by one who did not have a sufficient title to grant. Even those who had granted lands to another on the firm expectation that the grant would result in a marriage could use a writ of entry if that marriage did not then take place. In Felicia's case, the writ of entry specified that the Mortimer title was flawed because Robert and Joyce derived title ultimately from William de Whelton, who held Whilton only at the term of his life by virtue of a grant made by Nicholas de Whelton. That, of course, had been the description of the regrant made between Nicholas and William de Whelton when William returned to Whilton—assuming, of course, that Nicholas had gained valid seisin.

The form of a writ of entry depended not only on the wide choice among possible flaws in title but also on the description of the derivation of title. Writs of entry grew up cautiously out of the possessory writs of assize and the proprietary writs of right,[1] destroying what might have been a neat cleavage between possessory and proprietary actions. The caution with which they developed is best shown by the limitation of the writs, which persisted until 1267. This limitation originally had a rational base, but it came to be seen—and will be treated here—as prescribed by the mere form of the writ. Until 1267 the derivation of the title could extend no further than could be described with the use of the words *per* and *cui* ("by" and "to whom"). A lessor claiming directly from a lessee after a term had expired would not need to use either word to connect the present tenant with the claimant's line. A lessor claiming from the lessee's heir or assign would, however. Before 1267 Felicia could have sued only Roger de Whelton by a writ of entry, stating that he had no entry into Whilton except by (*per*) William de Whelton, to whom (*cui*) Nicholas her father had leased the land for a term that had expired. To sue William la Zouche or Joyce, Felicia would have needed another preposition, so that a writ of entry was not available. She would have had to resort to a writ of right, placing all her claim to Whilton on that one final verdict. In 1267, however, the Statute of Marlborough provided that writs of entry would be available also "in the *post*." Now Felicia could use a writ of entry specifying that Robert de Mortimer and Joyce had no entry into Whilton if not after (*post*) a lease, the term of which had now expired, that Nicholas her father made to William de Whelton. The Statute of Marlborough had opened up to people in Felicia's position that whole middle ground between possession and right which had been available for a half century or more to those who were suing parties closer to the point at which the defect in title had occurred.

The first writ of entry put forward by Felicia's guardian—a writ of entry in the *post* against Robert de Mortimer and Joyce for two-thirds of the manor of Whilton—was doomed from the start. Like all writs of entry, except for the few coming before an eyre, it initiated a case before the justices of the Court of Common Pleas; unlike the assizes of novel disseisin or mort d'ancestor, such cases were not meant to be heard in the countryside. The case came before the justices in January 1277, and the Mortimers immediately objected that Felicia was still underage. It was a longstanding and well-known rule of law that a minor could initiate only possessory actions. In 1277 Felicia was eleven or twelve years old; litigation by writ of entry and writ of right would have to wait until she reached the age of fourteen. Her guardian perhaps initiated the suit at this time to make it clear that Felicia had a recoverable right to Whilton. Only if other people believed that would the guardian be able to provide Felicia with a suitable husband. The husband or his father would have to pay the guardian in order to marry Felicia, of course, so that the guardian would be interested in asserting Felicia's claim at this time.

DOCUMENT 16
An Action of Entry: *Whelton* v *Mortimer*

Source: CP 40/18, m. 3d *Date*: circa 21 January 1277

Northamptonshire. Felicia daughter of Nicholas de Whelton seeks against Robert de Mortimer and Joyce his wife two-thirds of the manor of Whilton with appurtenances as her right by a writ of entry etc.

And Robert and Joyce by their attorney come and say that the abovesaid Felicia is underage. And he asks judgment if he ought to answer to such a writ until she attains majority.

And because the abovesaid Felicia is underage, this suit therefore remains without day until she does attain age etc.

*

The case was revived only in 1285, well after Felicia had gained her majority. The reason for the delay must be speculative. Her guardian had the right to determine whom she would marry and could exercise that right while she was underage and for up to two more years. During that period she was liable to severe penalties if she did not marry the guardian's nominated groom. There was only one condition: the marriage should not be a disparaging one. The designated spouse had to be at least of a similar rank or better. Although Felicia could claim easily enough to have a right to two-thirds of Whilton and thus to a very respectable spouse, such a spouse might be difficult to find, since her right might well come to nothing. It is possible, therefore, that her guardian could find no one suitable who was also willing to marry her or that Felicia herself, once she attained her majority, delayed bringing her suit until after the two-year deadline, so that her disadvantage as a prospective bride would continue until she could determine her own spouse. Had she recovered the land within the two-year deadline, a suitable spouse—one not of Felicia's choosing—would have been easy enough to find. Majority brought its own trials, however. She could now choose her own spouse, but she also had to provide for her own livelihood and legal expenses. She could, of course, have entered into an agreement with a lawyer whereby, if she won, he would receive a portion of Whilton, even though that kind of arrangement had been forbidden in 1275 by statute under the name of champerty. Apparently, however, she abided by the law. Perhaps she merely borrowed the money. It is, in brief, not known how Felicia paid for the suit she was able to bring finally in 1285.[2]

The case, when it was brought, came into the eyre of Northamptonshire, not into the Court of Common Pleas. An eyre was a special, omnicompetent session of the king's court designated to handle all kinds of cases for a single county for a limited period of time and to investigate royal officials and royal revenues in that county. While an eyre was in progress in a county, all the litigation in the central courts at Westminster from that county was adjourned into the eyre; furthermore, no new case from that county could be started in the central courts before the eyre had been completed. From the reign of Henry II, eyres had been considered so useful that an increasing number of responsibilities had been placed on justices in eyre. By 1285 eyres had become cumbersome and lengthy, and they would be completely discontinued after the four eyres in 1329-1331. On the whole, eyres were detested, because the close supervision by royal justices inevitably resulted in a multitude of amercements placed on individuals and on hundreds and the county as a whole. For Felicia herself, however, the eyre of Northamptonshire may have been a blessing. If she was short of money, the presence of the eyre in the county would at least have ameliorated the financial burden of litigating.

Felicia's writ was similar in its essentials to the one brought in 1277. She claimed once again the manor of Whilton as her right, excluding the one-third still held in dower and also fifty acres of cultivated land and nine acres of meadow. Named with Robert de Mortimer and Joyce were Nicholas de Lee and Alice his wife, who had been granted land in Warwickshire by Robert and Joyce and had subsequently been sued for that land. Robert and Joyce had properly warranted them, had lost the case, and, under the rules of warranty demanding compensation, had been obliged to grant them lands equivalent in value. Robert and Joyce had therefore granted them the specified lands in Whilton. Nicholas and his wife will reappear in later litigation, but for now they can be ignored. They merely vouched Robert and Joyce to warrant them once more; Robert and Joyce did so and thus assumed the burden for the whole claim. Felicia's writ was once again a writ of entry framed in the *post*, based on the grant for life said to have been made by Nicholas de Whelton to his father.

The pleading in the case immediately centered on the previous litigation. The Mortimers defended themselves by recounting the process of the assize and attaint and then by arguing that, since Nicholas's right to the land had already been discussed and dismissed by a verdict of twenty-four jurors, and since a judgment had been rendered on that verdict before the king himself, Felicia should not be able to make any use of Nicholas's supposed seisin of Whilton. Felicia countered by arguing that the part of the attaint concerning Nicholas was only incidental to the judgment and beyond the authority of the mandate that had initiated the case, which had only authorized discussion of her seisin. Furthermore, she argued that she had been unable to consent to such an examination anyway, because she had been underage. Clearly, the vital point in this case would be the binding power of the jury of attaint that had considered Felicia's father's title in order to discover whether she could have been seised through her father and thereafter disseised by the Mortimers.

The next stage in the pleading illustrates precisely the role of the justices. Felicia had not specifically contradicted the Mortimers, had not denied that there was a previous case of attaint or that it had annulled her father's seisin. Rather, she composed her own argument. It was the duty of the justices in this kind of case to rationalize the argument in court so that in a logical order each assertion was admitted or denied. In the process, of course, they determined some legal issues by overruling objections as legally invalid or by ruling that certain matters were more relevant to the case and thus to be answered first. By this judicially supervised argument the two sides were made to come to an irreducible and single point on which they disagreed and on which they were willing to have the case decided. If that point was a matter of law, the justices would have to decide it; if it was a matter of fact, the truth concerning that contested fact—and concerning that alone—would be asked of a jury of twelve men, who would be assembled only after the pleading had been completed. This jury, therefore, did not listen in court to pleading or to legal argument; it was merely assembled on a specific day to answer a specified question put to the jurors in advance. Until that question was known, however, it was the justices' duty to make the parties admit and deny in turn, interfering in the pleading minimally, acting as referees to facilitate the procedure when a problem arose about who should admit or deny what.

Felicia and the Mortimers had reached an impasse. The Mortimers maintained that Felicia's age during the attaint was not relevant. They thought the important legal issue was the repugnancy of allowing a jury of twelve men to reverse the verdict of an attaint that had been rendered by twenty-four men. Felicia maintained that her age at the time was vitally important, that no judgment made against her when she was a minor could now preclude her action. The justices agreed with Felicia and required the Mortimers to answer whether or not they would admit that she had been a minor at that time. The Mortimers steadfastly refused either to admit or to deny her minority, maintaining that her age was not the legally important issue. The justices, therefore, by the normal procedure that allowed them to break such a deadlock, held that the court considered the point to have been admitted. The pleading could therefore proceed. The Mortimers were required to alter their defense or lose the case.

The Mortimers were determined nevertheless to use the verdict and judgment that had been rendered in the attaint. They therefore denied specifically the basic point in Felicia's case: that Nicholas had held title when he granted Whilton back to his father for the term of his father's life. This, of course, was precisely the point Felicia wanted to have a jury decide. But the Mortimers did not aver—offer to verify and give proof for their denial—by jury trial. Instead, they offered averment by record, that is, by the record made of the case of attaint, which would be found in the plea rolls of the Court of King's Bench. The difference in their strategy was that they now were submitting to a new trial but using the attaint as the proof, whereas before they were maintaining that the legal action should be completely precluded. The record on which they wanted to rely, of course, would show that a jury of twenty-four had decided that Nicholas had never had seisin. The Mortimers also left themselves some room to maneuver; they allowed that they might consider another method of proof if the court decided that averment by record was not appropriate. Such a tactic put the problem squarely on the shoulders of the justices, so they adjourned the plea until 15 November 1285 in order to consider the proper course of action.

On that day the justices announced their decision: they agreed entirely with Felicia. They repeated, in essence, the arguments Felicia had used. The assize and the attaint had been concerned only with Felicia's own seisin. It would be improper, particularly since she had then been a minor, for her to lose whatever right might descend to her from her father because of such an assize and jury. Now, the Mortimers had not demurred on that point; they had not come to issue with Felicia on a point of law on which they wanted the whole case to be determined. The justices therefore ruled only that the issue suggested by the Mortimers should be proved by jury instead of by record. The question to be put to the jury, fundamentally, was whether or not Nicholas had been seised of Whilton in such a way that he could grant the manor to someone else. If he had been so seised, Felicia would recover, because she would have inherited the right to Whilton from Nicholas after the termination of William de Whelton's life estate. If he had not been so seised, the Mortimers would retain Whilton.

Proof by jury was never forced on litigants. The Mortimers still had a choice. They chose to stand by their argument and to refuse trial by jury. The conclusion of the case thus came very quickly, as the Mortimers would have expected. Since the only method of proof available to them was trial by jury, and since they refused it, they were essentially without a defense. Judgment was therefore given that Felicia recover Whilton and that Robert de Mortimer and Joyce be amerced. For the second time Felicia was to be restored to Whilton by judgment of the king's court.

The Mortimers were not put in a hopeless situation by that decision, and they firmly intended to challenge the justices' ruling. Processes of review were being expanded during the reign of Edward I. Attaint had been available for something less than a century on assize verdicts, and after 1275 it was also available, selectively, for normal jury verdicts, as, for example, might have been the result here had the Mortimers accepted trial by jury.[3] The Mortimers' complaint, however, was with a ruling made by the justices. The writ for reviewing this decision was not attaint but the milder writ of error. There were times, however, when serious problems arose in the process on a writ of error. The justices in the Court of King's Bench, before whom the case would come, would take the record written in the plea rolls of the justices in eyre at Northampton as the only precise account of the case. Only if the error alleged actually appeared in the plea roll could it be corrected. The plea roll record, however, was written by scribes in a normally conventional, stylized, and concise fashion. Most of the arguments rejected by the justices did not appear in the record. It would thus *not* have been abnormal, inefficient, or corrupt for the scribes merely to have entered Felicia's complaint, omitted all the argument made by the Mortimers, and noted only that they were undefended and that judgment was given for Felicia. In such a situation the Mortimers could not have challenged the justices' decision effectively: there would be no record of what they had said. The Statute of Westminster II, c. 31, enacted earlier that same year,[4*] provided a solution for that problem, and the Mortimers may well have been the first to employ the new procedure. They had drawn up, in precise and legal form, the challenge they had made, including the description of the attaint and its verdict and judgment, and their offer to aver the issue by record. This unofficial document was called a bill. The Mortimers submitted their bill to justice John de Vaux, who certified that it was an accurate account of what they had said by affixing his seal to the bill. That sealed bill could be used thereafter in a case of error. So soon after the statute, of course, the justices were somewhat sensitive to the matter and could be relied upon also to have their scribes include all that argument in the plea roll record. They in fact did so, and the scribes even included the full form of the bill of exception. The whole case, pleading and bill of exception, is contained in Document 17.

DOCUMENT 17
A Second Action of Entry: *Whelton* v *Mortimer*

Source: JUST 1/619, m. 39 *Date:* 1285

[Northamptonshire.] Felicia daughter of Nicholas de Whelton seeks against Robert de Mortimer and Joyce his wife two-thirds of the manor of Whilton with appurtenances except for fifty acres of land and nine acres of meadow in the same manor and against Nicholas de Lee and Alice his wife thirty acres of land and four acres of meadow with appurtenances in the same manor, in which the same Robert and Joyce, Nicholas and Alice do not have entry unless after a demise which Nicholas, son of William de Whelton and father of the abovesaid Felicia whose heir she is, made thereof to William de Whelton at a term which has expired, to wit, the term of the life of the same William etc.

And Robert and Joyce by the attorney of the same Joyce and Nicholas and Alice come. And Nicholas and Alice, for the tenements sought against them, vouch to warranty the abovesaid Robert and Joyce; and they warrant them. And both as to the tenements sought against them and as to the tenements they warrant to the abovesaid Nicholas and Alice, they deny her right when etc. And they say that they ought not to answer her thereof, because they say that the seisin of the abovesaid Nicholas, from whose seisin the abovesaid Felicia seeks the abovesaid tenements, was annulled by judgment of the court of the lord king. They also say that the same Felicia formerly in the court of the lord king before Geoffrey de Leukenore and John de Mettingham justices assigned at Northampton brought a certain assize of novel disseisin against them concerning those same tenements and recovered seisin thereof by recognition of that assize. And afterwards, before Ralph de Hengham and Walter de Hopton justices assigned to this, they arraigned a certain jury of twenty-four knights to convict the twelve jurors of the aforementioned assize. Before [that jury] they complained that the jury of the aforementioned assize made a false oath in that they said that the abovesaid Felicia was in seisin of the abovesaid tenements as of a free tenement by descent from the abovesaid Nicholas her father whose heir she is such that she could be disseised, whereas the same Felicia neither had nor could have any free tenement in those tenements, because she had nothing in those tenements except by an intrusion which she made in them by her guardians after the death of William la Zouche, father of the same Joyce whose heir she is, who died seised thereof in his demesne as of fee. And concerning this they sought the recognition of the twenty-four. And [Robert and Joyce] say that the same Felicia came before the same Ralph and Walter and answered them and said that the jury of the aforementioned assize made a good and legal oath, because she said that before the death of the abovesaid William la Zouche and afterwards she was in good and peaceful seisin of the same tenements as of her free tenement until the abovesaid Robert and Joyce unjustly [and without judgment] disseised her, and she asked that this be inquired by the jury. And [Robert and Joyce] say that the same Ralph and Walter, the reasons having been heard by turns, proceeded to the taking of the same jury.

Having heard the verdict of the same [jury], they adjourned the parties before the lord king and his council at three weeks after Michaelmas in the third year of his reign to hear their judgment thereof. At which day the parties came before the lord king himself. And [the court saw that] it had been found by the verdict of a jury of twenty-four that the abovesaid tenements at some time belonged to a certain William de Whelton who had two sons, to wit, a certain Roger firstborn and the abovesaid Nicholas born thereafter, between which certain William and Nicholas a certain agreement had been made that the same William would enfeoff the same Nicholas of these same tenements, but—whatever feoffment the abovesaid William made thereof to the abovesaid Nicholas—the same William never altered his estate but rather always continued his estate until the lord Henry, king, father of the present king, came with his army to Northampton. Whereupon [the court] proceeded before the lord king to the judgment that the estate of free tenement or fee which the abovesaid William was supposed to have made to the abovesaid Nicholas of the abovesaid tenements was null and that the jurors of the aforementioned assize made a false oath in this that they said that the abovesaid Felicia was in seisin of the abovesaid tenements as of a free tenement such that she could be disseised thereof, whereas the seisin which the abovesaid Felicia had in the same tenements after the death of the abovesaid William la Zouche yielded her no more free tenement than if a stranger had entered and that the same Robert and Joyce should recover their seisin and Felicia should be in mercy. And concerning this [Robert and Joyce] put themselves on the record of the rolls of the abovesaid Ralph and Walter. Wherefore, inasmuch as the seisin which the abovesaid Felicia says the abovesaid Nicholas her father, whose heir she is and from whose seisin she counts as of fee and right, had has been found null by the verdict of twenty-four and on this was annulled by judgment of the court of the lord king rendered in so solemn a place, which certain judgment has not been revoked as invalid but rather stands in its strength, [Robert and Joyce] seek judgment if they ought to answer her concerning such a seisin.

And Felicia says that the exception of the abovesaid Robert and Joyce ought not harm her, because she says that at the time of the taking of the abovesaid assize and similarly at the time when the abovesaid jury of twenty-four to convict [the twelve etc.] was taken, whereby the same Robert and Joyce recovered their seisin of the abovesaid tenements against her, she was underage. And this she is prepared to verify by the countryside [i.e., a jury]. Because, she says, although the jury of twenty-four etc. had been examined by the justices before whom the jury was taken concerning the seisin of the abovesaid Nicholas her father, this ought not harm her, because this was outside the articles of the writ and from the office of the justices. Nor could she have consented to an examination of this kind concerning the seisin of her father, because she was underage. Wherefore, inasmuch as the abovesaid jury was arraigned to convict the jury of the aforementioned assize and to affirm or annul her seisin which she obtained by the verdict of the same assize, she asks judgment if by an examination which was made by the justices on the seisin of her father from the office of the court and in which certain examination she could not put herself by reason of her minority, which she is prepared to verify as has been said above, she ought to be excluded from relying on the seisin of her father.

And Robert and Joyce, asked by the justices if they want to admit that verification which the abovesaid Felicia offers that she was underage at the time of the taking of the abovesaid jury, say that it does not seem necessary to them. They say that, whether or not that Felicia was underage at the abovesaid time, her father's seisin was annulled judicially as has been said. And this they are ready to verify as before. They also say that, if the same Felicia is allowed to claim from the seisin of her father notwithstanding their abovesaid reasons, it would be contrary to law, because thus it would follow that the abovesaid verdict of the jury of twenty-four etc. and the judgment rendered on that verdict might be annulled by a simple jury of the countryside, because the action of the same Felicia, if it is admitted, would have its termination by a simple jury of the countryside. Whereof, they ask judgment etc.

And Felicia says that the reasons of the same Robert and Joyce conclude on her father's seisin. [But] concerning his seisin etc., no question had ever been moved. Wherefore, if anything was examined from the office of the justices by a third party and outside the articles of the writ on the same seisin as has been said above, it ought not become prejudicial to her, because at the time of the taking of the same jury she was underage. She seeks judgment etc.

And because the abovesaid Robert and Joyce did not want to admit that verification which the same Felicia offers concerning her minority, this court here takes that point as conceded. And because the abovesaid Felicia was underage at the time at which the abovesaid jury of twenty-four was taken and examined on the seisin of the same Felicia and neither the assize nor the abovesaid jury had been arraigned concerning that seisin, it is considered that the abovesaid Robert and Joyce answer further to the seisin which the same Felicia said the abovesaid Nicholas her father had, if it seem to them expedient etc.

And Robert and Joyce deny the same Felicia's right. And they well deny that the abovesaid Nicholas was ever in seisin of the abovesaid tenements such that he could sell those tenements to another. And concerning this they put themselves on the record of the abovesaid rolls. And should the court consider that they ought not to verify in that way, they are prepared to verify that in another way as the court shall have considered etc.

Day is given to hear their judgment here on the Thursday after the feast of St. Martin [15 November 1285].

At that day the parties come. And because the abovesaid assize had been arraigned on the seisin of the abovesaid Felicia, by which she recovered her seisin of the abovesaid tenements with appurtenances and afterwards the abovesaid Robert and Joyce arraigned the abovesaid jury of twenty-four to convict the jury of the same assize concerning a false oath and to annul only the seisin of the abovesaid Felicia, by which jury the abovesaid Robert and Joyce recovered such seisin as they had before the taking of the abovesaid assize and because it is not consonant with justice that the right of the abovesaid Felicia which might accrue to her from the seisin of her ancestor be annulled either by the abovesaid assize or by the abovesaid jury arraigned and taken on the same seisin, particularly since the abovesaid Felicia at the time of the taking of the abovesaid assize and jury was underage, it is considered, notwithstanding the abovesaid judgment on the aforementioned jury taken only to annul the seisin of the abovesaid Felicia and to convict the jury of the aforementioned assize of a false oath as has been said above, that the court should proceed to a jury of the countryside to inquire whether or not the abovesaid Nicholas, father of the abovesaid Felicia whose heir she is and from whose seisin she counts as of fee and right, was ever seised of the abovesaid tenements with appurtenances such that he could demise them to another, if the abovesaid Robert and Joyce want to admit [this verification] etc.

And the same Robert and Joyce say that the seisin of the abovesaid Nicholas had been judicially annulled. And this they are prepared to verify by the abovesaid record which still stands in its strength. [Thus] they do not want to admit any verification by the countryside, because that would be contrary to the law, because from this it would follow that a judgment of the court of the lord king might be annulled by a jury of the countryside.

And the abovesaid Felicia asks judgment concerning the abovesaid Robert and Joyce precisely as of ones undefended, because they do not want to admit the abovesaid verification which she tenders.

And therefore it is considered that the abovesaid Felicia recover her seisin against the abovesaid Robert and Joyce as against ones undefended, and let Robert and Joyce be in mercy etc.

And therefore the same Robert and Joyce tender a certain

bill and ask that it be signed and handed to them, which bill they tender in these words:

> "And Robert and Joyce say that they formerly at Northampton on the Sunday on the octaves of St. Michael in the third year of the reign of the present king [6 October 1275] in the court of the same lord king before Ralph de Hengham and Walter de Hopton, justices assigned to this, brought a certain jury of twenty-four concerning the same tenements against the abovesaid Felicia. And they said that the jury of a certain assize of novel disseisin which was summoned and taken thereof in the court of the lord king at Northampton before Geoffrey de Leukenore and John de Mettingham between the abovesaid Felicia and the abovesaid Robert and Joyce made a false oath in that they said that the abovesaid Felicia had been disseised of her free tenement, whereas she neither had nor was able to have any free tenement in the abovesaid tenements. And Felicia responded to this before the abovesaid Ralph de Hengham and Walter de Hopton that the jury of that assize made a good and legal oath, because she said that a certain Nicholas her father, whose heir she is, was seised of the abovesaid tenements in his demesne as of fee and sold that same tenement to a certain William de Whelton to hold for the term of his life from the abovesaid Nicholas and his heirs and she was in good and peaceful seisin after the death of the abovesaid William de Whelton as daughter and heir of the abovesaid Nicholas by the form of his abovesaid feoffment until the abovesaid Robert and Joyce unjustly [and without judgment] disseised her; and concerning this she put herself on the jury. And the abovesaid Robert and Joyce similarly. By which certain jury it was found that the abovesaid tenements were the right and inheritance of a certain William de Whelton, which certain William wanted the advancement of the abovesaid Nicholas, father of the abovesaid Felicia, and made a certain seisin of the above-

said tenements over to the abovesaid Nicholas. And the abovesaid William, father of the abovesaid Nicholas, neither removed his goods from there nor ever changed his estate such that the abovesaid Nicholas had any seisin in the abovesaid tenements such that he could enfeoff the abovesaid William or anyone else thereof. On account of which, it was considered before the lord king and his council that the abovesaid Robert and Joyce should recover their seisin, and that the abovesaid Felicia should be in mercy. And inasmuch as formerly it was found by the abovesaid jury that the abovesaid Nicholas, father of the abovesaid Felicia whose heir she is and from whose seisin she now seeks, had no seisin in the abovesaid tenements such that he could enfeoff the abovesaid William or anyone else thereof, they ask judgment if they ought now to respond to this writ concerning the seisin of the abovesaid Nicholas, particularly since the abovesaid Felicia was present and party in the plea of the abovesaid jury before the lord king and his council, which certain judgment was never afterwards annulled but rather still stands in its strength. And this they are prepared to verify by the abovesaid record, and it seems to them that they ought not verify in any other way than by the abovesaid record. And on this they ask judgment as before etc."

And the abovesaid bill is delivered to them signed by the seal of John de Vaux etc.

*

The Mortimers, in losing this case of entry, had certainly lost a battle, but they fully intended to win the war.

This case of entry had a broader interest than is apparent from an examination of the plea roll record; the case was also reported. Yearbook reports of cases, completely distinct from plea roll records, had no official standing and were neither made nor preserved by the court. Rather, the reports were written by lawyers, presumably apprentice lawyers, as part of their training while they were present in court. Since these apprentices were interested only in the law and not in the personal concerns of the litigants, their reports were often careless about names of people and places and about the verdict rendered by the jury. For them, a jury verdict had little interesting legal significance; the proper legal strategy and the law determining it had all been laid out during pleading. As it happens, the two reports of this case correctly give the names and other relevant information, even though one lists John de Mettingham and the other William de Saham as the justice most involved with presiding over the pleading. Both justices were among the five sitting in eyre at Northampton. Since the earliest yearbook reports date from the 1270s, these are very early examples; in fact, they are almost the earliest reports to come from an eyre instead of from the Court of Common Pleas. Finally, reports contain material that is not recorded in the plea rolls. Lawyers, of course, would want to know which arguments had not worked, whereas the court scribes wanted to preserve only those pleas that had led to the issue that would be put before the jury. These reports, therefore, offer an informal and wholly different perspective on what was happening in court. The substantive difference between records and reports can thus be very great, though in this instance it is not.

The reports show that professional pleaders and not the parties themselves were responsible for the legal argument in court. It is convenient to say—as I have done until now—that the Mortimers defended themselves or put forward a certain legal argument; indeed, that is the way the plea roll records read. Nevertheless, the parties themselves almost never said anything in court. They left the legal business to their lawyers, of whom there were two distinct kinds: attorneys and pleaders. Attorneys stood precisely in their clients' stead and were legally equivalent to the parties themselves; they could make admissions and win or lose the case even in the absence of their clients. The pleader, on the other hand, was legally absolutely distinct from the client. Historically, the function of speaking on behalf of another derived from the duty of the lord to defend his man—to speak up, stand beside, and defend him when he needed aid. In Felicia's time that active duty had long since given way to the legal doctrines that had grown up around it and preserved it as a legal necessity. Courts had developed a very rigorous idea that anything a person—and therefore anything a person's attorney—said in court was binding on him, both in form and in substance. If the party or his attorney made a minor error in form—an error very easily made, given the formalism of early courts—he could lose his whole case. Therefore, a pleader did all the speaking. When the pleader had made the appropriate statement, he would be "avowed" by the client or by the client's attorney; that is, the statement would be accepted by the client as precisely what he wanted to say. A pleader was not often avowed during a case, perhaps only after the initial formal statement of the plaintiff's case and then again when an issue had been derived and was going to be submitted to justices or jurors. In between, the pleaders tested each other, striving to gain the maximum advantage for their clients, setting up every possible defense, challenging any flaw in form or process that might be to their benefit. Pleaders in the king's court tended to be men at the very top of the legal profession, so that they were well able to argue law before the justices. In this case the main pleaders were Gilbert de Thornton and William de Kellaway. Little is known about Kellaway, but Thornton would be elevated to the position of chief justice of the Court of King's Bench only five years after this case, replacing Ralph de Hengham, who was found guilty of corruption.

Yearbook reports held the same fascination for medieval English lawyers as do the games of chess masters for chess enthusiasts today. It was an opportunity to see how the real experts in the profession handled difficult situations and to compare their tactics. Moreover, the reports constituted something like a professional journal, providing every lawyer with material he might find useful in his own practice. The first report of this case is an excellent example of crisp analysis, albeit in dialogue form. It presents concisely the most important argument in this case—the binding effect of a case of attaint passed against a minor when the minor eventually reaches majority and brings a writ of entry—while noting by mention of the bill of exception that the decision might be reversed.

DOCUMENT 18

Report No. 1: *Whelton* v *Mortimer*

Source: Bodleian Library, Douce 139, fol. 188v *Date*: 1285

Felicia de Whelton brought her writ of entry against Sir Robert de Mortimer and Joyce his wife concerning the manor of Whilton and said that they had no entry except by William de Whelton, to whom Nicholas sold it at a term which has expired.

Sir Robert and Joyce deny wrong and force etc. "And we tell you that at another time there was an assize arraigned concerning the same tenements by this same Felicia, whereby she recovered. And this Robert and Joyce complained of this and brought the attaint before the council of our lord the king, by which jury of twenty-four it was found that the assize had made a false oath, wherefore it was commanded that Sir Robert recover his estate and his seisin. And inasmuch as this Felicia was party to this jury and was present and this judgment stands in its strength and is not annulled, we ask judgment if we ought to answer."

GILBERT DE THORNTON. "Sir, we tell you that when this attaint passed this Felicia was underage. Wherefore we ask judgment if, from this matter done while she was underage, she ought to be harmed and made unanswerable."

WILLIAM DE KELLAWAY. "And we ask judgment, inasmuch as [Nicholas's] estate whereby he was able to make a lease was found null by the twenty-four jurors and this Felicia was party and amerced, whether she is answerable."

GILBERT DE THORNTON. "Sir, whether they say that she was amerced or not, or party or not, we are ready to aver that she was underage when this jury passed."

WILLIAM DE SAHAM [justice]. "What do you respond to this averment that they tender you?"

WILLIAM DE KELLAWAY. "Sir, we tell you that the attaint was in the court of the king before his council, where Felicia was party and was amerced by the twenty-four jurors because Nicholas had no estate. And inasmuch as this judgment still stands in its force and we are ready to aver this by rolls and by record, we ask judgment if they can come to an averment by the countryside inasmuch as we tender a higher averment than that—the record of the council of the king—because, if they have an averment of the countryside, this would only be to reverse the verdict of a jury of twenty-four by an inquest of twelve, which seems to us the reverse order."

WILLIAM DE SAHAM [justice]. "Do you want this averment which Felicia tenders you that she was underage when the jury passed or not?"

And Sir [Robert's attorney] answers, "Sir, I pray the averment of the rolls of the king and his council, and I do not want anything else."

WILLIAM DE SAHAM [justice]. "And because Felicia tenders you an averment that she was underage when the attaint passed and tenders it by a good jury and we have asked you if you want to receive this averment and you wholly refuse, so this court considers that Felicia recover her seisin of this manor against Sir Robert and Joyce as against ones undefended; and let Robert and Joyce be in mercy."

And they put forward their exception written down, and they had it sealed by the seal of the chief justice.

*

In this way, then, the apprentice lawyer reported all of the case that was interesting to him.

The second report, by a different apprentice lawyer, is not

as concise as the first, but it shows much better the way lawyers thought and argued. It is obvious from both reports that precedent played no role in their argument. Nor, indeed, did the lawyers argue in abstract principles concerning justice or natural law or social policy. The whole discussion here, as in other medieval reports, is mired down in technicalities—procedure, methods of proof, the analysis of the relationships of one kind of litigation to another. English law was already such a mass of technicality and different modes of litigation that lawyers seldom raised their thoughts to clearly stated abstract principles: such would have had little relevance. Their worry was in reasoning correctly about what the law was, not what they should make it. Since there was no codification of the law and neither a body of finely reasoned precedents nor a mystique that would give one justice's mistake an aura that could bind his successors, they relied heavily on analogy to make sure their course in a current case was congruent with the law as a whole.

This absorption with the system is best shown in the second report by the arguments that Justice Mettingham used to prove to Mortimer's pleader that he was wrong. Every time Mettingham spoke at length, he reasoned from analogy, not from principle. In his first speech he put the case of a person who litigates to gain the wardship of a minor in which both a normal jury and a jury of attaint in turn return a verdict for him to the effect that he or his ancestors had been in possession of such services from the child's parents as would properly make him lord and therefore guardian. Mettingham then asked whether the guardian could thereafter use those verdicts instead of a new jury against the child after the child reached majority and denied owing him those services. The answer, obvious to any medieval lawyer, was that the child had not been involved in those verdicts and therefore could not be bound by them. Mortimer's second pleader then objected that the two situations were not really analogous. His reasoning was based ultimately on a seemingly major difference between the hypothetical case and the case involving Felicia: in the suit for wardship the child was merely the subject in contention between the two other parties; in Felicia's case, the child herself was involved as plaintiff. Mettingham proved his point nevertheless by noting that in certain situations a minor on reaching his majority would be able to defeat a previous assize with another assize, because the law had to presume that there could be collusion between the guardian, who was in complete control of the child, and the opponent. This was a very technical but also a very good argument to show that the Mortimers could not bar Felicia from a new jury by record of the attaint verdict. The other arguments recorded in the second report of the case are similarly technical but not impossible to follow. Mettingham, like others of his profession, was at his best when showing what must happen in one case by drawing a parallel instance in a different form of action. Any problem could best be solved by looking to its analogue, as if the law were a seamless web or an endless chain of congruent circles.

DOCUMENT 19

Report No. 2: *Whelton* v *Mortimer*

Source: British Library, Additional MS 31826, fol. 67v *Date*: 1285

[Two changes have been made in this document to aid the reader. The different phases of the argument have been artificially separated by an asterisk, and the pleader's client and the designations "C" for "claimant" or "T" for "tenant" have been inserted after each pleader's name.]

Felicia de Whelton brings a writ of entry against Robert de Mortimer and Joyce his wife concerning two-thirds of the manor of Whilton except etc., and says that they do not have entry unless after the lease which Nicholas de Whelton father of the abovesaid Felicia whose heir she is made thereof to William de Whelton at a term which has expired, after which term it ought to revert to her.

KELLAWAY (for Robert and Joyce) [Mortimer, T]. "Sir, she herself brought a writ of novel disseisin against them before Sir Geoffrey de Leukenore and John de Mettingham, and the assize passed for Felicia. And afterwards Robert and Joyce recovered their first estate. And we ask judgment if she can resort to seek from a higher seisin than that from which she sought before."

THORNTON [Felicia, C]. "Sir, she can seek from a higher seisin and not otherwise, as to seek from a lower seisin than before."

*

KELLAWAY [Mortimer, T]. "Sir, in the writ of novel disseisin she said that Nicholas her father leased this land to William for the term of his life such that she entered as Nicholas's daughter and heir after William's death. And by this title she claimed a free tenement. And Robert and Joyce his wife said that this was William's inheritance and that Nicholas never had a free estate whereby he could make a lease, but rather that William always continued his first estate and died seised as of fee and of right and that Felicia's entry was an abatement without title. On that the assize passed and said that she did have a free tenement. Therefore Robert and Joyce purchased an attaint. The attaint was taken and charged on the same matters as the assize had been, to wit, if she entered by abatement. Wherefore, we ask judgment if she can have an action against such a verdict, since her father's seisin has been defeated by the oath of twenty-four."

THORNTON [Felicia, C]. "Sir, the verdict—whether of twenty-four or of twelve—is only an assize. And such a verdict concerns solely the free tenement. And, even if the justices make a preparation to the assize concerning the title in the right, such a preparation is only incidental to judgment, because their verdict is only that of an assize. And we ask judgment that we can claim from the seisin of our ancestor, which is higher as of fee and of right, even though the assize said beyond the verdict of an assize what it ought not have said and even though we lost the free tenement by this verdict."

KELLAWAY [Mortimer, T]. "This was not an incident to the judgment. Rather, it was part of the plea, because we pleaded on the title. [This is so,] because in a writ of [novel] disseisin one can plead the right just as we did."

*

THORNTON [Felicia, C]. "Even were it true that in such a writ one could plead about the right, this would be no injury to Felicia, because she was then a minor."

KELLAWAY [Mortimer, T]. "Felicia's title was Nicholas's seisin, and we pleaded on that seisin. That seisin was found null by the twenty-four. And since no inquest can pass on what the twenty-four have said, we ask judgment if she can have an action concerning the seisin which was defeated by them."

METTINGHAM [justice]. "Suppose that you seek the wardship of a child and you are counterpleaded that neither you nor your ancestors were ever seised of royal service. And then you go to an inquest, which returns a verdict for you. And then an attaint is purchased against you for the child. And that attaint passes for you again, and thus the ward remains with you. Then [finally] the child comes of age, and thus he obtains his lands. And, before royal service runs whereby you have the writ of the king to levy services, you make a distraint. And he brings his writ, and the distraint is returned to him. You then plead and avow that the distraint was good, because it was made for royal service. And he answers you that you were never seised so that you could make a distraint. And you say that he cannot get to this response, because formerly an inquest passed on this between you and him and afterwards also an attaint, and both passed against him. And he answers you that this ought not harm him, because he was then underage. Do you think that the court will receive this averment or not?"

Thornton [Felicia, C] said that the child's averment ought to be received.

METTINGHAM [justice]. "Correct."

IDLE [Mortimer, T]. "Sir, it is not analogous, because thus

it would ensue that if one brought a writ of mort d'ancestor against an underage child and recovered against him, he could defeat that recovery when he came of age."

METTINGHAM [justice]. "I tell you indeed that if you bring a writ of mort d'ancestor against an underage child and the assize be taken on his default and pass against him, he will have his recovery when he comes of age. And this recovery will be by a writ of mort d'ancestor. And likewise I tell you that, if an underage child bring a writ of novel disseisin, he will not have license to seek a better writ. Rather, it is appropriate that the assize pass or that the writ be found vicious. And the reason for this is that there might be collusion between the tenant and the guardian."

*

KELLAWAY [Mortimer, T]. "Sir, the judgment which was so rendered on the attaint was rendered before the king himself. And since the attaint and the judgment took place in so solemn a place—which judgment is still in force and which judgment could be repealed were there error—we ask judgment precisely if she can have an action by this writ against such a judgment."

THORNTON [Felicia, C]. "If you want to say that Felicia was a party to this judgment, it behoves you to say that she was of age."

KELLAWAY [Mortimer, T]. "Grant the judgment and afterwards say that this ought not harm her because she was underage, and after you grant the judgment we will answer concerning the minority."

THORNTON [Felicia, C]. "An underage child does not know what a judgment is; therefore she can neither acknowledge nor grant such a judgment."

KELLAWAY [Mortimer, T]. "When she pleaded, she herself was present before the king and was amerced. Wherefore, she indeed knows how to grant the judgment."

METTINGHAM [justice]. "If by her presence she was able to plead, by the same token she could make an attorney, but she could not plead in her own proper person because of the delicacy of her minority. And because of this the king's court will give her a guardian, but she ought not acknowledge the one made her guardian. Therefore, we tell you to answer whether she was a minor or not."

KELLAWAY [Mortimer, T]. "If you adjudge that what she did while she was minor ought not injure her, we will answer further."

Mettingham said that it would not.

*

KELLAWAY [Mortimer, T]. "Then we will answer that Nicholas was never seised such that he could make a lease. And we are ready to aver that by whatever method you adjudge is appropriate after the verdict of an attaint; or we are ready to aver by record that such was the verdict of the attaint, if you adjudge that."

Day was given them to hear their judgment.

*

At that day Robert and Joyce said, "Nicholas was not seised, and this was found by the oath of twenty-four before the king. And, since the seisin was found null by their oath in so solemn a place, we ask judgment if any other averment than averment by record is appropriate."

THORNTON [Felicia, C]. "This matter was alleged previously, and you were ousted from it by adjudgment of minority. Therefore, you cannot now resort to it."

IDLE [Mortimer, T]. "That which we say now we said before in the form of an exception; now we say it as a response. Thus it will work for us as a response even if it was worthless as an exception."

METTINGHAM [justice]. "It will be worth no more now as a response than it was before as an exception, because of the minority. And I will show you further. Suppose an underage child brings a writ of novel disseisin, and the assize passes against him. He then brings an attaint on this and says that those on the assize made a false oath because his ancestor died seised in his demesne as of fee and that he entered as son and heir, and the attaint says that he had no free tenement and that his ancestor did not die seised in his demesne etc. When he comes of age, will he not have an action by a writ of mort d'ancestor? Certainly he will. In the same way in this case, that which she did while she was underage ought not harm her now. And, whereas you tendered averment by record or by the countryside or in another manner, it seems to us that averment by the countryside is appropriate."

*

KELLAWAY [Mortimer, T]. "Say first by your award that averment by record is not appropriate."

LOVEDAY [justice]. "The party tenders you an averment by the countryside. Do you want it or not?"

KELLAWAY [Mortimer, T]. "We ask as before. And we ask the attorney if he wants the averment by the countryside."

And the attorney says that he wants averment by record.

LOVEDAY [justice]. "Felicia demands against Robert de Mortimer and Joyce his wife two-thirds of the manor of Whilton etc. from the seisin of Nicholas her father. Robert and Joyce respond to her action that Nicholas was not seised, and concerning this they tender averment by record of the [verdict of the] twenty-four which was taken formerly while Felicia was underage—and the minority is granted by the recognition of Robert and Joyce—and Felicia tenders averment by the countryside. And the law does not bar one from an action because of a thing done while a minor. Wherefore, the verdict of the abovesaid twenty-four is no bar to Felicia. And Robert and Joyce refuse the averment of the countryside. Therefore the court considers that Robert and Joyce are undefended, that Felicia recover her seisin, and that Robert and Joyce his wife be in mercy."

*

Document 19 offers an excellent example of the kind of argument that became so mired down in recondite knowledge of technicality that reports of such proceedings often remain difficult even for those who have spent a lifetime working on them. But it is also this kind of argument that makes the reports so valuable, both for understanding the law itself and for understanding the individuals who worked with and used the law. These two reports (Documents 18 and 19), together with the official record (Document 17), provide different but essentially similar accounts of the proceedings on Felicia's writ of entry.

The Mortimers, by having the justice seal their bill of exception, had made clear their intention to challenge the justices' decision not to allow the use of the attaint verdict as a bar to Felicia's recovery of Whilton by the writ of entry. As soon as possible after the judgment had been given—that is, in January 1286—they were pressing their claim for redress. They initiated their claim by a writ of *certiorari* in the Court of King's Bench. *Certiorari* was and today still is part of the process for review of judgments. The review took place in early February and justified the Mortimers' expectations.

DOCUMENT 20

Certiorari: Mortimer v *Whelton*

Source: KB 27/96, mm. 19, 19d *Date*: circa 11 February 1286

Northamptonshire. The lord king ordered his beloved and faithful John de Vaux and his companions, justices itinerant late at Northampton, that, because for some certain reasons he wanted to be certified about the record and process of a suit recently held before them between Felicia de Whelton claimant and Robert de Mortimer and Joyce his wife concerning two parts of the manor of Whilton with appurtenances except fifty acres of land and nine acres of meadow in the same manor, they send to the king the record and process of the abovesaid suit with all corroborative evidences touching that suit here at this day. Which certain justices sent the record in these words.

[There follows a transcript of Document 17.]

Afterwards, before the lord king on the octaves of the Purification of blessed Mary in the fourteenth year of the reign of King Edward son of King Henry in the presence of the parties, after the abovesaid record and process had been read and heard and at the complaint of the abovesaid Robert and Joyce—who had complained that inasmuch as they vouched the rolls to warrant that the seisin of Nicholas the father of the abovesaid Felicia had been annulled by judgment, on whose seisin she counted against them, the justices before whom the suit had been handled less correctly and against the form of right had adjudged them as undefended, because they persisted in their voucher to warranty—the suit was examined by the justices of both benches and certain others. The reasons of certain of the justices who were present at that judgment were heard. Those reasons were thought about, and reasons on the other side were proposed. It then seemed that the abovesaid justices had less correctly proceeded to judgment before inspection of the record which the abovesaid Robert and Joyce vouched at their peril. Wherefore, it was considered that the abovesaid Robert and Joyce have back their seisin such as they had before the abovesaid justices adjudged seisin thereof to the abovesaid Felicia and that the abovesaid Robert and Joyce be quit of the mercy at which they were amerced. And the right of the abovesaid Felicia to prosecute her right, if she has any, by the original writ whereby the plea was moved between them or otherwise as it shall seem expedient to her shall be saved. And because the abovesaid Felicia married a certain Philip de Montgomery after she purchased her original writ, she sought license to withdraw from her writ and had license.

*

The writ of *certiorari* was designed to review decisions made by justices. In this case the Mortimers were fortified with their bill of exception, which evidenced their pleading, even though the justices in this instance had taken care that all the relevant material appeared also in the official court record.

After reviewing the record, the wide assembly of justices showed some understanding for both sides and gave a narrow holding in favor of the Mortimers. The justices' decision was not, as might at first seem, that the Mortimers could use the attaint verdict as a bar to Felicia's claim. Rather, they held only that the justices had been incorrect in not at least examining the record that had been vouched before going to judgment. Perhaps the impression was also strongly conveyed that such an attaint judgment would not be a bar, for when the case was reconvened, the Mortimers did not refer to the attaint judgment but rather put themselves on a jury. The effect of the *certiorari* in this case was to restore the parties to the standing each had had prior to the rendering of the judgment.

Nevertheless, the justices could not completely recreate the situation of 1285, for Felicia's personal position had changed radically since then. It was probably late in 1285 that Felicia married Philip de Montgomery. Philip was the king's hereditary steward of the forest of Cannock in Staffordshire, and he also held some lands in Lincolnshire.[5] He probably considered the marriage something of a gamble. If Felicia retained Whilton, his marriage would have properly improved his standing. If Whilton were lost, Felicia's position in Sussex would prevent his choice from being an unmitigated disaster. It is even possible, although one doubts such a thing, that Philip married Felicia without regard for her possibilities. Felicia, for her part, probably found in Philip a man of quite acceptable position. He was not a baron, but he was solidly positioned in Staffordshire. It remained true, however, that Joyce's marriage to Mortimer secured an advocate of higher standing and greater importance than Felicia had managed to gain in Philip. By this marriage, nonetheless, Felicia was in a better position, with greater resources and more influence, to defend her right. Thus, when the case was renewed, probably around May 1286, the claimants were Philip de Montgomery and Felicia his wife.

There are two different records of the ensuing trial. The

jury verdict recorded in both is almost identical. But there are other differences in the two accounts, and those differences are of some importance. The record in the plea rolls would make it seem that Philip and Felicia purchased another writ, that the Mortimers then appeared docilely and put themselves on a jury, and that the case was of no particular importance or difficulty.[6*] This record is almost certainly the product of the way in which scribes of the Court of Common Pleas reshaped the events into the form with which they were familiar. The other document, produced below as Document 21, describes the case as an assize. The case was most assuredly not a possessory assize; it had been begun by a new writ of entry. Yet it must have seemed like an assize, for the question to be put before the jury was known when the case started. It was probably known even at the end of the argument on the *certiorari*. The justices then had given a very narrow holding and probably also demanded that the Mortimers simply put themselves on a jury on the issue that had been settled previously at Northampton or else lose. There was thus probably no further pleading. Likewise, the second account shows that the case was being watched very carefully. It first appeared in June 1286. When the jury was supposed to appear in January 1287, all four justices of the Court of Common Pleas, the chief justice of the Court of King's Bench, all the Barons of the Exchequer, the Chancellor, and the Treasurer gathered together to preside over the taking of the verdict. The case was sufficiently difficult to command the attention of all the important royal judicial officials.

That judicial attention demanded that the jurors make the long trek to Westminster, there to be empaneled and to render their verdict. It was becoming normal, particularly after the Statute of Westminster II in 1285, for juries to be taken by *nisi prius* procedure. That procedure allowed a justice to tour the countryside, empanel the jury there, and take their verdict. The verdict would thereafter be returned to Westminster, and the judgment on the verdict would be given there in the central court. *Nisi prius* procedure was easier for the jurors, but it produced a spatial as well as a temporal distance between pleading and trial and between trial and judgment. In this case the justices wanted to oversee the process at the trial itself. Perhaps the Mortimers asked specially for this attention. They may have thought that jurors would be less likely to succumb to illicit pressure—or be more susceptible to the evidence the Mortimers brought concerning the previous cases—if they had to take their oath before such an assemblage of judicial majesty. They were mistaken.

The jury was finally assembled at Westminster in January 1287, more than two decades after the transaction between William de Whelton and his son Nicholas. One can well doubt that they knew anything about a transaction that had taken place so long before and about which so many contradictory things had been said. As the Mortimers had feared, this jury returned a verdict for Felicia. They decided that Nicholas had indeed done all those acts which previous justices had said were proper acts for establishing seisin and which previous jurors had specifically denied Nicholas had done. The jurors either recited very carefully the story as Felicia was now presenting it or else they willingly reshaped the facts in their verdict to obtain from the justices what they considered the proper judgment. They succeeded. Felicia and her new husband gained possession of the land and also the opportunity at least to figure out some way to safeguard it against the Mortimers, who, they must have feared, would now proceed to litigate by writ of right, the highest and final level of litigation.

DOCUMENT 21

The Action of Entry: *Montgomery* v *Mortimer*

Source: British Library, Additional MS 31826, fol. 161v

Date: January 1287

An assize taken at Westminster before Thomas de Wayland, John Lovetot, Ellis de Beckingham, Roger de Leicester, justices of the Bench; and before John de Kirkby, Treasurer; and before William de Hamilton, Chancellor of England; and before Ralph de Hengham, justice of the lord king; and all Barons of the Exchequer of the lord king on the Thursday on the morrow of St. Vincent in the fifteenth year of the reign of King Edward [23 January 1287] concerning two-thirds of the manor of Whilton by these jurors written below: A., B., etc.

Afterwards, on the octaves of St. Hilary in the fifteenth year of the reign of King Edward came the jurors, who say on their oath that the abovesaid William de Whelton enfeoffed Nicholas his son of the abovesaid tenements by his deed of feoffment which he made to him thereof. And he put him in full seisin. By that feoffment he was in good and peaceful seisin for fifteen days. And he cut down trees, fished in the fishponds, and marled the lands and took the fealty of his free tenants and villeins. And he took recognition of a half mark and more. And he removed the reeve and bailiffs at his will. Therefore they say that the abovesaid Nicholas was seised thereof as of fee and right.

Therefore it is considered that the abovesaid Philip and Felicia recover their seisin thereof and that Robert and Joyce be in mercy etc.

And let it be known that the abovesaid Robert and Joyce by their attorney challenged that more than twenty-four are placed in the writ of judgment against the form [of the statute].

*

The Mortimers' intention still to make every effort to reclaim Whilton was shown by the notation at the very end of the record. The Statute of Westminster II, c. 38, had provided that no more than twenty-four people should be summoned to make up an assize (and therefore any jury?) of twelve, because a sheriff could do that merely to harass his enemies. Yet more than twenty-four people had in fact been summoned, so the Mortimers made their complaint on the slight possibility—a possibility that did not materialize—that it might turn to their advantage. The dispute, obviously, would continue.

Further litigation, however, was necessarily delayed. After about fifteen years of marriage, Robert de Mortimer died, probably in February or March 1287, soon after the loss of Whilton to the Montgomerys.[7] Then from July to October 1287 Joyce could not sue the Montgomerys, because Philip was in Wales fighting for the king and therefore temporarily safeguarded from such litigation.[8] In the meantime, however, she could attend to securing her dower: a life estate in one-third of all the tenements of which her husband had been seised heritably at any time during the marriage. In July and November 1287 the king, as guardian of Hugh, who would stand as the lord from whom Joyce held her dower, allotted her the appropriate dower from the lands of which Robert de Mortimer had died seised. That amounted to two manors worth almost £50 yearly and the lordship of almost twelve knights' fees, from which she would derive income as from rents, wardships, marriage rights, relief, and so forth. She then sought her dower from those lands of which Robert had not died seised. Regarding such lands, I noticed only a suit for her one-third of two manors; that matter was apparently settled in January 1288. The current tenants of those lands were recompensed from the lands of the heir, Hugh. In addition, she retained all the tenements she had by inheritance; she had no need to ask for dower from those. She thus held four manors in her own right.[9] Had Robert de Mortimer during the marriage alienated any of those lands that were hers by right—unless it had been done by final concord and she had been personally questioned by the justices—she could reclaim them. Apparently Robert de Mortimer had not sold any such lands. There had been a grant of Norton, the manor just across Watling Street from Whilton, to Reynold de Hotot, made by the king with her consent; Joyce was able to regain that, apparently without litigation, by October 1287.[10] A conservative appraisal would estimate that Joyce was worth at least £150 yearly. She would have no problem financing further litigation.

As it turned out, however, Joyce never again brought suit about Whilton. During April and May 1289 she would once again have been unsuccessful, because Philip de Montgomery was away fighting for the king in Gascony.[11] Joyce was perhaps not then in the best of health anyway; she died in March 1290.[12] Neither she nor Robert de Mortimer had had time to start another major suit. Since Hugh, the heir, was still underage, he was unable to bring any suit more important than an assize; in effect, he was unable to proceed until he reached majority. Felicia and Philip de Montgomery thus had a few years to hold Whilton in peace.

Joyce had lived through the second phase of normal litigation. The action of entry and the litigation that depended on that action had determined specific matters of title. This level of litigation ended with Felicia in possession. Joyce, Felicia's mother, and Hugh, Felicia's half-brother, had been removed from the land. The first action of entry had been initiated while Felicia was still underage, in 1277. It had been renewed in 1285, had gone before the king's council, and had been finally settled by jury verdict in 1287. As at the possessory level, the Mortimers had fought every inch of the way, challenging even the ruling of the justices in eyre by using the bill of exception as the foundation for review by *certiorari*. The documents concerning the action of entry also provided a contrast between the official plea roll records and the yearbook reports. Finally, it should again be noted that the jury verdict of 1287 was at variance with the verdict of the jury of attaint taken a decade previously. One need not suspect corruption. Jury verdicts, then and now, are not truth itself, only the fallible perception of twelve individuals concerning something that happened in the past. Even so, the law seemed to work well. That both sides in this dispute persistently resorted to law courts instead of to violence—and both Robert de Mortimer and Philip de Montgomery were knights trained in combat—is a tribute to the perceived superiority of law over self-help or, at least, a tribute to the perceived danger of resorting to violence instead of to the courts.

Felicia, although in possession of Whilton at last, still could not rest easy. Even if she considered the law superior to violence, she had no illusion that the law would infallibly protect her title. It clearly behoved Philip and Felicia to forestall any further attempt to deprive Felicia of her inheritance.

CHAPTER 5

Securing Title to Whilton

THE MONTGOMERYS had succeeded in litigation against the Mortimers, but the judgment was only their first step in actually securing the title to Whilton. They still had to make themselves the effective lords of Whilton. The unfree tenants would cause little problem, but the Montgomerys would have to deal at length with the free tenants, who were much more able to resist. The litigation springing up between them and their free tenants should be seen as a clean-up operation following their victory over the Mortimers. But the Montgomerys also had to make it more difficult for the Mortimer heir to prosecute them. They could do so by attracting the interest of powerful individuals in their cause and by careful use of legal rules. All of these necessary steps toward securing actual title to Whilton show how much was often still to be done even after judgment was rendered. The law worked no miracles.

Philip and Felicia first had to enforce their position as lord and lady of Whilton. The opposition—William la Zouche, then Joyce and Robert de Mortimer—had been in possession of the manor for nearly two decades, with only brief interruptions. Moreover, Philip, as a new husband, was a total stranger. The villeins would have presented few problems. If they recognized the new lord and lady, their holdings would, as before, be protected fairly well by the custom of the manor. If they did not recognize the Montgomerys, the villeins would face immediate and unappealable forfeiture of their holdings. No demonstration of opposition from the villeins has left any record; there probably was none. The free tenants, however, were rather more secure and not as dependent on the lord of the manor. Philip and Felicia therefore set about making these tenants recognize them as lord and, in addition, removing the free tenants who had been granted land in Whilton by the Mortimers. It was not an easy matter. Three cases appeared in the Court of Common Pleas, showing the progress and problems associated with renewal of seisin after so long a time.

The free tenants, as far as Philip and Felicia were concerned, were of two kinds: those who owed their tenure on the land to the Mortimers, and those whose tenures, dating back at least to the time of William de Whelton, were traditional. The traditional tenants might have to be disciplined, but their holdings were secure. Those who owed their tenure to the Mortimers, however, could be removed. If the Mortimers themselves had possessed no real right to the land, they certainly could not sell or give it away. The title of all those to whom they had sold land in Whilton was thus open to challenge.

The Montgomerys had been obliged to proceed against some of these tenants while they were proceeding against the Mortimers. Tenants who held in fee (freely and heritably) could not be ignored in the main suit. When Felicia brought her writ of entry in 1285 (Document 17), she sued the Mortimers for most of the manor, and also Nicholas de Lee and Alice his wife. The Lees, it will be remembered, were holding thirty acres of cultivated land and four acres of meadow in Whilton as compensation (*escambium*) by warranty for some Warwickshire lands they had held from the Mortimers but had lost in litigation. After the judgment on the *certiorari*, Philip and Felicia continued their suit against the Lees as well as against the Mortimers. Summoned to appear in April 1286, the Lees essoined themselves—that is, they excused themselves for cause from appearing. Then in June they defaulted, so that the land was taken into the king's hands. They appeared in court two weeks later, and Philip and Felicia decided to try to win on that default, since any default after an essoin was sufficient to lose the case. Nicholas and Alice, however, said that they had never actually been summoned and that they had not essoined themselves. The court was always somewhat lenient with this kind of plea, though corruption was certainly possible. The court wanted to avoid situations in which individuals lost their lands without having received prior notice that their title was being challenged. The Lees were therefore allowed to make their law twelve-handed—to prove their excuse by their own oath and by the oath of eleven other lawful men.[1]* In the face of the Lees' willingness to undertake that proof, it seems that Philip and Felicia, not wanting to waste time, simply started the case over again. The delay experienced with the Lees may account for the delay between the *certiorari* judgment and the taking of the verdict between the Montgomerys and the Mortimers (Document 21).

The case against the Lees thus began again. In October 1286 they appeared in court and vouched the Mortimers to warrant them. But that voucher to warranty failed, because Robert de Mortimer died. One could not call on a dead person to warrant one's title. The Lees therefore had to revouch Joyce alone. When Joyce finally came into court in the summer of 1287, she refused to warrant them the land. A jury was thus necessary to settle the dispute between the Lees and Joyce as to whether Joyce should warrant them. During 1289 they were unable to assemble a jury, and early in 1290 Joyce died.[2] Nicholas and Alice therefore had to vouch a third time. They called on Hugh, the son and heir of Robert and Joyce, to warrant them their title. Hugh, however, was still a minor, so that the suit against the Lees had to be delayed until his majority. Philip and Felicia, for the time being, had been frustrated in their attempt to regain that part of Whilton.

DOCUMENT 22

Vouching to Warranty: *Montgomery* v *Lee; Lee* v *Mortimer*

Source: CP 40/82, m. 20d *Date*: circa 17 April 1290

Northampton. Philip de Montgomery and Felicia his wife by their attorney seek against Nicholas de Lee and Alice his wife thirty acres of land and four acres of meadow with appurtenances in the manor of Whilton as the right [of Felicia]. And Nicholas and Alice formerly in the court here came and thereof vouched to warranty Joyce who was the wife of Robert de Mortimer. That Joyce has now died etc. And the abovesaid Philip and Felicia by their attorney and the abovesaid Nicholas and Alice by their attorney now come. And Nicholas and Alice say that a certain John Engayne and Joan his wife in the king's court before John de Vaux and his companions, the lord king's justices last itinerating at Warwick, sought against the same Nicholas and Alice one messuage, one virgate of land, and ten marks of rent with appurtenances in Merton in the county of Warwickshire, such that the abovesaid Nicholas and Alice in the same court vouched Robert de Mortimer of Richard's Castle and the abovesaid Joyce his wife to warrant thereof against them. The same Robert and Joyce were summoned in the same court to warrant etc., and lost the abovesaid tenements by a certain jury there taken thereof between the same Nicholas and Alice and the abovesaid Robert and Joyce. Therefore it was considered in the same court that the abovesaid John [Engayne] and Joan should recover their seisin of the abovesaid tenements against the same Nicholas and Alice and that the abovesaid Nicholas and Alice have [land] from the land of the abovesaid Robert and Joyce to the value [of the land lost to John and Joan]. And because the abovesaid Robert and Joyce did not have sufficient lands in the county of Warwickshire whereof they could make the warranty, the same Nicholas and Alice recovered the abovesaid tenements now sought against them for the remainder of the warranty etc. Therefore, they vouch thereof to warranty Hugh, the son and heir of the abovesaid Joyce, who is a minor etc.

Therefore let the suit remain until he has reached majority etc.

*

This delay was a serious hardship for Philip and Felicia. No matter which party won in *Lee* v *Mortimer*, Philip and Felicia would have regained the land. *Lee* v *Mortimer* would have determined only whether the Lees would be compensated. If Joyce had lost and been obliged to compensate the Lees, she could not then have disputed the Montgomerys' claim to the land: she had surrendered that option by disputing her warranty obligation. As it turned out, however, neither party won. The delay resulting from vouching a minor—a delay seemingly to extend from April 1290 to December 1295—must have seemed needlessly unjust to the Montgomerys.

The delay finally became intolerable. Sometime in 1294 Philip and Felicia lost their patience and simply ejected the Lees. What finally moved them to take such a course of action is not known. Perhaps Philip, who died in May 1295, had been a moderating influence on Felicia. In 1294 Felicia may already have been managing the family affairs in a more ruthlessly righteous manner. Perhaps Philip himself was simply tired of waiting. At any rate, the Lees responded to their ejection by bringing an assize of novel disseisin.

DOCUMENT 23

An Assize of Novel Disseisin: *Lee* v *Montgomery*

Source: JUST 1/625, m. 19 — *Date*: 1294

Nicholas de Lee and Alice his wife who brought a writ of novel disseisin against Philip de Montgomery and Felicia his wife concerning tenements in Whilton do not prosecute. Therefore they are in mercy. And nothing from the pledges, because by faith etc.; they have nothing.

*

I was unable to discover what happened to the Lees in the end. They were obviously in a weak position to bring an assize of novel disseisin and did not have even the financial resources to find sufficient pledges, let alone to engage in such a risky suit. They therefore withdrew from the suit. It could be that Hugh Mortimer, soon to come of age, acknowledged his obligations to the Lees and gave them some kind of compensation; even less likely, Philip and Felicia, having asserted their right, might have come to some accommodation with the Lees. The Montgomerys, however, had no reason to compromise with these protégés of the Mortimers, even if the Mortimers had now chosen to ignore them. That portion of Whilton, the recovery of which had been long delayed by legal rules protecting minors, was recovered finally by force.

The Lees had claimed as tenants in fee. There was, however, another kind of free tenant in Whilton who had to be attended to: Felicia, the widow of William de Whelton. She did not claim a fee, but only a dower for the term of her life: namely, one-third of the manor of Whilton. Hence, the writs of entry between Felicia and the Mortimers specified only two-thirds of the manor as being in dispute. When William de Whelton died and the king's court decided that Roger de Whelton was the person who should be allowed to redeem the land, it was, at least in theory, Roger who assigned her that third of the manor as her dower. That assignment, however, was not similar to the grant made by the Mortimers to the Lees, for the widow's claim did not depend on the validity of Roger's title; it was established merely by the fact that William de Whelton had held Whilton heritably during their marriage. The assignment consisted merely of designating which third she was to hold. Unlike the Lees, therefore, when the Mortimers lost possession of the land by judgment of the king's court, Felicia the widow was as secure in her holding as she had been before the judgment.

A widow's dower, however, was considered to be held not directly from her husband's lord but from the husband's heir, and the assignment of dower was accompanied by her recognition of his lordship. The widow Felicia had thus in turn acknowledged Roger de Whelton, William la Zouche, and the Mortimers as lord. Unless something was done now, the widow Felicia's death and the consequent expiration of her life term of dower would cause her third of Whilton to revert back to those acknowledged to have the fee (the heritable interest) upon which the life estate had been based: Joyce and her heirs. Philip and Felicia could only view such a reversion as a major setback. Some arrangement had to be made with the widow Felicia.

The widow Felicia was not opposed to such an accommodation. It is true that she may not have been related to the younger Felicia, since William de Whelton had been married several times. Nevertheless, Nicholas de Whelton had named his daughter after his father's wife. And the widow had even less reason to favor Joyce. The younger Felicia thus sued the widow in 1285 at Northampton at the same time she sued the Mortimers.[3] That suit against the widow was mere formality. The widow apparently waited to see whether the younger Felicia or the Mortimers would prevail in the main suit. It is even possible that she supported the younger Felicia; the support of the aging widow, a probable eyewitness to the transaction between her husband and Nicholas de Whelton, could be expected to carry great weight with the jurors and might be one reason why the Mortimers feared to put themselves on a jury. There is no doubt that in general the widow supported the younger Felicia. When Felicia won against the Mortimers, the widow apparently declined to defend herself, thus surrendering her dower in Whilton. Undoubtedly by a prior understanding, Philip and Felicia then regranted her the same one-third to hold simply as a life estate. The widow need not have made that trade in tenure. Now she had committed herself to holding her third of the manor not as doweress but rather by virtue of a grant from the Montgomerys. From a legal viewpoint, the widow's interest now rested upon the Montgomerys' fee. For the duration of the widow's life, the Montgomerys would have the fee, even though the widow had a secure right to hold the land. At the widow's death, the Montgomery's rights in the land would automatically expand to include actual possession. That third of Whilton would no longer revert to the Mortimers. The change in the way the widow claimed to hold her third of Whilton was a blatant maneuver to make it more difficult for the Mortimers to gain any access to Whilton.

The Montgomerys themselves then set about trying to defeat a similar arrangement in regard to the manor of Norton (often called Norton-by-Daventry, sometimes shortened to simply Daventry in the documents). William de Whelton's father, Roger de Whelton, after whom two of William's sons were named, had held Norton. When Roger died, William de Whelton as heir had assigned Norton to Roger's widow, Margery, as her dower. William may also have tried to convey to his son Nicholas the right to the reversion to Norton after Margery's death. When William died and the Mortimers finally took possession of Whilton, they were able to come to an accommodation with Margery concerning Norton. Margery gave the Mortimers her dower in Norton, and the Mortimers gave her the Buckinghamshire manor of Emberton for the term of her life. This exchange gave the Mortimers immediate possession of Norton and would make a challenge from Felicia more difficult. Margery may in fact have retained her living quarters in Norton, but at least the titles had been arranged so that the manor belonged to the Mortimers. Margery then married Hugh de Tywe, who soon, following the example of the elder Roger de Whelton, left her once again a widow.

In January 1287 the Montgomerys sued Margery for Norton. Their suit began with a writ of besaiel, so that their action was possessory. Their claim was based on the fact that Felicia's great-grandfather (in law French, *besaiel*) had died seised and that Felicia was the nearest heir. Roger de Whelton had indeed been her great-grandfather, but this suit would have been difficult to maintain. Besaiel was most appropriate in those rare situations in which the great-grandfather outlived his son and grandson and died leaving an heir who was his great-grandson. The difficulty in the suit never surfaced, however, since in November 1287 the Montgomerys received permission from the justices to withdraw from prosecution.[4] Perhaps they had wanted only to discover what right Margery claimed in Norton. If that was their aim, they had already found out by November. Robert de Mortimer had just died, and a jury, assembled in October 1287 to inquire into his holdings in order to ascertain what rights of wardship might accrue to the king, had just determined that Margery had indeed exchanged Norton for Emberton.[5] Norton thus remained with Joyce. Felicia's side of the claim for Norton resurfaced as an action of entry in October 1298, May 1300, October 1309, and January 1311, but nothing was ever settled.[6]* The abortive 1287 action of besaiel may well represent the necessity at times for lords to prosecute tenants in order to find out if they actually claimed rights. Anyone partial to the Mortimers might well have been reluctant to provide the Montgomerys with any helpful information.

The Montgomerys had thus concerned themselves with the Lees, with the widow Felicia, and with the widow Margery. The Lees were tenants who had received their land from the Mortimers; they were thus to be rejected. The widow Felicia had a good claim, but the Montgomerys succeeded in altering the precise way she held the land so that their hold on Whilton would be more secure when she died. The widow Margery may have been prosecuted only to ascertain exactly what rights she claimed. None of these situations dealt with the "ordinary" free tenant in fee who had good and longstanding rights, who would have to be maintained in his holding, but who might have to be disciplined to render his services. That situation surfaced finally in 1293, when Philip de Montgomery pressured the prior of Daventry into bringing a writ of replevin against him.

As lord of Whilton, Philip de Montgomery had a court that his tenants were required to attend. In some ways, it was two courts: one for his free tenants, and one for his unfree tenants. Since Philip was not a man with very extensive holdings and numerous tenants, however, the meetings for the free and unfree tenants undoubtedly were the same. For the unfree tenants, the manor court was extremely important as the normal forum for resolving all disputes. For the free tenants, the court of Whilton's lord was not as important as it had been a century earlier. In the twelfth century it was generally the court that determined all disputes concerning the relationship between the lord and his men, but by the late thirteenth century those disputes seldom came before such a court. The court of Whilton, however, could perhaps still expect to arbitrate certain problems both with and between tenants and to bring to an amicable and satisfactory conclusion certain problems between free tenants. The attendance of those free tenants was a more important matter than such functions might indicate. Regular attendance was a continuing acknowledgment of tenurial subordination to the lord of Whilton, a recognition of his lordship, and was one of the specified services—the service of suit of court—by which the free tenants held their land. The service was fulfilled both by attending and by rendering the judgments of the court, which was a communal court. Philip had a controlling authority, but judgments on the free tenants would be rendered by the court as a whole. A tenant's nonappearance, then, was a matter of concern for both the lord and the court.

The prior of Daventry was a tenant who was not attending the court of Whilton. He held one virgate of land in Staverton, which was considered a part of the manor of Whilton, and was thus obliged to render suit of court. The Montgomerys had regained Whilton in 1287, and this particular prior had only been elected in 1289. It may well have been the certainty that the Mortimers were going to go to court again that prompted the new prior to refuse to attend court. Whatever his reason, his failure to attend was an open challenge to the Montgomerys. The court therefore took action against him and amerced him for his defaults. The amercement was enforced by distraint: two of the prior's horses found within Philip's lordship in Staverton were taken and held until the prior should appear to pay his amercement and explain his conduct. It was by this distraint that Philip precipitated the dispute, for the prior of Daventry did not then docilely attend the court of Whilton. Instead, he purchased a writ of replevin against Philip.

The procedure associated with the action of replevin was designed to lower the tension occasioned by a distraint and to put the dispute into peaceful litigation. By 1293 the procedure could be initiated either by a writ purchased from the king's Chancery or by mere complaint made to the sheriff. The prior chose to begin by purchasing the writ. The sheriff was thus ordered to return ("replevy") the distrained animals to their owner. In return, the prior had to give security first that he would prosecute in court his complaint about animals taken and unjustly detained and then that, if he lost, he would return the animals to Philip. If the prior won the case, Philip would have to proceed against him in some other way. Each party was thus assured an opportunity to air his grievance. The prior regained his animals for the time being. And Philip, when charged in court with taking the animals, would admit that he had done so and then set forth the reasons. The case would thereafter focus on whether Philip's reasons were sufficient and correct, and the issue would be put to a jury. All this was standard form in an action of replevin.

In the case between Philip de Montgomery and the prior of Daventry, the problem concerned the traditional rules for distraint—the way in which one could take and hold another person's chattels. Philip, as lord, was limited in what he could do. He could not, for instance, take the prior's animals if he found them on lands other than those held of him, as on the king's highway or in Daventry or in Northampton itself. Philip had obeyed this rule. In justifying the distraint, however, Philip had to affirm that he had been in seisin of that service of suit of court required of this same prior; that is, the prior had to have actually performed his suit at least once. Distraint by 1293 was allowed only against those who had acknowledged themselves to owe the services. The prior challenged Philip on that very point, stating that Philip had never been seised of the service of suit of court by his hands. They joined issue on that point, and the matter was to be submitted to a jury in May 1294.

Then the suit was simply dropped. It was not at all abnormal for a case to end in this way. Quite possibly, during the pleading attention had been focused on a part of the factual situation adverse to one party, forcing that party to abandon the legal configuration he had worked out. He knew he would lose the case and should compromise. In this case, there was probably some right on both sides. The prior probably did owe suit of court, but Philip had distrained him unlawfully. With the case so close to being settled by jury and judgment, both sides may have been willing to compromise a little. The case was dropped, but it is unlikely that Philip and the prior had agreed merely to disagree. We can be confident that Philip successfully disciplined the prior to render his service of suit of court, but we can also suspect that the prior might have been able to wheedle some concession from Philip in return for dropping the suit.

DOCUMENT 24
Action of Replevin: *Prior of Daventry* v *Montgomery*

Source: CP 40/102, m. 216 *Date*: circa October-November 1293

Northamptonshire. Philip de Montgomery was summoned to answer the prior of Daventry in a plea by one writ why he together with John Lylie took a certain horse of the same prior etc., and in a plea by another writ why the same Philip together with the abovesaid John took a certain other horse of the same prior etc. And thereof he complains that the abovesaid Philip together with the abovesaid John on the Saturday next after the feast of the Holy Trinity in the twentieth year of the present king [7 June 1292] at Staverton in a certain place which is called Othehil took a certain horse of the same prior etc., and on the Wednesday following [11 June 1292] at Staverton in a certain place which is called Lackfurlong took another horse of the same prior and unjustly detained them against gage [and pledges] until [the deliverance was made by the king's command], wherefore he says that he has suffered loss and has damages to the value of 40s and thereof he produces suit.

And Philip by his attorney comes and denies force and injury when etc. And he well acknowledges that he took the abovesaid horses and justly, for he says that the abovesaid prior holds from the same Philip one virgate of land with appurtenances in Staverton by fealty and the service of doing suit to the court of the same Philip at Whilton from three weeks to three weeks, of which service the same Philip was seised by the hands of the same prior. And he says that the abovesaid prior made defaults at many court sessions there held etc., wherefore he was amerced 2s for the abovesaid defaults etc., for which amercement and other defaults he took the abovesaid horses in his fee as he was well entitled to do etc.

And the abovesaid prior says that the abovesaid Philip cannot avow the abovesaid taking as just etc., because he says that the abovesaid Philip never was in seisin of the abovesaid suit by the hands of the same prior etc. And of this he puts himself on the countryside.

And Philip similarly.

Therefore the sheriff is ordered to make to come here at three weeks from Easter twelve [as well knights as other free and lawful men, of the county of Northamptonshire], by whom [the truth of the matter can be best known and who are related neither to the prior of Daventry nor to Philip de Montgomery in any affinity etc.] because both [the aforesaid prior of Daventry and the aforesaid Philip de Montgomery, between whom there is litigation therein, put themselves on an inquisition etc.].

❋

The judgment of the king's court that restored Felicia to Whilton in 1287 obviously did not assure her of a quiet and complete re-entry. She and her husband had to continue to prosecute her right vigorously. First they had to eliminate tenants who had been granted lands by the Mortimers. The Lees and others like them could receive—at least in theory—compensation from the Mortimers elsewhere; it would have been unfair for the Mortimers to be able to fulfill their own obligations by dissipating Felicia's inheritance. Proper tenants like Felicia's grandmother and the prior of Daventry had to be made to acknowledge Felicia's right, either by gentle persuasion or by distraint and litigation. The case of replevin brought by the prior is precisely the kind of litigation that could be expected at a re-entry. The judgment in 1287 gave Felicia only an immediate recovery of the land and the manor house and a basis on which to recover all other rights associated with the manor. The social bonds that would have grown up between the tenants and the Mortimers probably created obstacles to the immediate recovery of such rights that would have to be overcome slowly one by one. Finally, the dealings with Felicia's grandmother show a more long-range concern. Not only did the judgment of 1287 have to be actualized; precautions had to be taken to make it more difficult for the Mortimers to challenge her title once more at law.

Gaining the protection of influential individuals was much more important as a precaution than the arrangement with Felicia's grandmother. There was literally no way in which the Mortimers could forever be prevented from challenging the Montgomerys again. But if Philip and Felicia had enough support in the right places, the Mortimers might find it prudent to delay bringing their suit for some time. And when they finally did bring it, the judicious application of influence by friends of the Montgomerys might reveal ways to hinder the Mortimers even during such litigation. The person whose favor the Montgomerys felt they needed was Robert Burnel, bishop of Bath and Wells, Chancellor of England, and undoubtedly one of the most influential and powerful men in the realm.

Burnel had already been involved with the family for some time prior to 1290. In 1273 he had been one of the clerks who had witnessed Roger de Whelton's release to Alelm of his claims to Toternhoe.[7] In or around 1280, Roger de Whelton had enfeoffed Burnel of the services due him from the manor of Churchill.[8] Then, in 1289, the Montgomerys established some link with Burnel. In that year Philip acknowledged a debt of nearly £20 to Burnel. That recognition was entered into the close rolls and thus became a matter of record. Burnel could then make use of a particularly expeditious procedure. If the debt was not paid on schedule, depending on circumstances, he could simply get either an order for the sheriff to levy the money from the Montgomerys' lands and chattels—and Philip had designated the Northamptonshire lands for such an eventuality—or a peremptory order for Philip to come into court to explain why the money should not be so levied. Such process thus avoided a plea of debt. As it happened, the debt was paid without recourse to such procedures.[9] Nonetheless, the debt recognition establishes some bond between the Montgomerys and Robert Burnel.

Any real intermingling of Burnel and Montgomery interests had to be established by something more significant than a debt. Outright bribery, of course, was always an option, but a poor one. Just at the time that Philip was making contacts with Burnel in 1289 and 1290, Edward I was taking action against judicial corruption. The king's campaign resulted in the dismissal and fining of most of the justices, including Ralph de Hengham, Chief Justice of the Court of King's Bench, and it also brought the elevation of John de Mettingham to the office of Chief Justice of the Court of Common Pleas. In such an atmosphere, an official of the king would likely have been slow to accept a bribe. Moreover, bribery is most effective to obtain an individual favor, whereas Montgomery was more interested in long-term protection. Another option open to Philip was a grant of an annuity, a common enough method to form an alliance. But such a grant might in the end prove very costly. What size annuity would be appropriate to gain the Chancellor's long-term regard? Neither an outright bribe nor an annuity would have been the optimal means of interesting the Chancellor in the fate of Whilton.

In fact, the most efficacious method would cost little or nothing but would give Burnel reason to protect and defend the Montgomery hold on Whilton: a grant and regrant transaction by which Burnel received the fee simple as a reversionary interest, while the Montgomerys continued to hold Whilton in fee tail. The way in which this transaction worked was somewhat more complicated than the grant and regrant between William de Whelton and his son Nicholas. The first part of both kinds of transaction was exactly the same: the grant of the fee to Burnel was a grant of the whole heritable and alienable interest in the land. The regrant from Burnel to the Montgomerys in fee tail, however, was a grant of rather more than a life estate. The fee tail was a "cut-down" or limited fee. It was limited in the two essential aspects of the fee: heritability and alienability. With a full fee or a fee simple, the land was inheritable either by one's direct descendants or, if there were none, by distant relatives. The fee tail was inheritable only by one's direct descendants, and heritability here could even be limited to a specific class of descendants, such as male heirs. Again, with a fee simple, the land was alienable. Alienability had increasingly been a mark of the fee during the thirteenth century; the statute *Quia Emptores* in 1290 eliminated even theoretical restrictions to alienation of the fee simple.[10*] The fee tail, however, was characterized by the inability of its holder to sell the land for any longer than his own life. That restriction on the fee tail was made clear by the statute *De Donis Conditionalibus* (Statute of Westminster II, c. 1) in 1285.[11*] The law thus recognized two distinct ways in which one could hold land heritably. One could hold land either in fee simple, with all rights of alienation and inheritance even for remote heirs, or in fee tail, with restricted rights of alienation and inheritance only for direct descendants.

The reason why this grant and regrant could give Burnel an interest in Whilton was that the two kinds of fees could, for any given piece of land, exist simultaneously. One person could hold the fee simple; the other, the fee tail. If inheritance for a fee tail was restricted only to direct heirs, the land must clearly go to someone if there were no direct heirs. That someone was the person or the heirs of the person who had originally given the fee tail to the holder. Thus, any holder of land in fee simple could give another a fee tail but still retain a continuing interest. At some date far in the future he or his descendants might take the land by reason of default of heirs—that is, he retained a reversionary interest. In the present, the person with the possibility was no better off, for he had no use of the land at all. But if the holders in fee tail had few or no children, possibility would seem a probability that could blossom forth into full ownership of the land. Similarly, the holder in fee tail was little worse off than if he held in fee simple. Unless he needed money desperately and wanted to sell the land for longer than his own life or wanted to endow his daughters, he would normally not even feel the restrictions. Thus, in this grant and regrant transaction Philip and Felicia were able to give Burnel a future possibility that he would value greatly and protect—while they retained full use of the land.

Given the factual situation, this kind of grant and regrant was particularly desirable. Robert Burnel had every right to think that he might take Whilton by reason of default of heirs. Philip and Felicia did have a son, but around the beginning of 1290 young Thomas was killed by misadventure.[12] At that time, there was no other child. Philip and Felicia, like Burnel, would find the deal sensible. No serious financial trouble was pressing them to sell Whilton; on the contrary, they were trying to retain it. Morever, this transaction preserved the right to inherit of their own children, if they were to have any more. There was even some reason for them to want to limit the rights of inheritance. Most likely, when Roger de Whelton and William la Zouche settled with the younger sons of William de Whelton concerning Wymington and Totternhoe, those sons yielded their rights to Whilton by quitclaim. If Philip and Felicia died without children, therefore, the land would go to the Mortimers. With the animosity there must have been by now between mother and daughter, that result would have been Felicia's last wish. The grant and regrant was both a precaution against the future and an overt act of hostility against the Mortimers.

After the transaction, the Montgomerys held the land as a grant from Robert Burnel. Since the Montgomerys did not want to diminish their own resources and only intended to give the reversion to Burnel, the service they rendered to Burnel for the land was minimal: for one year only they had to give him a chaplet of roses on 24 June, a date only three weeks after the transaction. Beyond that, the Montgomerys were to continue to render the services due the Stutevilles as chief lords of the fee. In that way, neither Burnel nor the Montgomerys were more benefited or burdened by way of services after the transaction than before. Since the land was Felicia's inheritance, it was settled in fee tail on her and her husband and the heirs procreated from her body. Felicia's line, including all of her children by any future marriage, would thus have priority. It was also specified that, if Felicia left no such heirs, Whilton, instead of reverting immediately into the hands of Burnel, would remain in fee tail to Philip and the heirs of his body, that is, his heirs from any previous or subsequent marriage. Finally, if both Felicia and Philip died without children, the land would revert to Burnel. Whilton was thus settled on Felicia and Philip in fee tail to the heirs of her body, with a remainder in fee tail to Philip and with the reversion back to Burnel, now legally the original grantor of the land to the Montgomerys.

The transaction was carried out by means of a final concord. That was the only way it could have been done, because Whilton was Felicia's inheritance. While she was married, her husband had complete control over her resources, but that control endured only for the husband's life. He could not so alienate her lands that she would not have them after his death; if he did, she could reclaim them even from an honest purchaser by litigation. A woman was indeed subjected to her husband, but her rights were rigidly preserved. The only way a married woman could sell her lands was by final concord. The justices who presided over the concord would interrogate her in private to determine if she really wanted to alienate the lands. If they determined that she did, the final concord was made, and the land was effectively conveyed. Absolutely any other kind of conveyance of a married woman's landed property, regardless of assertions about her consent, could be rendered null and void by the woman after her husband's death. Likewise, because the justices were sure about the care that surrounded the making of such a conveyance, a final concord would be rigidly enforced against a widow. This final concord, then, was the only way in which Philip and Felicia could give Burnel the reversion.

DOCUMENT 25
A Final Concord: *Burnel* v *Montgomery*

Source: CP 25(1) 175/56, no. 89 *Date*: circa 5 June 1290

This is the final concord made in the court of the lord king at Westminster on the octaves of Holy Trinity in the eighteenth year of the reign of King Edward son of King Henry before John de Mettingham, Robert de Hertford, Elias de Beckingham, William de Gisleham, and Master Robert de Thorp, justices, and others of the lord king then present there between Robert, bishop of Bath and Wells, plaintiff, and Philip de Montgomery and Felicia his wife, impedients, concerning the manor of Whilton with appurtenances and four messuages and 100s rent with appurtenances in Staverton whereof a plea of warranty of charters was summoned between them in the same court, to wit: the abovesaid Philip and Felicia recognized the abovesaid tenements with appurtenances to be the right of the same Robert as those tenements which the same Robert has from the gift of the abovesaid Philip and Felicia. And for this recognition, fine, and concord, the same Robert grants the abovesaid Philip and Felicia the abovesaid tenements with appurtenances to have and to hold to the same Philip and Felicia and to the heirs procreated from the body of the same Felicia [to hold] from the abovesaid Robert and his heirs in perpetuity by rendering thereof for one year a chaplet of roses at the feast of the nativity of St. John the Baptist [24 June] for all services, customs, and exactions pertaining to the abovesaid Robert and his heirs and by doing thereof all other services which pertain to those tenements to the chief lords of that fee for the abovesaid Robert and his heirs. And should it happen that the abovesaid Felicia die without heir procreated from her body, then after the death of the same Felicia the abovesaid tenements will remain to the abovesaid Philip and his heirs procreated from his body to hold from the abovesaid Robert and his heirs by the abovesaid services in perpetuity. And the abovesaid Robert and his heirs will warrant to the same Philip and Felicia and the heirs of the same abovesaid Felicia and also the abovesaid heirs of the same Philip, should the abovesaid Felicia die without heir procreated from her body, the abovesaid tenements with appurtenances by the abovesaid services against all men in perpetuity. And if it should happen that the abovesaid Philip die without heir procreated from his body, then after the death of the same Philip the abovesaid tenements with appurtenances will revert wholly to the abovesaid Robert and his heirs quit of other heirs of either the same Philip or Felicia to hold from the chief lords of that fee by those services which pertain to those tenements in perpetuity.

[Endorsed:] Hugh son of Robert de Mortimer puts forward his claim.

*

The endorsement in the final concord demonstrates both its force and its limitations. The concord did have some preclusive effect on third parties; that is, within limits and under conditions that changed from time to time in the thirteenth and fourteenth centuries, a final concord would bar claims made by outsiders. One firm limitation on this extraordinary power of the concord, as Felicia well knew, concerned minors and those abroad; their claims could not be barred because they had been unable to object. Another limitation worked in favor of those who actually objected. By putting forward his claim now, Hugh Mortimer preserved his right to sue for those lands on the basis of facts before June 1290. In any case, the purpose of this final concord had not been to bar the Mortimers from further litigation; nothing could do that, if the Mortimers remained vigilant. The transaction was intended rather to secure a powerful ally, and that aim had been accomplished. Burnel's lawyers would henceforth keep track of that reversionary right as part of Burnel's property and guard it as such. It was now in Burnel's own interest to safeguard the Montgomery claim to Whilton. A more powerful ally would be difficult to imagine, except perhaps the king or queen.

Thus, the final concord, the arrangement with the widowed grandmother Felicia, and the actions taken against the various tenants constitute the Montgomery strategy for securing Whilton up until about 1292. In that year their hold on Whilton tightened. Robert Burnel's death in October 1292 might seem a setback, because the Montgomerys lost the personal protection they had sought, and it is true that they could no longer count on the protection of the Chancellor of England. But the guardians of the Burnel heir would continue to protect that reversion. Indeed, as will be shown in the next chapter, Burnel dead proved better protection than Burnel alive. Probably also in 1292 a better arrangement was made with Felicia, the now elderly widow of William de Whelton. In 1291, perhaps late in the year, another child was born to Philip and Felicia: a girl named Anne.[13] She, of course, became the prospective heiress to the fee tail in Whilton. The widow Felicia had previously exchanged her dower for a simple life estate to be held of the Montgomerys. Now, perhaps influenced by the celebrations surrounding Anne's birth, she was prepared to go even further: she surrendered her life estate. If she was acting according to any normal pattern, she was not thereby left without resources. Just as she had surrendered her dower for a life estate, she probably gave up her life estate in land as part of a formal agreement whereby Philip and Felicia would be obliged to give her shelter, food, and care for the remainder of her life. The details of such agreements could be quite specific, but neither documentary proof nor hints of details have survived to indicate the nature of the settlement with her. It is nevertheless probable that there was one. Any change, however, would have been only in legal title. The Mortimers, for instance, need not have known and perhaps could not have observed any difference. The Montgomerys, finally, held all of Whilton in their own right. Burnel's death, the birth of an heiress, and the further accommodation with the widow all secured the Montgomery claim to Whilton.

The year 1295 witnessed a similar degree of Montgomery reverses. The misfortunes began with the death of Philip de Montgomery in May. Financially, Philip's death did not destructively curtail Felicia's resources. The manorial complex in Whilton and Staverton was her own property, and she would retain its income undiminished. The inquest taken by royal officials on the occasion of Philip's death confirmed her right. Had the land been held only by Philip, of course, the lord could have claimed wardship, and the inquest was taken on the possibility that the lord might be the king. He was not, of course, but the inquest incorrectly determined that the Wakes were the lords of whom Felicia held. By the concord of 1290, she held rather from the Burnels. Since Burnel then held of John Wake (son of Baldwin Wake), who held of the king, and since Felicia would be rendering the services directly to Wake, the finding was accurate enough.

DOCUMENT 26

Inquisition *Post Mortem* on Philip de Montgomery

Source: C 133/70, no. 27, m. 2 [and m. 9] — *Date*: 4 June 1295 [7 July 1295]

Inquisition made at Northampton on the fourth day of June in the twenty-third year of the reign of King Edward by the oath of William Bretun of Tekne, William de Stowe, Adam

Capys of Thorpe, William de Fodrinheye, John de la Chambre of Flore, William Flemyng of Heyford, Simon de la Sale of Daventry, Walter de Molendino of Thorpe, Thomas Boterels of Welton, William de Brochole, Adam le Glazun of "Brunton" and John Dolfin of Newnham. They say on their oath that Philip de Montgomery held nothing in chief of the lord king in the county of Northamptonshire on the day he died. They say also that the same Philip and Felicia his wife held the manor of Whilton jointly in chief of John Wake by the service of one knight's fee. Likewise, they say that the chief messuage with the garden is worth 17s yearly and the dovecote is worth 3s yearly. Sum: 20s. Likewise, they say that there are there nine virgates of arable land in the demesne lands, and they are worth £6 yearly. Likewise, they say that the separable pasture is worth 13s 4d yearly. Likewise, there are there twenty acres of mowable meadow, and they are worth £4 yearly. Likewise, there are there from the fixed rent of those holding freely by equal portions at the term of St. Thomas the apostle, the Annunciation of the Lady, St. John the Baptist, and St. Michael £4 10s. Likewise, [there are there from the rent of customary tenants eight virgates of land, of which each virgate renders 20s yearly at the abovesaid terms and a half virgate renders 12s at the same terms]. Likewise, from the rent of cottars at the same terms 12s 8d. Sum: £25 8s. Likewise they say that the abovesaid Philip and Felicia held jointly in Staverton 56s 4d of annual rent to be taken yearly at two terms, doing therefor 30s to the chief lords. And there remain 26s 4d.

*

Felicia also held in her own right the rents worth 23s 7½d in Whatlington, Sussex, although she apparently seldom visited Sussex. Finally, she and Philip had acquired lands in Thorpe jointly, so that at Philip's death she was entitled to retain the lands completely instead of seeking a third as her dower.[14] Her own income thus probably amounted to a little less than

£40 annually—a substantial sum in itself. She would eventually receive further income from the one-third of Philip's lands that would become her dower. Financially, Felicia could manage quite well.

Nevertheless, she was now more burdened than before. Legally, a widow had the same securely entrenched property rights as a man and was as capable of bringing a lawsuit. But medieval England did not have even a lurking suspicion that women as persons might be equal to men. In such a world, the practical and effective exercise of power was determined by forces other than legal rules. In this sense, Felicia was now more vulnerable at law because she was less able to influence people. Felicia was, moreover, burdened by the consequences of Philip's death. Fortunately, she found that she did not have to sue immediately to obtain her dower. But her daughter, Anne, could at will be taken from her and put into her lord's wardship, just as had been done with Felicia herself and with Hugh Mortimer during their minorities. And she was involved in litigation. As normal, Felicia was appointed one of the executors by her husband's will. That will, of course, did not concern land, because land descended only by the rules of inheritance, not by will. Executors were concerned only with distributing Philip's chattels and collecting or paying off his debts. Such affairs often resulted in litigation; indeed, Henry de Bray did sue the executors in 1296 for £8 16s that Philip had owed him.[15] Finally, Felicia's grandmother, the elder widow Felicia, seems to have died at about the same time as Philip. The newly widowed Felicia was sufficiently distracted and burdened that she would now seem more vulnerable to attack.

It was thus unfortunate for Felicia that Hugh Mortimer was due to come of age in December 1295.[16] In fact, Hugh decided in May that the situation was sufficient reason for him to renew his family's claim to Whilton even before he had come of age. In regard to the two-thirds of the manor regained by Felicia and Philip from Joyce and Robert, he had to bring a writ of right; that will be treated in the following chapter. In regard to the one-third that had been the elder widow Felicia's dower, he could still bring a writ of entry. The time for taking precautions had passed.

The action of entry proceeded in the usual manner. Hugh purchased his writ in May, and the sheriff was ordered to summon Felicia to appear in the Court of Common Pleas in June 1295. At that date the sheriff reported that he had not had enough time to summon her; his excuse may well have been true, even though it would be pleasant to believe that he had omitted his duty out of compassion.[17] The summons was therefore reordered, and Felicia appeared in court in November 1295. Hugh's claim, cast in the form of a writ of entry by intrusion, alleged that Felicia had intruded into the land after the death of Felicia the grandmother, who had held the land only as her dower. The reversion would thus belong, he thought, to him as the heir of Joyce, who was the heir of William la Zouche, to whom Roger de Whelton, heir of William de Whelton, had granted the land. This was essentially the same claim that Roger and Joyce had raised when defending themselves against Felicia. Felicia did not have to answer his claim right away. Since she held other land in the area—the remaining two-thirds of Whilton—she was entitled to have pointed out to her the precise lands claimed by Hugh. The court therefore ordered the sheriff to give her the view of the land, and the parties were ordered to reappear in court in June 1296.[18]* Only in November 1296, however, was the case finally pleaded to issue.

Felicia's defense in November 1296 revealed all the maneuvers that had been taken since 1286 in regard to that one-third of Whilton, including the transformation of the widow's dower estate into a life estate and then the surrender of the life estate. Hugh's writ alleged a particular kind of wrongful entry. Since these writs were designed to determine particular issues and not general title, Hugh's version of the way in which Felicia came onto this one-third of Whilton had to be correct in order for him to win. Felicia, of course, denied the alleged intrusion. That was the issue to be submitted to the jury, on which the case would be won or lost. If the jury was of the opinion that the two Felicias had reached the accommodations described by the younger woman, the earlier preventive precautions would have proved successful. The change in the widow's estate would result in the frustration of this suit brought by Hugh Mortimer.

DOCUMENT 27

Action of Entry: *Mortimer* v *Montgomery*

Source: CP 40/114, m. 139d *Date*: circa 12 November 1296

Northamptonshire. Hugh de Mortimer seeks against Felicia who was the wife of Philip de Montgomery one-third of the manor of Whilton with appurtenances as his right etc., and in which the same Felicia has no entry unless by an intrusion which she made in it after the death of Felicia who was the wife of William de Whelton who held it from William la Zouche in dower from the gift of the abovesaid William de Whelton her late husband. [And the abovesaid Hugh claims] from the assignment which Roger son and heir of William de Whelton made thereof to the aforementioned William la Zouche and to the heirs of the same William la Zouche and which after the death of the abovesaid Felicia who was the wife of William de Whelton ought to revert to the aforementioned Hugh, kinsman and heir of the abovesaid William la Zouche by reason of the abovesaid assignment etc.

And Felicia by her attorney comes and denies his right when etc. And she well denies that she intruded into the abovesaid third of the abovesaid manor after the death of the abovesaid Felicia who was the wife of the abovesaid William de Whelton as the abovesaid Hugh asserts etc., because she says that the same Felicia who was the wife of the abovesaid Philip recovered before the justices itinerant last at Northampton in the same county the abovesaid one-third against the abovesaid Felicia who was the wife of the abovesaid William de Whelton as her right. And afterwards the same Felicia who was the wife of the abovesaid Philip together with the same Philip, then her husband, granted the abovesaid third with appurtenances from her own seisin to the abovesaid Felicia who was the wife of the abovesaid William to hold at the term of the life of the same Felicia who was the wife of the abovesaid William etc., which same Felicia afterwards, three years before her death, rendered the abovesaid one-third with appurtenances to the abovesaid Felicia who was the wife of the abovesaid Philip as the right of the same Felicia who was the wife of the abovesaid Philip, so that the abovesaid one-third never afterwards devolved into the seisin of the abovesaid Felicia who was the wife of the abovesaid William etc. And this she is prepared to verify by the countryside etc.

And Hugh says that the abovesaid Felicia who was the wife of the abovesaid William held the abovesaid one-third in dower on the day on which she died and had a free tenement in the same one-third on the same day, after whose death the abovesaid Felicia who was the wife of the abovesaid Philip intruded into the abovesaid one-third etc.

And Felicia who was the wife of the abovesaid Philip says that the abovesaid Felicia who was the wife of the abovesaid William long before her death rendered the abovesaid one-third, as is said above, to the same Felicia who was the wife of the abovesaid Philip etc. such that the abovesaid Felicia de Whelton did not have a free tenement in the same one-third on the day on which she died etc. And the same Felicia who was the wife of the abovesaid Philip has entry into the abovesaid one-third by that rendering and not by intrusion as the abovesaid Hugh says etc. And of this she puts herself on the countryside.

And Hugh similarly.

Therefore the sheriff is ordered to make to come here at three weeks from Easter twelve [as well knights as other free and lawful men, of the county of Northamptonshire etc.] by whom [the truth of the matter can be best known and who are related neither to the abovesaid Hugh de Mortimer nor to the aforementioned Felicia who was the wife of Philip de

Montgomery in any affinity etc.] because both [the aforesaid Hugh de Mortimer and the abovesaid Felicia who was the wife of Philip de Montgomery, between whom there is litigation therein, put themselves on an inquisition etc.].

❋

As it happened, no jury ever rendered a verdict on that issue, though a jury was originally summoned for May 1297. Since successive panels did not come to Westminster, jurors were summoned also for October 1297, January 1298, and June 1298.[19] Such delays in assembling a jury were not abnormal. Had both parties been serious about the matter, however, they could have asked for a jury by *nisi prius* procedure, which would have allowed the jury to be taken in Northamptonshire instead of at Westminster and would surely have given them results. Instead, both Felicia and Hugh were probably biding their time, delaying as the companion case brought by writ of right slowly proceeded toward proof. The case on the writ of entry was postponed finally for an indefinite time in May 1299. The reason for the postponement will be covered in detail with the action in the right. It need only be said here that the postponement was the result of the final concord that Philip and Felicia had made to safeguard their seisin of Whilton. The measures they had taken were sufficient to preserve Whilton in the hands of Felicia for the rest of her life.

CHAPTER 6

Litigation by Writ of Right

IN SEPTEMBER 1295, about four months after the initiation of the action of entry alleging intrusion and more than a year before that case was to be pleaded, Hugh de Mortimer purchased his writ of right close. If this action were to come to a conclusion, the dispute itself would be concluded, because the issue in a writ of right did not focus merely on one aspect of the title but was framed in the broadest possible form to determine which of the parties had the greater right to hold the land. After that issue was decided, there could be no more litigation between them or their heirs relating to any complication in title concerning facts prior to the action in the right.

A transcript of the writ of right has survived. It was a writ of right close, a *precipe* (so called because of the first word of the body of the writ: "command") in the form *quia dominus remisit curiam suam* (because the lord has remitted his court). Only about a century before, it had still been assumed that determination of title belonged most properly to the feudal court—such as was held by the lord of Whilton for his free tenants—of that lord from whom both parties claimed to hold the land. But the bond between a lord and his accepted man was an almost sacred thing; it was difficult for an outsider to persuade a lord to reconsider a tenure already held of him. To some degree, then, as a simple practical statement of fact, but increasingly also as an abstract rule of law, the demandant had to obtain a royal order to bring the case before the lord's court. This mandate was a writ of right patent (Document 1). When the king himself was the lord of whom the parties claimed to hold, the case of course could come immediately into the king's court. The writ mandating jurisdiction to the king's court was a writ of right close, a *precipe*. The Chancery, however, had been in the habit of issuing *precipe* writs in other cases also. Access to the *precipe* had even been guaranteed to certain privileged individuals by charter. Such charters and other similar practices were rightly seen as detrimental to a lord's authority, so that Magna Carta, c. 34, promised that the writ *precipe* would not be used in such a way as to deprive a free man of his court. Henceforward, writs of right could be issued only in three broad forms. The first form was the writ of right patent, which initiated the case in the lord's court, although the case might subsequently be removed into the county court and then into the king's court. The second form was the *precipe* for those who claimed to hold of the king himself. The third form was the *precipe* that, eighty years after the Magna Carta, Hugh was to purchase: the *precipe quia dominus remisit curiam suam*. It brought the case immediately into the king's court and included in itself the reason: the lord to whom the case would ordinarily have belonged had remitted the case to the king, had waived his right to hear the case.

DOCUMENT 28
The Writ of Right: *Mortimer* v *Montgomery*

Source: British Library, Additional MS 31826, fol. 161v — *Date*: September 1295

King to the sheriff, greetings. Order [*precipe*] Felicia who was the wife of Philip de Montgomery that justly [and without delay] she return to Hugh de Mortimer two-thirds of the manor of Whilton with appurtenances which he claims to be his right and inheritance and whereof he complains that the abovesaid Felicia deforces him. And if she does not and the abovesaid Hugh shall have given you security [for prosecuting his claim], then summon by good summoners the abovesaid Felicia that she be before our justices at Westminster on the quindene of St. Michael to show why she does not. And have there the summoners and this writ. Witnessed by me myself etc., the [?] day of September in the twenty-third year of our reign. Because John Wake, chief lord of that fee, remitted his court thereof to us.

*

Although procedure on a writ of right could be extremely cumbersome, in this case the preliminaries were accomplished very expeditiously. Felicia was originally summoned for October 1295; she appeared in January 1296 and prayed the view of the land. She appeared again in court in November 1296 to defend her title. Hugh's formal exposition was fairly simple. The descent of the right from William la Zouche to Joyce to himself was fairly straightforward. Were one to judge the case solely from that opening statement, Hugh had the legal right to hold the land. Hugh was the son of Joyce, whereas Felicia was Joyce's daughter. The rules of inheritance demanded that the son inherit to the complete exclusion of daughters. But Hugh's conceptualization assumed that title flowed from Zouche to Joyce, whereas Felicia's title flowed from her father, not her mother. It might seem that Hugh was being less than honest in the way he formulated his claim, but in fact he was not allowed to make any mention of William de Whelton or Roger or Nicholas. He only had to put forward a general reason why the court should entertain his claim; he was thus required to describe his right as descending from his own ancestors, beginning with the ancestor first in possession and ending with himself. Since possession had passed directly from father (William) to daughter (Joyce), Hugh's claim as daughter's son was very simple.

The nature of Felicia's reply should have been equally simple. She was not the only person who would be injured if she lost the case. Edward Burnel, the nephew of Robert Burnel, was also an interested party. Robert Burnel, of course, had been not only the Chancellor but also a bishop and was thus unable either to marry or to have children whom the courts would recognize as heirs. When he died, his nephew Edward inherited his real property, including the interest in the reversion of Whilton gained by the final concord of 1290. All that stood between young Edward and possession of Whilton was Anne, a seven-year-old girl; it would not have been surprising for both Felicia and Anne to have died with no further heirs. Edward thus had not only a legal but also an actual interest in Whilton. The proper course for Felicia was to assert that she had only a fee tail in Whilton and then pray aid of Edward Burnel, the reversioner. In that way Edward would be called into court to defend her case with her. If only because the Burnel resources were so vast, that would have been excellent strategy. Even had it been bad strategy, it was the legally proper course.

Aid prayer of the Burnel heir was in this case extraordinarily desirable. Edward Burnel was still a minor. If he were associated with Felicia, the case could not be tried until he attained majority in 1307. For anyone actually in possession of land, postponement of such a case for a whole decade would be an undoubted advantage. Anything could happen in that length of time. Felicia herself might acquire greater resources. The Mortimers could be ruined. Hugh Mortimer might die, leaving a minor as heir, so that the plea would have to be further postponed. Felicia herself might die, so that she would have retained Whilton to her death without further litigation.

Although aid prayer was the proper course, it was not the course Felicia chose. Instead, she answered Hugh's count and thereafter continued to ignore Edward Burnel's right. The final concord that established Burnel's right was not included among the vital documents collected to present to the grand assize. Felicia must have viewed that final concord as a mere legal maneuver. Knowing that it neither restricted her present use of the land nor prevented her from doing anything she wanted to do, she must have concluded that it could be simply forgotten. Furthermore, the fact that she ignored this valuable defense must also mean that Philip and Felicia were bargaining in 1290 for a relationship with Robert Burnel only, not looking into the future and the possibility of a reversioner who was only a minor.

Felicia thus passed by this opportunity and denied Hugh's right. Had she been claiming as the descendant of some elder brother of Joyce, she could have pointed out that the alleged descent of the right was faulty. Since that was not her claim, she did not have to express the nature of her right. At this point, there was not even procedure for her to explain the way in which her title had descended to her. She could only deny Hugh's right and choose her method of trial, the way to prove her denial. That limitation on Felicia might seem unfair, and it would have been so if the matters alleged and denied at this point had served like evidence at trial, if the decision would be made on the basis of what was said here. But that was not the case. Felicia's unembroidered denial was perfectly adequate as a defense.

As the method of proof, Felicia could choose either trial by battle or the grand assize. By 1295 trial by battle was becoming unusual as a method of proof in disputes over property, although it was not unknown. Had Felicia made this choice, the champions of both parties—by this date, probably specially trained ruffians—would have determined the outcome by judicially supervised combat. Felicia, like most other tenants, preferred a less whimsical procedure. The grand assize—a panel of twelve men put under oath to tell the truth concerning a matter—had been available since 1179, when it was provided specifically as a tenant's alternative to trial by battle. Felicia thus made her mise to the grand assize; that is, she chose and formulated the broad issue for the grand assize. The verdict of the grand assize would thus determine whether Felicia or Hugh had greater right to hold Whilton.

The process for assembling a grand assize was not as simple as that for taking a normal jury; the procedure had been formulated before taking a jury was considered a normal happening. Four knights were first chosen to assemble at Westminster and choose the twelve who would be sworn to form the panel of the grand assize. The four knights were supposed to appear in court in May 1297. It was normal to experience some difficulty in securing their appearance; in fact, they did not appear in May 1297 or on the following appointed dates (October 1297 and January 1298).[1] Then Hugh had to absent himself to fight for the king in Scotland in the latter part of 1298.[2] Nothing more could happen in the case until May 1299.

Precisely what would have happened had the four knights chosen the twelve and the twelve had assembled as a grand assize is difficult to ascertain. Legal attention was so riveted on pleading that, for lawyers, the trial was something of an afterthought. Unlike the pleading, trial was expected to be brief, relatively informal, and not legally demanding. It is clear nevertheless that evidence could be presented both to petty assizes and to a grand assize. This evidence, as far as is known, would not be in the form of sworn and cross-examined witnesses. One of the few relevant cases to have survived shows a lawyer merely reciting the words that had been used in a transaction concerning land—a relatively casual provision of information to an assize of novel disseisin, designed perhaps simply to call their attention to a version of the facts.[3*] Two others show that important documents could be given to an assize, but only if the jurors so requested.[4*] The jurors, by and large, were supposed to be self-informing. The law was still far away from even pondering on any set of formal rules of evidence.

Between the time that Hugh purchased his writ and May 1299, one party or the other was busy assembling relevant documents, probably with a view both to informing the pleader and to persuading the jurors of the grand assize, either before or at trial. The documents that the party planned to submit were reliable transcripts of the claim for redemption by Roger de Whelton (Document 4), the first jury on the transaction between William de Whelton and Nicholas (Document 6), the jury on the participation of William de Whelton at the Battle of Northampton (Document 7), the assize of novel disseisin *Whelton* v *Mortimer* (Document 13), the attaint *Mortimer* v

Whelton (Document 14), the action of entry *Whelton* v *Mortimer* (Document 16), and the writ of right *Mortimer* v *Montgomery* (Document 27).[5] The work spent in collecting these documents, although they were never used, was not wasted. They remained interesting to lawyers and were therefore transcribed into a large volume containing legal treatises and yearbook reports. Their presence there finally attracted the attention of a modern historian.

Felicia also was busy fortifying her standing. Sometime before September 1298 she married William de Nevill.[6] Though she was in that society no longer a young woman—she was somewhat over thirty years old—Felicia was nevertheless a desirable spouse. In addition to her own holdings, she retained a third of Philip's properties for the rest of her life as dower. Her new husband, after Felicia's own death, would be entitled to keep her lands held heritably as curtesy until his death, at which time those lands would descend and revert to the proper heirs. Marriage to Felicia would have much enhanced a young man's prospects. Marriage for Felicia would also have been desirable from the strictly practical point of view. The law would maintain, of course, that her marital status had nothing to do with legal advantage and the defense of her rights against Hugh de Mortimer. There is no doubt, however, that a man could normally wield power much better than a woman. William de Nevill—or Felicia through him—could be expected to impress the countryside better with his wife's right and take a more aggressive stance than she could have taken alone. He could influence people she could not hope to touch. Whether love was involved in this marriage—or, for that matter, in her marriage with Philip de Montgomery or in Joyce's marriages to Nicholas de Whelton and Robert de Mortimer—is not known. It is clear, however, that for both Felicia and William this marriage was a profitable venture. In marrying, Felicia was taking a prudent social step in defending her rights.

When the case was resumed in May 1299, the king intervened on behalf of Edward Burnel and Anne. His intervention raises the question concerning the kind of interest in Whilton that Anne and Edward had. It is clear, for instance, that had Whilton been held in fee simple and had Anne thus been the prospective heir to a fee simple, she would have had no present interest. Felicia would have been able to give or sell the land without any intervention being possible, because one could intervene only on behalf of a person with a present interest. In some sense, of course, Anne would have been injured, because she would no longer have been able to inherit. But she would have been only a prospective heir anyway. Not until her mother died could she be determined as a true heir and obtain any actual right to a fee simple. The development of the fee simple had been completely in the direction of binding the heir to warrant his ancestor's grants, so that all the powers of alienation had been accumulated in the person of the current tenant: the prospective heir had no rights until the current tenant died, at which time he received both the inheritance and the warranty obligations.

The development of the fee tail was quite different. Before the statute *De Donis Conditionalibus* in 1285, grants made in the form "to A and the heirs of his/her body" were construed to have conferred a life estate on A that would become a fee simple if A had such heirs. In such a situation, the heirs still had no rights, because A would have a fee simple after the birth of the heir and could not be restrained from selling. The statute *De Donis Conditionalibus* altered this situation. The effect at first was not to create a new entity, a "fee tail"; rather, it restricted A from selling, making sure that the land would descend to the heir. The statute conceptualized that A had only a life estate. Once an heir was born, that heir was considered to have the heritable interest, the fee simple, while his parent retained only the life estate. The heir thus had a present interest while the parent was still living, and intervention could thus be made on his behalf.[7]

This conceptualization was, of course, shortsighted and thus short-lived. Suppose a grant made "to Felicia and the heirs of her body." She might have a child, Anne, who would then be deemed to have the fee simple. Felicia might then remarry and have another child, whom we shall call Joan. Suppose further that Anne died. The form of the gift would indicate that Joan should become the new holder of the fee simple while Felicia continued to hold only the life estate. But Joan's interest would surely be contested. Anne had possessed the fee simple, so that at her death the fee simple should properly pass to her heirs. A person related only in the half-blood—that is, through but one of the parents and thus a product of a remarriage—could not be a person's general heir. The fee simple would thus pass not to Joan but to some cousin. That outcome would frustrate the intention of the grant, because of the intrinsic difficulty of construing that any prospective heir held any present right to the inheritance. That difficulty had not yet been faced at the time of this case, however, since the king intervened not only on behalf of Anne but also on behalf of Edward, a remainderman. Both were thus considered to have a present interest—a situation at least as difficult as the one involving a child of a second marriage. That way of conceiving of tailored fees could not survive.

Only after 1312 did the law begin to regard such tailored fees as a new entity, as a fee tail. The parent and original donee was thus considered to have not a life estate but a new thing: a fee tail, a heritable estate that could not be permanently alienated. The heir had no present interest; indeed, there was no reason to think about who the heir would be until the parent died. But it was absolutely sure that, when the parent died, the heir, whoever it might be, would inherit.

Hugh's action of right, however, came well before 1312 and thus still at a time when Anne and Edward Burnel were considered to have a present interest. In May 1299, therefore, the king sent a mandate to his justices in the Court of Common Pleas reciting the terms of the 1290 final concord and his duty to his wards. He then ordered the justices to terminate all proceedings on that writ until Anne and Edward attained majority, provided, that is, that the justices found that the final concord—a transcript of which had also been sent to the justices—was such as it seemed. It was, of course, and the case would therefore have to be adjourned until both children reached their majority, Anne at age fourteen in 1306, and Edward at age twenty-one in 1307. Felicia was thus saved by royal action.

DOCUMENT 29

Action of Right: *Mortimer* v *Montgomery*

Source: CP 30/127, m. 131 *Date*: circa 11 May 1299

Northamptonshire. Hugh de Mortimer formerly by his attorney before the justices at Westminster sought against Felicia who was the wife of Philip de Montgomery two-thirds of the manor of Whilton with appurtenances as his right etc. by a writ of right "because John Wake chief lord [of that fee] remitted to the lord king his court thereof" etc. And wherefore he said that a certain William the ancestor of the same Hugh was seised in his demesne as of fee and right in time of peace in the time of the lord King Henry, father of the present king, taking thereof esplees to the value of etc. And from the same William descended the right etc. to a certain William as son and heir. And from the same William, because he died without heir from himself, the right descended etc. to a certain Joyce as sister and heir; and from the same Joyce, to this Hugh who now [demands] as son and heir. And that such is his right he offered [suit and good proof].

And Felicia by her attorney came and denied his right when etc., and likewise the seisin of the abovesaid William, ancestor etc., from whose seisin [he demands] as of fee and right, and all etc. And she placed herself on the grand assize of the lord king and asked that a recognition be made whether she or the abovesaid Hugh had greater right in the abovesaid tenements etc.

Day was given them there at three weeks from Easter. And then came the four knights etc. And afterwards, process having continued, the parties had day at this day. And now come the parties by their attorneys. And thereupon the lord king ordered his justices here in these words:

"Edward by the grace of God king of England etc., to his justices of the Bench, greetings. Whereas Robert Burnel, late bishop of Bath and Wells gave and granted to Philip de Montgomery and Felicia his wife the manor of Whilton with appurtenances to have and to hold in perpetuity from the aforementioned Robert and his heirs to the same Philip and Felicia and the heirs coming forth from the body of the same Felicia such that, if the said Felicia should die without heir coming forth from her body, then that manor with appurtenances after the death of the same Felicia would remain to the aforementioned Philip and the heirs proceeding from his body and that, if the same Philip should die lacking an heir of this kind, then the same manor with appurtenances should revert to the aforementioned Robert and his heirs, as is more fully contained in the fine levied thereof in our court before you in the abovesaid Bench between the abovesaid Robert, plaintiff, and the aforementioned Philip and Felicia, impedients, and [whereas] we now understand that Hugh de Mortimer after the death of the abovesaid Philip impleads the aforementioned Felicia concerning two-thirds of the abovesaid manor by our writ of right before you and that the same Felicia—not mentioning before you that the manor with appurtenances by virtue of the abovesaid fine ought to descend to Anne the daughter and heir of the same Felicia who is now underage and in our wardship and, if the issue of the same Felicia's body should fail, then it ought to revert to Edward son of Philip Burnel and cousin and heir of the abovesaid Robert who is similarly underage and in our wardship—put herself on our grand assize thereof fraudulently and in manifest disinheritance of the same heirs and to the enervation of the same fine. Wishing to preserve [*consonere*] the above heirs as well as other underage heirs in our wardship in strength as we are obliged, we order you to inspect the tenor of the abovesaid fine and, if you shall have found that fine to have been levied in the abovesaid form and that no other deed has followed afterwards which could or ought to annul that fine, then in no way to proceed in that plea by the taking of that kind of assize before you or in any way whereby there might arise either a danger of disinheritance of either of the abovesaid heirs thus underage and living in our wardship or damage to us on account of the wardship which thereby might accidently happen to us in future times. Witnessed by me myself at Westminster the eleventh day of April in the twenty-seventh year of our reign [1299]."

And the Treasurer and Chamberlain by a writ of the king which came thereof to them sent the justices here a transcript of the abovesaid fine in these words: [There follows an accurate transcription of the final concord, Document 25].

And, the tenor of the abovesaid fine having been inspected, the justices asked the abovesaid Hugh by his attorney if he had anything or knew of anything to say why the justices ought not thus supersede the abovesaid plea according to the abovesaid order of the lord king etc. He says that he is not aware of any deed subsequent to that fine which ought to void that fine nor does he know anything else to say concerning this etc.

Therefore, let the parties go without day etc.

*

There is no doubt but that Felicia had made a thoroughly bad job of defending herself by neglecting to obtain the king's assistance earlier. Nevertheless, she had been saved in time, and not only in this suit. A corresponding writ and transcript of the fine were sent in regard to the action of entry (Document 26), and that suit likewise was indefinitely postponed.[8] It may be that we can credit William de Nevill with this intervention. He had just married Felicia in 1298 and had undoubtedly gone through the family papers. There he would have found a copy of the final concord. Felicia, of course, could no longer reverse her own course after putting herself on the grand assize, but Nevill could have brought the matter to the king's attention. The action then taken would have been the same as if the king's own officials had noticed the cases. Litigation concerning Whilton was now securely delayed until 1307. No one could have foreseen that serious litigation between the two sides about Whilton would not reappear until 1329.

CHAPTER 7

The Interlude

✻

BETWEEN the adjournment in 1299 and the reappearance of the dispute in 1329, no real progress was made in settling the title to Whilton or in reconciling the various descendants of Joyce. By the 1320s, of course, all the original parties to the dispute were long since dead; but they had bequeathed their descendants an inheritance of litigation. In such a family, it was unlikely that litigation would simply cease until 1329. Certain auxiliary disputes, such as that concerning the manor of Norton, would inevitably continue. More important were the cases of debt, detinue, annual rent, and trespass, which demonstrate the legal transactions of the family and the minor disputes that arose at least partly in connection with the problem of Whilton.

Anne's situation altered drastically between 1299 and 1308. In 1299 she was apparently still living with her mother; perhaps the king had not bothered to take bodily possession of his ward. He was, however, keenly aware of her value. Her wardship and marriage had been assigned to Edmund, earl of Cornwall, along with other wardships in payment of various debts. Then, in 1302, when she was about ten years old, one of the earl's executors sold Anne's marriage to John de Haldenby for £40, a sum to be expected only for a woman with substantial prospects. In accord with the sale, William de Nevill, Anne's stepfather, was ordered to hand the girl over to Haldenby to be married.

DOCUMENT 30
The Sale of Anne's Marriage

Source: PR, 1302-1307, p. 34 [altered] *Date*: 1 May 1302

Acceptance of the sale by Walter de Aylesbury, one of the executors of the will of Edmund, sometime earl of Cornwall, to John de Haldenby of the marriage of the daughter and heir of Philip de Montgomery, tenant in chief, for £40, whereof John has paid Walter £20 and will pay the remaining £20 at Michaelmas next to the said executors, to whom the marriage was assigned among other wardships and marriages, in part payment of the king's debts to the earl.

By K. on the information of J. de Drokenesford.

Mandate to William de Nevill of Whilton to deliver to the said John the body of the heir to be married.

Despite the tone of Document 30, this sale in itself did not do much to change Anne's situation. It may have been disturbing to her, in that she was taken away from her mother, but John de Haldenby was no stranger. Anne would henceforth be staying at Holdenby—less than five miles from Whilton—where her stepfather as well as her new guardian held part of the manor. Nevertheless, the sale would have driven home the fact that she was coming close to marriageable age. Anne, however, did not marry immediately. Late in 1304 her various guardians—William de Nevill and Felicia for her lands in Lincolnshire and Robert de Bruce for her lands in Staffordshire—were summoned to court to join with the king, who had some other lands in wardship for Anne, to provide proportionately the dower for Alice, the new wife of William Passelawe, from her late husband. The dower would amount to something over £1 5s in rents and two-thirds of an acre of woodland. Anne also was to be brought to court, and this order was conveyed to John de Haldenby. He was still listed at that time, when Anne was thirteen years old, as the guardian of the body,[1]* indicating that Anne remained unmarried.

The real change in her status came from the birth of a son to William de Nevill and Felicia: James de Nevill. Anne would, of course, remain Philip's heir, but the rules of inheritance dictated that, for any lands descending from Felicia herself, a son from whatever marriage entirely excluded her daughter. Anne was thus subordinated in regard to Whilton and the Sussex manor to this new male heir, who was born probably after 1302 and the sale of Anne's marriage to Haldenby but before 1308. Her attraction as a spouse was thus limited to her status as the Montgomery heir to the stewardship of the forest of Cannock. That inheritance, however, was sufficient to attract the attention of John de Swynnerton. His marriage to Anne late in 1305 or early in 1306 made him a substantial person in Staffordshire.[2] Whether or not James had been born by the time of the marriage, thereby limiting Anne's prospects, is not known. That birth may have been a severe blow to John de Swynnerton's expectations.

The birth of James was not the only circumstance that made William de Nevill and Felicia seem a burden for the newly married couple. No sooner had the stewardship of the forest of Cannock been delivered to Swynnerton than William and Felicia were able to sue for Felicia's dower from the stewardship. She apparently had to wait so long to sue because the stewardship was an office; ordinarily she could have claimed immediately on her husband's death. Her claim for dower in 1307 was thus for one-third of the stewardship in forty-five named places in Staffordshire. At the same time, she and her husband claimed her dower from a much lesser but reasonably substantial holding in Derbyshire.[3] Felicia's dower rights, although they stemmed from her previous marriage, were not altered in the least by the fact that she had married again.

Anne's actual ties to Whilton were progressively severed. It was probably in 1311, after almost five decades of her life had been consumed in fighting for Whilton, that Felicia died.[4]

By 1314 William de Nevill had taken another wife, Constance.[5] William, of course, would continue to hold Whilton, by the right of curtesy, until his death, when the manor would descend to James as heir of the fee tail. Anne would not lose interest in Whilton, however. Neither William nor James de Nevill could completely alienate the land—the former because he held only for life, the latter because he had only a fee tail and not a fee simple. Anne and her descendants would keep careful track of James, for if he died childless, Anne or her heirs could still inherit Whilton. Anne's interest, moreover, was not merely economic. She had been born, baptized, and raised at Whilton.[6] Furthermore, unless I am far mistaken about the personalities involved, Felicia had instilled in Anne a determination not to yield Whilton. There would be little chance that Anne would neglect any claim she had to Whilton. Years later, both Anne's son and her grandson—the latter the great-great-great-grandson of William de Whelton, the last undisputed tenant of Whilton—would claim the estate. In addition, then, to the main conflict between the Nevills and Hugh de Mortimer and his descendants, there was the further tension between the Swynnertons and the Nevills. Rights, like rabbits, tended to proliferate.

Likewise, although such judgments are hard to make from legal records, the men involved seem to have been fairly disagreeable characters. For William de Nevill, I have no evidence but have come to think of him as a harsh and domineering person John de Swynnerton, Anne's husband, was accused with others of the rape and detention of Joan, the widow of Peter de Greseleye, in 1310.[7] He received a pardon for his part in the deed. Although "rape" here may have meant only "abduction," that pardon did not ignore Joan's claims, and Swynnerton acknowledged a debt of £200 to her.[8] One must suspect a rather more grim side to his character. Indeed, in the next few years it became apparent that Swynnerton was eminently capable of using violence to obtain his ends.[9*] It is thus not surprising that William de Nevill and Felicia had to sue John de Swynnerton and Anne for Felicia's dower from the profits of the stewardship of the forest of Cannock in 1308.[10*] Finally, it must be said that Hugh de Mortimer was probably little better. A poet did mention Hugh for his part in the seige of Caerlaverock in 1300: "Hugh Mortimer, who well knew how to make himself beloved."[11] Whether the poet was being ironic or Hugh simply never used his talent with his wife, Matilda, is not known, but she killed him by poison on 5 August 1304. Queen Margaret seems to have thought that action not entirely reprehensible and interceded to obtain a pardon for her.[12] It is thus likely that the personalities involved would only have exacerbated the difficult legal situation.

Hugh de Mortimer was poisoned at the age of thirty-one, leaving his wife and two daughters, Joan and Margaret. The inheritance divided between the girls amounted to about sixteen knights fees each—a fact that in itself emphasizes the difference in stature between the Mortimers and the Nevills. Furthermore, the girls were not long burdened by the provision of dower to Hugh's widow: Matilda died in 1308.[13] Joan had married Thomas Bykenore before Hugh died in 1304; she would later have a second marriage with Richard Talbot.[14] Neither husband will partake in the dispute, although Joan herself will. Margaret was already married by the time Matilda died. Her husband, Geoffrey de Cornwall, was the son of an illegitimate son of Richard, earl of Cornwall and king of the Germans.[15] Joan and Margaret were thus not insignificant people. They and their husbands would be prepared to claim their respective halves of Whilton.

After the adjournment of 1299 there followed several unrelated suits involving the Nevills. In 1299 Richard de Montgomery brought an action of debt against William de Nevill and four others, claiming £10 from each of them.[16] Also in 1299 William and Felicia brought an assize of novel disseisin against William le Bretun for certain tenements in Whilton, presumably two acres of meadow and 40s rent with appurtenances. The suit was dropped, apparently, because William le Bretun merely brought a countersuit in the Court of Common Pleas, demanding that the Nevills warrant him that land. He claimed to have their deed, so that there was nothing much William and Felicia could do to dislodge him.[17] Then, in 1300, William and Felicia brought an assize of novel disseisin against Jordan, son of John le Mouner of Whilton. Jordan had apparently flooded some land to make a pond, and the Nevills objected. Their show of determination most likely caused Jordan to back down, because William and Felicia did not bother to prosecute further in 1301.[18] These suits represent merely the normal run of litigation that would be expected for any family of the Nevills' station.

In 1301 William de Nevill apparently fell behind in paying his lawyer, Adam de Harwedon. Lawyers at this time often functioned simultaneously in the king's court and a county court and could thus serve fully as a family lawyer. They were often retained and paid by an annuity supplemented only by payment of expenses. Such an annuity was a life grant conditioned on service rendered when required. It functioned very much like the grant of a fee to a knight, except that an annuity did not become hereditary and could be revoked readily if the lawyer failed to serve. In this situation, however, it was probably William who failed to pay. In January 1301 he acknowledged a debt of 9½ marks to Harwedon in the Court of Common Pleas. The schedule for payment was 60s due in October, 33s 4d at Christmas, and 33s 4d at Easter 1302, with the provision that, if the payments were not made, the sheriff could levy the value from William's lands and tenements. By 1302 Harwedon was doing just that. He sued out a writ *scire facias* ordering the sheriff to levy the money unless William produced proof of payment.[19]

Adam de Harwedon was a fairly popular lawyer. He had been retained by John de Plessy with an annuity of 20s and a robe. John de Ferlington had likewise retained him with an annuity of 20s. Robert de Crevequer saw fit to grant him an annuity of 40s. And the town of Northampton finally valued his services sufficiently to grant him an annuity of 4 marks (53s 4d) and a robe.[20] The robes specified in such annuities were not inexpensive; often the value of the robe was specified as 20s, so that it could easily double the value of the annuity. All these annuities, of course, would have been for legal services. Furthermore, in Michaelmas term 1309 in the Court of Common Pleas—the only term I examined for Harwedon—he was appointed the attorney in eleven cases.[21] His yearly caseload was therefore probably double that figure at least. The difficulty between Harwedon and Nevill in 1301 and 1302 did not terminate their relationship. Harwedon continued with Nevill until about 1312.[22] By then he may have become much too expensive, and Nevill began appointing John de Braunfield as attorney around 1314.[23]

The Nevills also found that they had to deal with a stubborn villein. In June 1303 they brought an action of neifty against one Richard, brother of Thomas son of William of Staverton. Not much can be known about the case, but the writ would have looked much like that hypothesized in Document 31. The writ of neifty, to modern ears, has a cold and aristocratic tone that properly conveys the proprietary attitude of the lord of the manor to his villeins.

DOCUMENT 31

A Hypothetical Writ of Neifty: *Nevill* v *Richard*

Source: Based on *Early Registers of Writs*, R. 244 *Date*: June 1303

The king to the sheriff, greetings. We command you that justly and without delay you cause William de Nevill and Felicia his wife to have Richard the brother of Thomas son of William of Staverton, his villein and fugitive, with all his chattels and all his brood wherever he is found in your jurisdiction, unless he be in our demesne, who fled from his land since the coronation of the lord Henry, king of England, our father. And we prohibit, upon our penalty, that any one detain him unjustly. Witness etc.

*

Richard came from that portion of Staverton which was united to the manor of Whilton. William and Felicia were asserting that Richard was a villein and their unfree tenant, a claim that Richard was in some way resisting. He may have attempted to flee Staverton to live in Northampton. He may have resisted seigneurial exactions that the lord of the manor was entitled to take from his villeins. He may even have been trying to establish himself as a free tenant at common law. Whatever was happening, the action of neifty was supposed to settle, once it was in the king's court, whether Richard was their villein or not. To establish his villeinage, William and Felicia would have to produce several of Richard's relatives who admitted to being villeins—villeinage was a matter of blood—and the case could eventually be settled merely in that way or might, in certain circumstances, be determined by jury. The case, however, was merely continued until January 1305 and then disappeared.[24] Perhaps Richard finally despaired of getting his freedom. Neifty was the kind of action necessary for the lord to maintain his domination over his more substantial or more restive unfree tenants, a particularly valuable portion of the aggregate of rights and land that formed a manor.

A peculiar threat to William de Nevill's hold on Whilton materialized early in 1312, and it is this threat that raises the presumption that Felicia had just died. William now claimed to hold the manor by curtesy as a free tenement until his death. The threat was presented by a strange coalition: Roger and Joan—the children of Alelm de Whelton and thus Felicia's cousins—and John de Nevill. John de Nevill was related in some way to William. As mentioned before, the lord of the manor had the right to nominate to the bishop of Lincoln the person who would be appointed the parish priest of Whilton. William had provided for John de Nevill in this way. John would thus have a secure living for life and would have been expected to bolster the family hold on Whilton. Nevertheless, he and Felicia's two cousins were alleged to have broken into William's close at Whilton and cut down and carried away trees worth 100s. Such activities were a common way to assert outside of court a right to land. William brought a suit of trespass against them in the Court of Common Pleas.

DOCUMENT 32

An Action of Trespass: *Nevill* v *Nevill & Whelton*

Source: CP 40/190, m. 96d *Date*: January 1312

Northamptonshire. William de Nevill by Adam de Harwedon his attorney presented himself on the fourth day against John de Nevill, Roger son of Alelm de Whelton and Joan sister of the same Roger in a plea why with force and arms they broke the close of the same William at Whilton and cut down trees growing there and took and carried away those trees and other goods and chattels found there to the value of 100s and did him other enormities to the great damage of the same William and against the king's peace etc.

And they did not come. And the sheriff had been ordered to attach them etc.; and the sheriff did nothing thereof. But he replied that the abovesaid Roger and Joan have nothing by which they can be attached. Therefore the sheriff is ordered to take them if [they shall be found in his jurisdiction] and [keep them] safely so that he have their bodies here at the quindene of Trinity term [to answer to the same William de Nevill etc.]. And concerning the abovesaid John the sheriff replied that he is a cleric and does not have a lay fee where he can be summoned. Therefore the bishop of Lincoln is ordered to make him come here at the aforementioned term [to answer etc.], and whereof [our sheriff of Northamptonshire replied that he had no lay fee etc.].

*

At the same time he brought this action of trespass, William also brought actions of detinue and debt, which further delineate what was happening at Whilton. Detinue was the action for claiming certain objects that had come into another's possession. Unlike trespass, in which normally only damages were awarded, detinue properly ended in the return of the items detained. John de Nevill was alleged to have gotten possession of two deed boxes containing diverse chirographs (among which would have been the final concords relating to Whilton), charters, obligatory deeds, covenants, and quitclaims. They would thus have contained, among other things, William's evidences concerning title to Whilton. Alelm's children might well have wished to lay their hands on these to determine the feasibility of challenging William's title. They would have been none too sure of the nature of the litigation that had gone before, and William de Nevill was not the kind of person who would have helped them to obtain the information.

John de Nevill's interest in the whole matter is less clear. It would not have been abnormal for a dependent relative merely to have become restive. The action of debt that William brought against John would indicate that John, in addition to being obliged to William for his appointment to the parish of Whilton, also owed him £22 8s 8d. That sum is suspiciously close to the annual revenue of Whilton, but it cannot be known whether or not John had been acting as one of William's estate managers. Whatever the precise nature of the happenings in 1312, the detention of the deed boxes and the cutting down of the trees indicates some collusion in an attempt—quite abortive, as it turned out—to oust William de Nevill from Whilton.

DOCUMENT 33

Actions of Debt and Detinue: *Nevill* v *Nevill & Whelton*

Source: CP 40/190, m. 57d *Date*: January 1312

Northamptonshire. William de Nevill by Adam de Harwedon his attorney presented himself on the fourth day against John de Nevill parson of the church of Whilton in a plea that he return to him two strongboxes, two deed boxes with diverse chirographs, charters, obligatory deeds, covenants, and quitclaims found in the same strong deed boxes which he unjustly detains etc.

And he did not come. And the sheriff was ordered to summon him etc. And the sheriff did nothing thereof but returned that he is a cleric and does not have a lay fee where he can be summoned etc. Therefore the bishop of Lincoln is ordered to make him come here at the quindene of Trinity etc. and whereof etc.

The same William by the same Adam his attorney presented himself on the fourth day against the abovesaid John de Nevill parson of the church of Whilton in a plea that he return to him £22 8s 8d which he owes him and unjustly detains etc. And he did not come. And the sheriff was ordered to summon him etc. And the sheriff did nothing, but returned that he is a cleric and does not have a lay fee where he can be summoned etc. Therefore the bishop of Lincoln is ordered to make him come here at the quindene of Trinity etc., and whereof etc.

*

Little came of this disruption. Alelm's children did not, in the end, lodge a claim to Whilton, and William de Nevill severely disciplined John. It seems that William made John seal a bond of indebtedness for £1,000. William could thus destroy John at will. When John de Nevill once more got out of line in 1314, William sued him for the return of thirteen charters and for the debt of £1,000.[25] The new round of litigation ended without conclusion. John de Nevill undoubtedly settled down when faced with certain disaster. However close John may have been to the Wheltons, he now saw very clearly that he was William's subordinate.

To a medieval lawyer, this set of litigation—trespass, debt, and detinue—would have presented a definite contrast to all the other cases considered thus far. In English law, pleas related to land were sharply distinguished from all others; they were the real actions, because they dealt with real property.

Trespass, debt, and detinue were classed as personal actions; they were seen as claims against a person rather than as claims to a thing. For trespass, this was an easy perception. It contained an allegation that another had done one a wrong—a personal injury, a taking away of one's goods, a breaking of one's close. Debt and detinue, although both claimed the return of something, were focused on a personal relationship between individuals. The actions enforced those commonly assumed obligations that adhered to the individuals involved. Trespass thus concerned a nonconsensual relationship; debt and detinue, a consensual relationship. In each case, the persons involved were to be forced to live up to their obligations. That was a clearly different matter from establishing who had proper title to land or rents. Despite such lawyerly distinctions, however, these cases demonstrate that, as far as the litigants were concerned, personal actions could be very much part and parcel of a dispute about land.

From 1314 to 1321 the litigation relating to Whilton was not concerned with the main dispute. In 1315, 1317, and 1320 William had to sue his officials to render account for the money they had collected on his behalf.[26] Such suits, like the action of neifty, constitute the normal run of litigation necessary for any lord. More exceptional was an action taken against William in 1319. He had been sheriff of Warwickshire and Leicestershire from May to November 1318; he would be sheriff of those same counties again from December 1319 to October 1321. As sheriff he was responsible for collecting moneys due the king—for which he accounted at the Exchequer—and for executing the numerous royal mandates sent him, including all the legal procedure for cases coming from those counties into the Court of King's Bench, the Court of Common Pleas, and the Exchequer of Pleas. Furthermore, he was in charge of the county and hundred courts of those two counties. Most of his tasks were handled by a substantial staff of clerks and bailiffs, and William's most important duty was the selection and supervision of that staff so that it would function efficiently. It was as sheriff of Warwickshire that he had been ordered to levy some money from the lands of Robert le Belleyetere. Robert had had enrolled in the plea rolls of the Court of Common Pleas an acknowledgment of a debt of £22 to Robert Ernefast, and the debt was now to be levied for default of payment. When William left office in November 1318, he had still not turned over 40s of that money to Ernefast, who therefore sued William. The sheriff of Northamptonshire was ordered to levy the 40s from William's lands and chattels in Northamptonshire, perhaps, thus, from Whilton.[27]

In 1321 Joan and Margaret, the daughters of Hugh de Mortimer, and their husbands hesitantly renewed the dispute. Why they chose this time is not clear. If James de Nevill had been born in 1300, he would have just come of age. That might have been a reason to sue, but James was more likely born around 1308. Margaret, the younger of Hugh's daughters, had herself been of age and married for about a decade already. Edward Burnel, the reversioner by the 1290 concord, had died in 1315, leaving Matilda, his sister, as his heir. She also was of age. Thus, it was not the end of a minority that suggested further litigation in 1321. Likewise, in 1321 William de Nevill was sheriff of Warwickshire and Leicestershire. Had he been sheriff of Northamptonshire, there would have been every reason to avoid suing him. It took a hardy litigant to sue a sheriff in his own county. But one might also expect that litigation would be marginally more difficult against a sheriff even outside his jurisdiction. Whatever the reason, however, the Cornwalls and Talbots, heirs to the Mortimer claim, seem to have thought, for a moment at least, that Nevill was vulnerable. Perhaps their strategy was related to the political disturbances in 1321. Pehaps they hoped that Nevill, like William de Whelton so long before, would end up on the losing side.

DOCUMENT 34

Renewal of the Dispute: *Talbot & Cornwall* v *Nevill*

Source: CP 40/236, m. 95d *Date*: circa 28 January 1321

Northamptonshire. The essoiner of William de Nevill presented himself on the fourth day against Richard Talbot and

Joan his wife and Geoffrey de Cornwall and Margaret his wife in a plea concerning the manor of Whilton with appurtenances. And they did not come. And they were the demandants. Therefore the above essoiner [go] hence without day. And the abovesaid Richard and others and their pledges to prosecute, to wit Adam de Houghton and Thomas Golafre, be in mercy.

*

The 1321 case was the only Mortimer resumption of the dispute between 1299 and 1329. Since Hugh's daughters decided very quickly that their strategy would not work and dropped the case, even the 1321 resumption occasioned William de Nevill little problem. William, then, held Whilton with Felicia for about thirteen years and, after her death, remained as a tenant by the curtesy for another eighteen years. For most of that time no serious challenges came against him for Whilton. Between 1312 and 1314, right after Felicia's death, there had been some problems, but not from the Mortimers; even those annoyances William was able to put down. When Felicia married Nevill to help her protect Whilton, she chose wisely.

CHAPTER 8

Resumption and Compromise

THE MANOR of Whilton had now become a traditional subject of litigation between Felicia and her heirs and Joyce and her heirs. It had been no real surprise that Hugh de Mortimer's daughters had remembered to revive the dispute in 1321; it was to be expected that they would try again. Nevertheless, some of the emotional content of the dispute must have disappeared. William de Nevill was the second husband of the half-sister of the father of Margaret and Joan; James de Nevill (William's son) was their (half) first cousin. It was no longer a contest between mother and daughter. Both because William had been closely bound to Felicia and because he had no reason to feel a personal bond with Felicia's relatives, he could be expected to defend Whilton resolutely. It was too valuable an asset to relinquish lightly. The time was nevertheless coming when compromise and reconciliation would seem better than an uncertain outcome by judgment.

In 1329, as in 1285, the king appointed justices in eyre for the county of Northamptonshire—justices commissioned to reside in the county for a period and to hear and determine all manner of pleas arising in the county. For the most part, William had avoided litigation since 1321. The coming of the eyre must have seemed to him like a personal catastrophe. The bishop of Ely, to begin with, sued him for a debt of 40 marks that had been due in 1321. Since William could not deny his written obligation, the bishop was awarded the 40 marks and £10 damages—£36 8s 8d in all.[1] Then Philip de Nevill claimed that William should warrant him eleven messuages in Holdenby—that is, eleven houses and their surrounding closes.[2] That action also represented the renewal of an old dispute: there had been a final concord on the matter back in 1315.[3] Thomas Botereus then sued William for ten acres of arable land and two acres of meadow in Whilton.[4] These three suits together with the two suits that follow, must mean that William de Nevill finally appeared to be vulnerable.

The first of the two relevant cases in the eyre was brought by William le Spenser, the descendant of the Lees, who had been granted their land by the Mortimers. The kind of writ he brought was a writ of aiele. The principle behind the writ of aiele was similar to that behind mort d'ancestor. In the simple form, mort d'ancestor defended the child and heir's right to the land of which his parent (or sibling, aunt, or uncle) had died seised in demesne as of fee (in personal possession of the land, claiming a heritable estate). Aiele was appropriate when the relative on whose death and seisin one claimed was a grandparent. The determination in aiele was considered, as in the assize of novel disseisin, to be only possessory, so that either a writ of entry or a writ of right could reverse the result. Spenser thus claimed that Alice, his grandmother, had died seised in demesne as of fee and that he should be put into the land as heir. William de Nevill first prayed aid of his son, but James, for reasons to be explained, declined to join himself to the suit. William then challenged the crucial point in the writ: he denied that Alice had died seised. If she had not died seised, then there was no prima facie reason for Spenser to gain seisin. His whole case would fail. The matter was thus ready to be sent to a jury.

DOCUMENT 35

An Action of Aiele: *Spenser* v *Nevill*

Source: JUST 1/633, m. 18 *Date*: 23 February 1330

William le Spenser seeks against William de Nevill, knight, one messuage, one carucate of land, six acres of meadow and 10s rent with appurtenances in Whilton of which Alice who was the wife of Nicholas [de] Lee, grandmother of the abovesaid William le Spenser whose heir he is, was seised of the abovesaid tenements in her demesne as of fee on the day on which she died etc. And wherefore he says that the abovesaid Alice was seised of the abovesaid tenements in her demesne as of fee in time of peace in the time of the lord Edward, king, grandfather of the present lord king, taking therefrom esplees to the value etc., and from that Alice the fee descended [and ought to descend] to a certain John as son and heir etc. And from the same John the fee descended [and ought to descend] to this William who now claims as son and heir etc. Of which etc. And thereof he produces suit etc.

And William de Nevill comes and formerly in court here he said that the abovesaid tenements now sought against him are parcels of the manor of Whilton and that he holds the abovesaid manor by the law of England [i.e., by curtesy] from the inheritance of a certain James de Nevill, to whom the reversion of the same manor pertains after the death of the same William. And he sought aid of the abovesaid James etc., so that the sheriff was then ordered to summon him to be here on the Monday next after the quindene of the Purification of the Blessed Mary [19 February 1330]. At which day the sheriff did nothing, wherefore as formerly the sheriff was ordered to summon the abovesaid James to be here at this day, to wit the Friday next after Ash Wednesday [23 February 1330], and he does not come. And the sheriff returns that he summoned etc. Therefore let the abovesaid William de Nevill answer without [the abovesaid James etc.]. And the same William denies his right when etc. And he says that the abovesaid William le Spenser can claim no right in the abovesaid tenements, because he says that the abovesaid Alice, grandmother etc., of whose death etc., did not die seised of the abovesaid tenements as the same William le Spenser by his writ supposes. And of this he puts himself on the countryside.

And the abovesaid William le Spenser similarly.

Therefore the sheriff is ordered to make to come here on the Saturday in the first week of Lent [3 March 1330] twelve [as well knights as other free and lawful men, of the county of Northamptonshire], by whom [the truth of the matter can best be known] and who [are related neither to the abovesaid William le Spenser nor to the abovesaid William de Nevill in any affinity etc.] to recognize [whether the abovesaid Alice atte Lee, grandmother etc., died seised in her demesne as of fee of the messuage etc.] because both [the aforesaid William le Spenser and the abovesaid William de Nevill have put themselves on the countryside thereof etc.].

*

At the same time that Spenser brought his action of aiele, the suit for Whilton proper was renewed, but very cautiously. It was brought only by Joan, the elder daughter of Hugh de Mortimer. Unlike the situation in 1321, Margaret, Joan's sister, and Geoffrey de Cornwall, Margaret's husband, declined to join themselves to the claim. Hence, Joan's claim was for only her share of the portion that had been the dower of William de Whelton's widow—a half of a third of the manor. Her suit could still be made by writ of entry. Except for the additional generation, her claim was the same as Hugh de Mortimer's had been: a claim alleging an intrusion after the widow's death and tracing the right from William de Whelton to Roger de Whelton, then by sale to Zouche, descending to Joyce, then to Hugh, and now to Joan and Margaret.

William de Nevill was not ready to surrender the land. He appeared before the justices and explained that he held only by curtesy; thus he prayed aid of his son. James once more declined to appear. Joan and William thus were allowed to continue the case, the one without her sister, the other without his son. William asked for proof of Roger's sale to Zouche. Joan proffered a transcipt of the 1270 final concord (Document 8). William then challenged her on a technicality. He pointed out that she had submitted a mere transcript, whereas she should have proffered a transcript verified by seal. Joan and William asked the justices to decide whether such an unsealed transcript was sufficient to make William answer Joan's claim. The justices decided to give their ruling at another day.

DOCUMENT 36

Action of Entry by Intrusion: *Talbot* v *Nevill*

Source: JUST 1/633, m. 126 *Date*: 12 March 1330

Joan who was the wife of Richard Talbot by Thomas de Tochewyk her attorney seeks against William de Nevill, knight, a half of one-third of the manor of Whilton with appurtenances as her right and inheritance and in which the same William does not have entry except by Felicia who was the wife of Philip de Montgomery who demised it to him and who intruded herself in that tenement after the death of Felicia who was the wife of William de Whelton who held that tenement from William la Zouche in dower from the gift of the abovesaid William de Whelton her late husband. [And the abovesaid Joan claims] from the assignment which Roger son and heir of the abovesaid William de Whelton made thereof to the aforementioned William la Zouche, great-grandfather of the abovesaid Joan whose heir she is etc. And whereof the same Joan says that the abovesaid Roger was seised of the entire one-third part in his demesne as of fee and right in time of peace in the time of King Henry, great-grandfather of the present king, taking therefrom esplees to the value etc., which certain Roger assigned the same one-third part to Felicia who was the wife of William de Whelton to hold by name of dower. And afterwards he granted the reversion of the abovesaid one-third part to the aforementioned William la Zouche, great-grandfather etc. By virtue of which concession the same Felicia attorned herself to the same William la Zouche, great-grandfather etc. From the same William great-grandfather etc., descended the right etc., to a certain Joyce as daughter and heir, and from the same Joyce descended the right etc., to a certain Hugh as son and heir, and from the same Hugh descended the right etc., to this Joan who now claims and to a certain Margaret now the wife of Geoffrey de Cornwall as to daughters and heirs, which certain Geoffrey and Margaret now are summoned to follow with [the abovesaid Joan etc.]. And they do not prosecute for her part. Therefore let the same Joan follow without etc., and in which etc. And thereof she produces suit etc.

And William by John de Braunfield his attorney comes and denies her right when etc. And he says that he holds the abovesaid half by the law of England [i.e., by curtesy] after the death of a certain Felicia his wife from the inheritance of James son and heir of the same Felicia without whom he cannot put the same half part into judgment. And he prays aid of the same James. Therefore let him be summoned to be here on the Monday in the third week of Lent [12 March 1330] to answer together with [the abovesaid William de Nevill]. The same day is given to the abovesaid parties here in the eyre etc.

At which day the abovesaid Joan came by her abovesaid attorney; and similarly came the abovesaid William by his abovesaid attorney. And the abovesaid James summoned and solemnly called did not come. Therefore let the same William respond without [the abovesaid James etc.]. And the same William says that the abovesaid Joan seeks the abovesaid tenements by reason of a certain assignment made thereof to the abovesaid William la Zouche great-grandfather etc., in which case he ought not answer without a special deed or record which testifies to that assignment. Wherefore he asks that she show in court if she has anything from that assignment etc.

And Joan says that formerly in the court of King Henry, great-grandfather of the present king, before Martin de Littlebury and his companions, justices of the same King Henry etc., at Westminster, three weeks from Michaelmas in the fifty-fourth year of the reign of the abovesaid King Henry [circa 20 October 1270] a certain fine was levied between the abovesaid William la Zouche, plaintiff, and Roger de Whelton, impedient, concerning the manor of Whilton with appurtenances, whereof there was a plea of warranty of charters summoned between them in the same court, to wit, that the abovesaid Roger recognized two-thirds of the abovesaid manor with appurtenances as in lordships, homages, and the service of free men etc., to be the right of the same William as those parts which the same William had from the gift of the abovesaid Roger to have and to hold to the same William and his heirs from the abovesaid Roger and his heirs in perpetuity. And in particular the same Roger conceded that the one-third part of the abovesaid manor with appurtenances which Felicia who was the wife of William de Whelton held in dower from the inheritance of the same Roger on the day on which the concord was made and which after the death of the abovesaid Felicia ought to revert to the abovesaid Roger and his heirs should remain after the death of the abovesaid Felicia wholly to the same William and his heirs to hold together with the two-thirds part of the abovesaid manor with appurtenances. And she proffers here a transcript of the abovesaid fine which testifies to the abovesaid [fine etc.].

And William says that since the abovesaid Joan does not show here any special deed nor any other thing which is of record which proves the abovesaid assignment except only the abovesaid transcript, whereas she ought to have had the abovesaid fine under the foot of a seal so that she would have been answerable thereof to this writ by the abovesaid fine. And he asks judgment if he ought to be put to answer the abovesaid Joan by that writ etc.

And Joan asks judgment if this is not sufficient for her by right to make the abovesaid William answer her at this abovesaid writ etc., since she is prepared to verify by record that the abovesaid fine was levied in the abovesaid form, by which fine the abovesaid assignment is sufficiently proved.

And thereupon day is given to hear their judgment here on the Wednesday next after the quindene of Easter [10 May 1330] etc., saving to the parties their reasons etc.

*

As with most legal cases, there was more happening here than would appear from just these records. William de Nevill was dying; by 10 May 1330 he was dead.[5] He had remained intransigent to the very end, and with him died the last personal link with the original problem. James de Nevill, Felicia's heir, unlike Anne, her daughter, had hardly known his mother. Hugh de Mortimer's daughters had had little enough time to know their own father, let alone Joyce, their grandmother. William de Nevill was thus the last remaining barrier to compromise.

That compromise had already begun to take shape before William's death. Although William remained unyielding, he could not force James to adopt the same opinion. Since William was only a tenant for life in Whilton (and even more so, since Whilton was held in fee tail), James would inevitably inherit. There was no way in which William could disinherit his son from that manor. He could, of course, have sold the other lands and tenements he held in fee and thus diminished James's inheritance, but that would have been an extreme measure indeed. Neither James nor anyone else was willing to alienate the elderly William to that degree. James, at any rate, was not particularly worried about departing from the stand his father had taken.

James planned to marry Joan de Cornwall, the daughter of Margaret, the niece of Joan Talbot, the great-granddaughter of Joyce. This marriage, in fact, had probably already taken place. However, it need not yet have been solemnized. At this date, a marriage could be validly contracted by the exchange of words of present consent by the concerned man and woman without any ecclesiastical assistance. It then became immediately an enforceable marriage. Ecclesiastical officials would thereafter insist only that it be solemnized in church. Such a marriage would explain why James de Nevill had declined to join with his father in defending Whilton: he had made his arrangements by marrying into the opposition. Such a marriage would also explain why the Cornwalls declined to join in suing William: there was little need for an all-out assault on the failing father of their son-in-law. Even the suits of Joan Talbot and William le Spenser were probably aimed not at successful prosecution but rather at bringing William de Nevill around to consenting to the arrangements being made by James and the Cornwalls. Neither suit was reinstated against James. Furthermore, Joan Talbot's claims, after William de Nevill's death, were decisively forgotten: she probably yielded whatever claim she had to her neice as a wedding present. It seems, then, that James, Joan Talbot, William le Spencer, and the Cornwalls were pressuring William de Nevill to accept the union of James and Joan.

Preparations for the solemnization went forward. I think those preparations can be seen in part of the plea rolls of the eyre—timed, one might think, indecently soon after William's death. On 27 April 1330 Geoffrey de Cornwall made two debt recognizances to William le Hunte, a merchant of Northampton, for a total debt of £15 17s 8d.[6] Then, on 15 June 1330 Geoffrey de Cornwall and James de Nevill jointly made a further recognizance to Thomas de Staunforde, another merchant, for £13 6s 8d.[7] These expenditures to merchants were probably for the marriage celebration. Some of that money may also have been needed to obtain a dispensation from the Church. James was marrying his (half) first cousin once removed. Now, marriages within the fourth degree were prohibited. James de Nevill was only in the second degree from Joyce (it had taken two acts of generation to go from Joyce to James), and Joan was only in the third degree from Joyce. Since one used the longer line for these purposes, measuring from the common ancestor, James and Joan were related in the third degree, well within the four-degree prohibition. For the wealthy, of course, fourth-degree marriages readily received dispensation. A third-degree dispensation would have required rather more effort and expense. Perhaps the fact that Felicia and Hugh were related only through Joyce and not through their fathers was of some assistance; the laudable purpose of the marriage, familial reconciliation, would certainly have helped. Whatever difficulty they may have encountered has not been recorded in documents yet printed. It is even conceivable, but hardly likely, that no one even raised the issue. The fact remains, however, that they were married.

The most important preparation for the marriage was the compromise over Whilton. The central element in the agreement was that Whilton would be given to the couple in fee tail. But there were complications. Joan Talbot would have to surrender her claim to half of Whilton, or else James would not surrender his own independent title. Apparently she did, probably by written and sealed quitclaim. Then, account had to be taken of the other Cornwall children. Geoffrey and Margaret had three sons, each of whom would be entitled to inherit the claim to Whilton before Joan. It was decided that James simply would not acknowledge the opposition's claims, so that the arrangement was not an implicit recognition of Joan's brothers' right to the inheritance based on the Mortimer descent. James also compromised, because he surrendered his independent title, although he surrendered it in such a way that he still held Whilton securely. The compromise thus demanded a substantial reordering of claims to Whilton; it was not a mere capitulation by either side.

The settlement was arranged once more by final concord, made on 23 May 1330. In the eyre plea rolls there is only the typically short notice of the making of a fine, listing Joan already as James's wife.

DOCUMENT 37
License to Concord: *Nevill* v *Cornwall*

Source: JUST 1/633, m. 172d *Date*: May 1330

James son of William de Nevill and Joan his wife give one mark for a license to concord with Geoffrey de Cornwall in a plea of covenant concerning the manor of Whilton with appurtenances. And let them have a chirograph by Robert de Scardeburgh, pleader etc.

*

In the fine itself James and Joan granted Whilton to Geoffrey de Cornwall. Geoffrey then regranted Whilton to James and Joan and the heirs of their bodies—thus, to them in fee tail. The specification limited the inheritance to the children of the marriage, with children of either James or Joan by different and later marriages excluded. If James and Joan should die without such an heir, remainders in fee tail were provided for the two younger Cornwall children: first to John and the heirs of his body and then to Hugh and the heirs of his body. The reversion, should James and Joan, John, and Hugh all die without leaving an heir of the specified class, would be to Geoffrey de Cornwall and his heirs. The fine thus gave a clear advantage to Geoffrey. He was not, admittedly, to receive the full possession of that half of Whilton for which he might have hoped when he married Margaret; nor, since the service for the holding was only a rose, would he receive significant annual services for the land. He had, however, endowed his daughter with Whilton and had thus acquitted himself, at least in part, of providing for his daughter at little actual expense. Furthermore, he had secured the underlying title for himself and his children, a title that, for all he knew, amid the personal catastrophes of successive deaths might blossom suddenly into full possession. James, on the other hand, would no longer have to worry about defending Whilton; his title would now be unchallenged. By this settlement, James was secure in Whilton, although henceforward title to the manor would flow from Geoffrey de Cornwall, not from Felicia or from the Mortimers.

DOCUMENT 38
A Final Concord: *Nevill* v *Cornwall*

Source: CP 25(1) 176/73, no. 60 *Date*: 23 May 1330

This is the final concord made in the court of the lord king at Northampton on Wednesday next after the feast of the Ascension of the Lord in the fourth year of the reign of King

Edward, third of that name since the Conquest, before Geoffrey le Scrop, John de Cambridge, John de Radenhale, Thomas de Louth, Peter de Middleton, and Thomas de Radeclyve, justices in eyre there, and others faithful to the king then present there between James son of William de Nevill and Joan his wife, plaintiffs, and Geoffrey de Cornwall, deforciant, concerning the manor of Whilton with appurtenances whereof there was summoned a plea of covenant between them in the same court, to wit: that the abovesaid James acknowledges the abovesaid manor with appurtenances to be the right of the same Geoffrey as that which the same Geoffrey has from the gift of the abovesaid James. And for this recognition, fine, and concord, the same Geoffrey grants to the abovesaid James and Joan the abovesaid manor with appurtenances and renders it to them in the same court to have and to hold to the same James and Joan and the heirs proceeding from the bodies of the same James and Joan from the abovesaid Geoffrey and his heirs in perpetuity by rendering each year thereof to the abovesaid Geoffrey and his heirs one rose at the feast of the nativity of St. John the Baptist [24 June] for every service, custom, and exaction pertaining to the abovesaid Geoffrey and his heirs and by doing thereof to the chief lords of that fee for the abovesaid Geoffrey and his heirs all other services which pertain to that manor in perpetuity. And if it happen that the same James and Joan die without heir proceeding from the bodies of the same James and Joan, then after the decease of the same James and Joan the abovesaid manor with appurtenances will remain to John son of the abovesaid Geoffrey and to the heirs procreated from his body to hold from the abovesaid Geoffrey and his heirs by the abovesaid services as is said above in perpetuity. And if it happen that the same John die without heir procreated from his body, then after the decease of the same John the abovesaid manor with appurtenances will remain wholly to Hugh, brother of the same John and the heirs procreated from his body to hold from the abovesaid Geoffrey and his heirs by the abovesaid services as is said above in perpetuity. And if it happen that the same Hugh should die without heir procreated from his body, then after the decease of the same Hugh the abovesaid manor with appurtenances will revert wholly to the abovesaid Geoffrey and his heirs quit of all the heirs of James and Joan, John, and Hugh to hold from the chief lords of that fee by the services which pertain to the abovesaid manor in perpetuity.

[Endorsed:] John de Haudlo and Matilda his wife put forward their claim.

The events of 1330 were directed toward putting to rest a dispute that had endured for over sixty years. Up until 1330 the law had been used as a means of crushing the opponent. Every opportunity for gaining advantage, both legal and social, had been taken. Strategy had been carefully planned to delay the opposition and retain possession of Whilton for as long as possible. In short, up until 1330 litigation functioned as a peaceable and acceptable mode of conflict. In 1330 the parties began to use litigation in quite another way: as an integral part of an effort toward reconciliation and compromise. Joan Talbot and William le Spenser had each used litigation to pressure William de Nevill to accept the inevitable. All William's prospective in-laws tactfully declined to join suit against him. Even his son declined to join himself to William's stubborn defense of Whilton. When William died, the marriage and compromise promptly fell into place. The conflict was to be buried, as it were, in the mounting pile of final concords in the king's court.

CHAPTER 9

Formedon and the Use

THE FINAL concord of 1330 and the marriage between James and Joan effectively resolved the dispute between the Nevills and the Mortimers, but only at the expense of the rights of others: the descendants of Felicia's daughter and the heirs of Robert Burnel. In the final concord James granted a fee simple to Geoffrey de Cornwall, from which Geoffrey then regranted James and Joan the more limited estate of the fee tail. The problem was that James purported to give Geoffrey more than he himself had. The final concord of 1290 (Document 25) had established a fee tail for Felicia and her descendants. It was clear by 1330 that a fee tail would limit the holder's powers of alienation and the method of inheritance at least until the fourth generation. James de Nevill was only the second generation. By the 1290 final concord, the Burnels and their heirs had the reversion in fee simple, but in 1330 James, in effect, attempted to switch that reversion from the Burnels to the Cornwalls. Matilda, the wife of John Haudlo, was the Burnel heir. She and her husband duly entered their claim, which was endorsed on the final concord and thus preserved. At least to that extent, then, the final concord of 1330 did not end the possibilities for litigation.

Anne, Felicia's daughter and James's half-sister, had also been ignored. To a certain extent, this was legitimate. Neither the Haudlos nor Anne could really complain about anything so long as James or his descendants lived. By the terms of the 1290 fine, neither Anne nor the Haudlos could profit from Whilton until one of the remainders established by the 1330 fine took effect in the Cornwall children. If James died without surviving children, Anne's children could claim as descendants of Felicia; the Haudlos could only claim after Anne's line similarly failed. Therefore, Anne's descendants, the Swynnertons, were those most concerned in observing the fortunes of the new Nevill household.

The success of the compromise of 1330 depended on the survival of the son soon born to James and Joan: James de Nevill the younger. In 1362 James, Joan, and James were still alive and at Whilton. On 28 June of that year Robert Syer complained that they had assaulted and variously oppressed him and had killed his animals. Syer felt the matter to be of sufficient urgency that he was willing to pay to have a commission of *oyer* and *terminer*. Those commissioned were a special session of the king's court assembled to hear and determine the case right there in Northamptonshire. The limitation of their jurisdiction to the one case clearly distinguished such commissions from the general eyres, the last of which had been held in 1329-1331.

DOCUMENT 39

A Commission of *Oyer* and *Terminer: Syer* v *Nevill*

Source: CPR, 1361-1364, p. 284 [altered] *Date*: 28 June 1362

[Commission of *oyer* and *terminer*] to John de Verdon, John Knyvet and John Lyouns, on complaint by Robert Syer that James de Nevill knight, Joan his wife, James his son, John Packesson of Henkeston, Robert Packesson of Henkeston, William le Warde hayward, Henry Howeman and others assaulted him at Brockhall, Northamptonshire, and afterwards threatened him with death so that for a great time he dared not pass from the said town to his own dwelling house, impounded his cattle at Whilton without cause until he made fine by 100s for their deliverance, and hunted 100 of his sheep there with dogs urging on the dogs to bite the sheep so that by the hunting and biting twenty of them, worth 40s, died.

For 2 marks paid in the hanaper.

*

Such charges were often exaggerated simply to obtain the commission. Any reading of the case, however, clearly shows that the Nevills were still exercising power in and around Whilton in 1362.

The situation changed dramatically in 1375. James, son of James and Joan, had already died, leaving no children. James and Joan had no further children. James de Nevill himself then died in 1375 or thereabouts, not quite seventy years old. If the 1330 final concord was valid, Joan could continue to hold until she also died. By the terms of the 1290 final concord, however, the most she could hope for was a third of Whilton as dower. Either she suspected and wanted to avoid the imminent claim by the Swynnertons or else she was no longer able to manage Whilton herself. In 1375 she sold the manor to John Holt and John the parson of Whilton.[1] They in turn put the manor into the hands of some reliable friends. This series of transactions precipitated the claim by Anne's descendants.

Anne's husband, John de Swynnerton, turned out to be even more active than William de Nevill in local affairs. He served as sheriff of Shropshire and Staffordshire, as escheator, and often in Parliament as a knight of the shire from Staffordshire. He died in 1340. Anne outlived him and is last mentioned in 1347.[2] Perhaps she fell victim soon thereafter to the first widespread occurrence of the Black Death. Their son, also named John de Swynnerton, had been born around 1309. It was he who brought suit for Whilton in 1376, at the age of sixty-seven. His suit, however, was not pursued resolutely. He first failed to find pledges to prosecute; then, in 1377 his case disappeared.[3]* He died in 1379 without having resolved the matter.[4]

John de Swynnerton, his son and thus Felicia's great-grandson, immediately renewed the litigation. The writ he purchased, like the writ his father had purchased, against Holt's reliable friends was a writ of formedon—the word itself means "form of the gift"—in the descender, a writ specially tailored for those claiming a fee tail as a descendant of the original recipient of the gift.

DOCUMENT 40

A Hypothetical Writ of Formedon in the Descender: *Swynnerton* v *Latymer et al.*

Source: Modeled on *Early Register of Writs*, R873 *Date*: 1380

Richard, by the grace of God King of England etc., to the sheriff of Northamptonshire, greetings. Command William Latymer, knight; Richard Stury, knight; William de Thorpe, knight; Richard de Treton, cleric; William Thirnyng; and John Wade, parson of the church of Hemmingford Abbots that justly and without delay they render to John son of John de Swynnerton son of Anne daughter of Philip de Montgomery and Felicia his wife the manor of Whilton with appurtenances in Staverton which Robert late bishop of Bath and Wells gave to Philip de Montgomery and Felicia his wife and the heirs proceeding from the body of the same Felicia and which, after the death of the aforesaid Philip and Felicia and of James the son and heir of the same Felicia and of Anne the sister of the abovesaid James and John son of the abovesaid Anne ought to descend by the form of the abovesaid gift to the aforementioned John de Swynnerton son of the same John son of Anne and cousin and heir of the abovesaid James, as he says. And if they do not and the said John son of John de Swynnerton shall have given you security to prosecute his claim, then summon by good summoners the aforesaid William Latymer, knight, etc., that they be before our justices at Westminster one month [?] from Easter to show why they have not done this. And have there the summoners and this writ. Witness, etc.

*

Such a writ was the only remedy available to Swynnerton. Had he chosen to bring, for instance, a writ of right, he would automatically be regarded as claiming a fee simple, whereas he could only claim a fee tail. He had to rely on the entailed nature of his estate, based on the 1290 final concord, in order to make a claim, or else James de Nevill would have had every right to make the 1330 final concord and exclude the Swynnertons from Whilton forever. John could conceivably have attempted to use a somewhat different form of formedon writ: a writ of formedon in the remainder based on the remainder that had been given to Philip de Montgomery and the heirs of his body if Felicia's line should fail. That would have been somewhat ludicrous, however, because the claim as a descendant was both prior and stronger. It is even likely that any claim by Swynnerton as a remainderman would seem not only ludicrous but also invalid. He therefore claimed as a direct descendant of Felicia, the original grantee of the gift. The resolution of such a plea was considered to be as binding on the parties as the resolution in a suit begun by writ of right.

John de Swynnerton, as Felicia's great-grandson, would stand as a fourth-generation holder of the fee tail. Had he been claiming immediately after the statute *De Donis* in 1285, it is probable that James de Nevill would have been allowed to alienate the manor. Moreover, since Swynnerton stood in the fourth degree, and since neither his parents nor his grandparents had died seised, he would not have been granted a writ of formedon.[5*] He would not have had any valid claim. During the fourteenth century, however, with no explicit discussion of the matter that has survived, the fee tail came to be perpetual like the fee simple. But the effect of perpetuity was completely different in the two situations. For the fee simple, the absence of any limitation on the duration of the title made the land alienable. For the fee tail, because of its direct restrictions on alienation, perpetuity meant that the land could never be alienated for longer than the current tenant's life, or at least for as long as there continued to be heirs of any of the specified classes. This extension of the duration of the fee tail was countered by the development of formal methods to bar or break the tail, so that the land would not inevitably be tied up forever. The fee tail in Whilton, however, had not been broken. John de Swynnerton was thus the beneficiary of the extension of the fee tail.

In certain situations John de Swynnerton might have found it financially worthless to try to reclaim the fee tail. The worst case would have involved the complexity of the general as against the special heir—that is, if John were not only the heir in the tail (the special heir) to James de Nevill but also the heir general, the person who would inherit James's lands by the ordinary laws of succession to real property. In such a situation John would have to warrant James's real property transactions to the value of the lands he inherited as heir general: he would thus receive both the burdens and the benefits of inheritance in carefully maintained balance. The result would have been that, although he might receive Whilton by litigation, he would have to give other lands in exchange; nothing would have been gained. But Swynnerton was related to Nevill only in the half blood; general heirs had to be related in the full blood. Swynnerton's only claim was thus by virtue of the tail, and he had no warranty obligations. Nothing therefore prevented his claim.

DOCUMENT 41

An Action of Formedon in the Descender: *Swynnerton* v *Latymer et al.*

Source: CP 40/478, m. 252d *Date*: April/May 1380

Northamptonshire. John de Swynnerton of Hilton in his own proper person seeks against William Latymer, knight; Richard Stury, knight; William de Thorpe, knight; Richard de Treton, cleric; William Thirnyng; and John Wade, parson of the church of Hemmingford Abbots, the manor of Whilton with appurtenances and four messuages and 100s rent with appurtenances in Staverton which Robert late bishop of Bath and Wells gave to Philip de Montgomery and Felicia his wife and the heirs proceeding from the body of the same Felicia and which after the death of the abovesaid Philip and Felicia and James the son and heir of the same Felicia and Anne the sister of the abovesaid James and John son of the abovesaid Anne ought to descend by the form of the abovesaid gift to the aforementioned John de Swynnerton son of the same John son of Anne and cousin and heir of the abovesaid James etc. And wherefore he says that the abovesaid Philip and Felicia gave the abovesaid manor and tenements with appurtenances to the aforementioned late bishop etc., to hold to him and his heirs in perpetuity. And then, to wit, on the octaves of the Holy Trinity in the eighteenth year of the reign of the lord Edward son of King Henry late king of England in the court of the same Edward a certain fine was levied here between the same late bishop, plaintiff, and the abovesaid Philip and Felicia, impedients, concerning the manor and tenements abovesaid and by which fine the same Philip and Felicia acknowledged the abovesaid manor and tenements with appurtenances to be the right of the same bishop as those which the same bishop had from the gift of the same Philip and Felicia and for that recognition etc., the same bishop granted to the aforementioned Philip and Felicia the same manor and tenements with appurtenances to have and to hold to the same Philip and Felicia and the heirs proceeding from the body of the same Felicia, by which gift the same Philip and Felicia were seised thereof, to wit, the same Philip in his demesne as of free tenement and the aforementioned Felicia in her demesne as of fee and right by the form [of the gift etc.] in time of peace in the time of the abovesaid Edward, king, son of King Henry, taking thereof esplees to the value etc. And from the same Felicia the right descended by the form [of the gift etc.] to a certain James as son and heir etc.; and from the same James, because he died without heir proceeding from his body, the right descended by the form [of the gift etc.] to a certain Anne as sister and heir etc.; and from the same

Anne the right descended by the form [of the gift etc.] to a certain John as son and heir etc.; and from the same John the right descended by the form [of the gift etc.] to this John de Swynnerton who now seeks as son and heir etc., and which after the death [of the abovesaid Philip and Felicia and James the son and heir of the same Felicia and Anne the sister of the abovesaid James and John son of the abovesaid Anne ought to descend by the form of the abovesaid gift to the aforementioned John de Swynnerton son of the same John son of Anne and cousin and heir of the abovesaid James etc.]. And thereof he produces suit etc. And he proffers here in court the tenor of the foot of the abovesaid fine under the foot of the great seal of the lord king which testifies to the abovesaid gift in these words: [Document 25 follows in full].

And the abovesaid William Latymer and all the other tenants by Henry de Getyngton their attorney come and deny his right when etc. And they say that a certain John Holt and John parson of the church of Whilton were formerly seised of the manor and tenements abovesaid in their demesne as of fee and thereof enfeoffed the same William, Richard, William, Richard, William and John Wade to hold to themselves and their heirs in perpetuity. And saving to them their advantages and action by virtue of the same feoffment in future times if etc., they say that they cannot deny that the abovesaid manor and tenements were given to the aforementioned Philip and Felicia by the abovesaid fine in the abovesaid form nor that the same manor and tenements are the right of the abovesaid John de Swynnerton as by the writ and the count of the same John de Swynnerton is supposed. Therefore it is considered that the same John de Swynnerton recover against the abovesaid William, Richard, William, Richard, William, and John his seisin of the abovesaid manor and tenements with appurtenances.

And no amercement of the same William Latymer and the other tenants because they came by summons on the first day etc.

*

On the face of it, Document 41 is absolutely startling. This action of formedon should have raised once more the whole Whilton problem, particularly the events prior to 1290. The Mortimer endorsement on the 1290 fine had preserved their right to delve into those matters, so that an argument as to whether the Montgomerys had been so entitled to Whilton that they could make the 1290 fine would almost certainly have arisen. Instead, the tenants—recipients of the Zouche-Mortimer-Cornwall claim—hurried into court without any delay at all and surrendered up the land without putting up an argument. They did not even bother to vouch Holt and the parson to warranty and thus would not be compensated for the loss of Whilton. The most they did was to stipulate that if, at some future date, they saw things differently, they could litigate then. However, that clause, by the reign of Richard II, was a regular stipulation in pleading and a sign of lawyerly caution, not a real indication of intent. This superficially strange result raises questions about the nature of the tenure claimed by these particular tenants and the reason they so willingly surrendered it to Swynnerton.

The explanation for the tenants' behavior is that, although they held the land in fee simple, they received no benefit from it. The benefits went altogether to John Holt and the parson. This was an arrangement known as a use, because the holders of the fee simple held the land only for the use of another. The working of the use can best be understood in the context of the grant and regrant relationships that played so large a part in the Whilton case. It will be remembered that land could not be left by will, even though it could be sold before one died to anyone, even to the person to whom one would have devised the land had that been possible. For that reason, William de Whelton had to give Whilton to Nicholas before he died, and Nicholas had to regrant Whilton to William for life so that William would not lose the proceeds during his lifetime. By the grant and regrant, William tried to make use of the legal rules so that Nicholas would succeed him in Whilton. Likewise, grant and regrant situations had long been used for the purpose of changing one's estate. The final concords between Burnel and the Montgomerys (Document 25) and between Cornwall and James de Nevill (Document 38) show such situations institutionalized in the king's court. Similarly, when a man and woman were to be married and wanted to put the woman's holdings into the man's name—they could thus be sold if necessary during the marriage without levying a final concord—the prudent method of performing the transaction was for the woman to grant the land to a trustworthy friend, who would establish himself in the land and then, perhaps after the marriage, grant the land to the husband. The friend merely performed a service that took precautions against the marriage perhaps not taking place as expected and also against the possibility, because of related legal rules, of the transaction being ruled null and void at a later date. Nevertheless, the friend for a time was the holder of a fee simple. Grant and regrant relationships were an accepted part of the way in which individuals satisfied both their own desires and the demands of the law.

A more sophisticated grant and regrant than that between William de Whelton and Nicholas could be used, in effect, to leave land by will. A tenant in fee simple—say, John Holt—could grant the land to trusted friends on the understanding that they would do with it whatever he requested. John could continue to take the profits or even live on the land, could instruct them to sell the land to whomever, or could, in his will or otherwise, request them to grant the land to one of his younger sons. This arrangement had the advantage of great flexibility, since John could change his mind about his sons at any time before his death. The grant and regrant between William de Whelton and Nicholas, if performed properly, had quite the opposite effect: William could not change his mind thereafter. This trusting grant of a fee simple to friends was thus attractive to fathers who wanted to promote a younger son or a daughter but still retain control.

John Holt would have seen further financial advantages in such an arrangement with friends. Felicia and Anne, Hugh de Mortimer and his daughters had all been minors when their fathers died; their lords thus had the rights of wardship and of marriage. These were rights beneficial to the guardian in that the guardian took all the income from the estates not required for the upkeep of the heir. But if John Holt granted the fee simple to his six friends, and if they held it until the designated recipient was of age before regranting the land, there would be no rights of wardship or of marriage. The friends—as a group called the feoffees to uses—were the tenants of the lord; their heirs would have been in the lord's wardship had they all died at once. That eventuality, however, was exceedingly improbable. The recipient had no estate in the land while he was underage and thus had no tenurial relationship with the lord; therefore the lord had no rights over him. And when the designated recipient received, he received not by inheritance but rather by a grant from strangers. The recipient would thus not have to pay the lord the traditional charge for inheriting: relief. The profits of the land that would have gone to the lord could be redirected as Holt, the feoffer, stipulated: to pay off his debts, to give alms for the good of his soul, to increase the value of the estate for his descendants. Such an arrangement thus had enormous advantages.

The disadvantage, of course, was that Holt had given the land away completely. He no longer had legal title to Whilton. One might think that this situation was the occasion of many sleepless nights for Holt, but the arrangement was not as precarious as it might seem. Even had he entrusted only a single individual with the land and not a group, one might well expect that the friend could usually be trusted. We who spend our lives reading court cases tend to devalue the trustworthiness of individuals, because we are daily concerned with breaches of trust. Not every man is a thief. Moreover,

Holt had entrusted the land not to one individual but to a group. More likely than not, the group would respect the arrangement. Indeed, one is forced to conclude that trustworthiness was the normal state of affairs, because such arrangements were becoming commonplace in the 1370s and 1380s. Finally, the character of the individuals was such that they were unlikely to want to become regarded as infamous and untrustworthy. William Thirning, a justice of the peace in Northamptonshire, was also a pleader in the king's court and would become a justice of the Court of Common Pleas in 1388. Richard de Treton was the keeper of the writs and rolls of the Court of Common Pleas. William de Thorpe was a justice of the peace in Northamptonshire. Richard Stury was a knight retained by King Richard II. William Latymer was probably the William Latymer who was one of the king's councillors.[6] To expect that such people, acting, as it were, as a board of trustees, would keep one's trust may not have been expecting too much. If one chose the feoffees to uses properly, one may well not have had to worry much about the necessity of enforcement through courts.

Even had things gone awry, Holt could have resorted to some formal enforcement. The Court of Common Pleas would have done little. The most Holt could expect there would be the court's toleration of his self-help, of his entering onto the land and taking it back on his own initiative. There was no court procedure at common law for Holt to use to regain Whilton if his feoffees proved untrustworthy. The greater problem would be enforcement by the beneficiary Holt designated to take the land after his death. Such a beneficiary would have found some recourse in the ecclesiastical courts, which treated the matter as a question of conscience relating to probate of wills: Holt's stipulation of the beneficiary would be treated as a will, the fulfillment of which was incumbent on the feoffees. At the time Holt made his feoffment, Chancery was beginning to undertake the same function. Here also, however, it was not a question of enforcement of property rights. The Chancellor would enjoin the feoffees to do what they should because it seemed the moral thing to do, because it was a matter of conscience and right. Propriety with regard to the conduct of feoffees to uses had not yet been distilled into a set of rules clearly known and strictly and regularly enforced. Prudent choice of one's feoffees, however, together with what judicial toleration and enforcement existed, were adequate to make the granting away of one's legal title in such a manner not particularly hazardous.

John Holt, moreover, had less reason to worry than most people. Holt was no ordinary person. He had been a serjeant-pleader in the Court of Common Pleas since 1366, one of that elite group of lawyers who argued cases and shaped the law. In 1382 he would be made a justice of that court. In 1376, when the elder John de Swynnerton sued in formedon, it was probably the prospect of fighting Holt in court that had made it seem better to drop the case. Challenging a serjeant-pleader's title to land, even when that title was theoretically in his feoffees, was sure to be a risky and expensive business. That case, however, put Holt on notice. Thereafter, probably some effort was made to find a mutually satisfactory compromise. By 1380 that compromise had been found. John de Swynnerton thus brought his case, confident that Latymer and his companions would merely surrender the land, for he had already struck his bargain with Holt. Immediately after his recovery, Swynnerton granted Whilton back to Holt and his wife, Alice, for their lives and for one year further to their executors.[7] The parson apparently had no substantial interest in Whilton, for he was not mentioned. John Holt was destined to live another thirty-eight years. The life grant of Whilton might seem a very expensive compromise for Swynnerton, but the latter might have felt that he could afford to be generous. He had at least secured title to Whilton by making his recovery a matter of record in the Court of Common Pleas. Furthermore, he was himself a man of affairs, and by his generosity he had secured a friend and ally in the Court of Common Pleas. Swynnerton must have counted that life grant as resources well spent, particularly when Holt became a justice only three years later.

Whatever benefit Swynnerton had hoped to derive from this relationship abruptly disappeared, however, when once more the rights to Whilton got caught up in the larger affairs of the realm. King Richard II had been humiliated by the Parliament of 1386 and its imposition of a commission to oversee the governance of the realm. In 1387 he secretly consulted his justices about the validity of that Parliament's actions. The justices, among whom now sat John Holt, replied that those who had been involved deserved death and that those most deeply involved deserved to be treated as traitors. Their advice became known and proved distinctly unpopular. The Merciless Parliament of 1388 condemned those justices. Holt himself was condemned to death, but he was pardoned and sent into exile in Ireland with an allowance for his maintenance. He nevertheless forfeited his lands to the Crown—a forfeiture of Whilton that came 124 years after the Battle of Northampton. Holt, however, could not forfeit to the Crown any other estate or rights than those he in fact possessed. The Crown would retain Whilton only for Holt's life. Had Holt been executed, Swynnerton would have recovered Whilton in short order. With Holt in exile, Swynnerton was deprived both of Whilton and of influence. Swynnerton's only real gain from his compromise was the recognition of his title. Full possession would have to wait until Holt died.

The forfeiture of Whilton would have been relatively straightforward. It is interesting to examine Holt's other forfeitures, because they throw light on the way in which Holt's feoffees in Whilton had been expected to act. The Crown sold those lands, even though they were in the hands of feoffees and Holt did not hold the legal title. In 1392 his feoffees were called into Chancery to be examined about their title, so that the sale could be completed. Richard Treton and John Wade were two of the feoffees for these lands, as they had been also for Whilton. They testified that they had taken no profit from the lands and had always held themselves ready to perform Holt's will in regard to those parcels.

DOCUMENT 42
Chancery Examination of Feoffees

Source: CCR, 1389-1392, p. 540 [altered] *Date*: February 1392

Memorandum of a gift made by the king by advice of the council by letters patent of 12 February 13 Richard II [1390] to John Devereux knight, William Brynchesle, Nicholas Tye and Nicholas Peten, their heirs and assigns, for 400 marks then and at set terms paid by the said John, of the manor of Lyveden, 300 acres of land, 100 acres of pasture, two dovecotes, twelve acres of meadow, twenty acres of wood and £12 of rent in Lyveden, Oundle, Churchfield, Warmington, and Alyngton, and all other lands in those towns and hamlets which Richard Treton, John Wade clerks and John Fossebroke or others had to the use of John de Holt knight and of all manors, lands, rents, and services there which John de Holt had, being forfeit to the king by reason of a judgment rendered against him in the Parliament holden at Westminster in 11 Richard II [1388], with the knight's fees, advowsons, wards, marriages, reliefs, escheats, suits of court, issues and profits thereof since Michaelmas then last; also that by divers writs the king after commanded Richard de Treton and John Fossebroke to be in Chancery on the octaves of the Purification 15 Richard II [1392], and they appeared at Westminster and delivered those writs to the courts, whereupon they were asked by Thomas Archbishop of York the Chancellor whether at any former time they had or claimed any estate in the premises or no, and if so what estate and right they pretended. And the said Richard acknowledged in court that long ago he was thereof enfeoffed to the use and at the will of John de Holt. And being asked whether he now has or claims any estate or right therein, freely and of his own motion he said that he claims none, but made a quitclaim in court to John Devereux and the others, their heirs and assigns. And John Fossebroke confessed that in 7 Richard II [1383-1384] John de Holt purchased the manors of Lyveden, Churchfield, Oundle, and Warmyngton in Northamptonshire from Richard Stoke and Roger Wymondesham, clerks, to be held by himself, the said Richard, John Wade and John Fossebroke and by the heirs and assigns of John de Holt to his use, that John Wade died in 9 Richard II [1385-1386], that John de Holt occupied the same, taking the issues and profits, that in 10 Richard II [1386-1387] John de Holt made a release with warranty thereof to John Fossebroke, his heirs and assigns, which release John Fossebroke had in his custody and delivered to John de Holt, who charged him to make a feoffment to Richard son of John de Holt and to the heirs of his body, with remainder to Walter brother of Richard son of John and to the heirs of his body, remainder to Hugh brother of Walter and to the heirs of his body, remainder to Peter brother of Hugh and to the heirs of his body, remainder to John de Holt, his heirs and assigns, that without gainsaying of John Fossebroke and Richard Treton John de Holt took all the profits of the premises, that he was ready to do the will of John de Holt and make such feoffment or another according to the limitation of John de Holt, and that he never took issues or profits thereof, further saying freely of his own motion that he has or claims no right or title in the premises, but by word of mouth made a quitclaim thereof in court to John Devereux and the others, their heirs and assigns; whereupon Richard Treton and John Fossebroke had leave to depart from the court.

*

Document 41 thus yields an extraordinary picture of the relationship between Holt and his feoffees, a picture but slightly different from that which seems to have pertained to Whilton prior to Swynnerton's recovery. In the case of Lyveden, John Holt had purchased the land, receiving it as part of the group, so that he was himself one of the feoffees and so that the other feoffees gained title, theoretically, not directly through him (although by his purchase) but rather from the vendors. Such a precaution would assure Holt even greater security during his own life, although he would still have to rely on the other feoffees to carry out his will after his death. When John Holt was required to advise the king, he realized that the situation was growing dangerous, and he took steps to secure his family. His release to the other feoffees would put him, in the normal course of the law, safely removed from the succeeding transaction. With the legal title firmly distanced, Holt still could control, because he retained the document that evidenced the release. That document would be safeguarded for the beneficiaries. Then he instructed the feoffees to enfeoff one of his sons, with successive remainders to his other children and with reversion ultimately to himself and his heirs general. Events, however, apparently moved too fast. Holt was caught up in the turmoil of the Merciless Parliament before the feoffees carried out their instructions. Even worse, Parliament decided to ignore the normal course of the law in this instance and to look beyond the mere legal title. Holt was to forfeit not only those lands to which he had legal title; he was also to forfeit those lands that he had alienated after advising the king and that were now held by others to his use.[8] Legal rules and technicalities were not allowed to stand in the way of penalties for, as his act had been described, treason.

Richard II, of course, remained favorable toward those he had been forced to disown and condemn. In 1390 he was able to grant some of Holt's land to Holt's son, also named John de Holt. Included in that restoration was Whilton, to be held for the life of John de Holt senior.[9] John de Holt senior himself was able to return to England in 1397 and was fully pardoned in 1398. He was then obliged to spend several years in recovering his other lands.[10]

The story of what happened to Whilton thereafter is clear, at least in the long term. After Holt died and his executors had held for the year further, the Swynnertons regained their possession of Whilton. The manor then descended to Thomas de Swynnerton, one of whose daughters, Alice, inherited Whilton and married Richard Beaufo. Alice died in 1472, and her heirs, the Beaufos, held Whilton until 1664.[11] What remains unknown is whether there was any interruption to their title, whether there was any litigation between the Cornwalls and the Swynnertons in the fifteenth century. Whatever the form of the resignation of claims that the Cornwalls gave to James de Nevill, it almost surely never reached the hands of Anne's descendants. By the 1330 final concord, which set up a new fee tail with Cornwall remainders and reversion, the Cornwalls might have launched a new round of litigation. Whether or not such litigation occurred, however, the general result is known. After litigation and legal expenses running over more than a century, Felicia and her descendants had won out, but more by compromise than by judgment.

CHAPTER 10

Conclusions

THE WHILTON dispute is but one example of dispute resolution. It is not so much typical as archetypical. No one would assert that the normal dispute over real property was so complicated. Many disputes were settled quite satisfactorily completely without resort to the law courts; many others were effectively settled merely with an assize. How frequently such litigation might become so prolonged is unknown. My guess is that the Whilton dispute was unusually long but that many cases were at least similar to it in that the single entry on the plea roll represents a much more intricate legal and social reality than might at first be supposed. But if the dispute is not strictly typical, it is archetypical. The Whilton dispute demonstrates the potential available at law in medieval England. As an embodiment of the legal system in that sense, the Whilton dispute constitutes a basis for several observations on the way in which law functioned in medieval England and on the way in which alterations in legal patterns reflect an increasingly more integrated society.

The law was not an ardent seeker after truth. The records we have must always be treated with caution. It is impossible to be sure of what happened between William de Whelton and his sons in the 1260s. The different verdicts on that subject are contradictory and force the historian to formulate some composite picture. The final verdict, in particular, seems false. It was shaped not according to facts the jurors knew or, at least, not in accord with what happened in 1264. Rather, it was framed either in accord with what they thought must have happened or with a view toward eliciting from the justices a judgment that would conform with their idea of justice.

Any particular verdict, thus, may be a peculiar composite of rendition of fact and reshaping of fact to fit legal rules, although one can expect that reshaping to resemble the facts substantially. That jurors acted in this way indicates that when they swore to tell the truth they perhaps felt that their oath had more to do with justice than with a historian's conception of truth. This kind of concern on the part of the jurors provided that community input which assured that the lawyer's law never completely corresponded with societal reality.

Likewise, the law was not a prescriptive standard to which individuals conformed in a simplistic manner. Some actions, particularly those related to the rights and disabilities of minors, are indeed fairly predictable. But James de Nevill's final concord of 1330 is mildly disturbing. Both law and logic would seem to dictate that a tenant in tail could not give away a fee simple when he possessed only a fee tail: one cannot give more than one has. It would be nice to believe that such things happened only by mistake or fraud. James de Nevill must have known that he was merely a tenant in tail: the final concord of 1290 must have been in the Nevill deed box. Yet, if his grant of a fee simple was not a mistake, neither was it a fraud. It is unlikely that the Cornwalls were unaware that James held only a fee tail, since the final concord of 1290 had delayed their prosecution for years on end. Moreover, James did not thereby perform an illegal act in the sense that he would be punished, for he would not. Nor, even in the broader sense, was his act immoral. He was working out an amicable compromise. It may indeed have been better had he bought out other outstanding rights, but it was not totally reprehensible or senseless that he did not. By that fine the Cornwall interests were legally enforceable against all but the claimants under the 1290 fine. If those earlier claimants ever died out, the Cornwall interests would be enforceable against anyone. James, of course, need not look so far. He probably did not expect to die without an heir descending from his body. If he left such heirs, no other claimant would matter, and the heir would have been freed from the possibility of the Cornwall claim. The restrictions on the fee tail could thus be ignored with impunity, and final concord could be piled on final concord until it happened by ill fortune that someone had some legal right that was presently enforceable. It was a hazardous game, but not for the current tenant who wanted to convey the fee simple he did not have. Furthermore, it was sometimes desirable that such things take place, and the amicable resolution of the Whilton dispute would have been a good thing. On the other hand, the result could also be bitter and long-lasting litigation.

Other key elements in the law functioned in such a way as to promote compromise. One of these was the tiered system of litigation. In present-day systems repeated trials are unusual. Normally, there is a trial, and the facts as they will thereafter be deemed to have happened are determined. Appeals can follow, but an appeal can be denied by a superior court if it feels there are insufficient grounds to reconsider the case. Moreover, it is relatively infrequent that the resolution of an appeal will result in a new trial. In medieval England there was no mechanism in the secular courts for even trying to determine all the facts in the first foray into litigation. Litigation by assize was restricted in scope. Judgment in such a case could not prevent the dispute from appearing again in a somewhat different perspective by a writ of entry and then in a much broader way by a writ of right. Nor were those later trials appeals: they were in no way based on what had been found in the assize. In certain situations a cautious person might even sound out his opponent with an action of trespass prior to proceeding by assize. Such a series of legal cases originating from a single dispute produced delay, exhaustion, and, more fortunately, compromise.

The protection of minors contributed to this delay. Minors could not sue or be sued concerning their rights to inherited land at any level higher than an assize. This protection was carefully balanced and was solidly rooted in sound judicial principles. But the way in which it worked created considerable delay. Given circumstances little different from those of the Whilton dispute, claimants or tenants in succession could be minors for decades on end. The litigation itself took time and money. And as the claimant's line grew more and more detached from the land and as the parties became more distanced from the original protagonists, there was greater chance for emotions to cool off. Litigants could more easily decide the fight was no longer worthwhile. The protection of minors thus also contributed to the possibility of compromise.

That conclusion may seem pure sophistry. Another point of view would insist that such delay only created and exacerbated injustice. After all, the rightful owner might live and die without being able to come into possession; the wrongful possessor could keep his ill-gotten gains by hiding behind the law. There was indeed that side to the matter. But it is also true that disputes were seldom that one-sided. In the Whilton dispute it is easy to see that Felicia had a justifiable claim; it had clearly been the intent of William de Whelton to give the land to Nicholas, her father. But Roger de Whelton and those claiming from him also had a justifiable position: William de Whelton, after all, had been trying to evade the rules of inheritance and had done a poor job of it. A theorist would maintain here that society had little interest in who won so long as the matter was settled; the parties concerned, of course, would take a slightly more partisan position. One must even consider that in those situations in which delay continued longest, it was usually the case that the claimant was not penniless and starving. Those with land had land by several different titles. Certainly neither Hugh Mortimer nor John de Swynnerton can have much claim on our sympathy, for they were among the privileged of their society. Felicia may have been a more sympathetic character, but she had been provided for and even as a minor had had her chance in court. Settlement of disputes among the more powerful members of society by compromise, even long delayed, may be beneficial.

All of these beneficial results, of course, were not intended; no far-sighted king or prudent chancellor laid down such a structure for the law. Such things grew up slowly and with other and more immediately justifiable rationales. Yet contemporaries surely recognized the relativity of rights to land. The grand assize, after all, did not ask who owned the land but who had *more* right. Many lawsuits, likewise, were undertaken, then as now, solely with the expectation of compromise: a lawsuit was the only way in which an intransigent possessor could be made to acknowledge that the claimant had some right. Of course, the desire for and intention to reach a compromise often cannot be seen in a legal record; the parties state their cases as strongly as possible in their own favor. But it is the very absoluteness of their claims and defenses and the one-sidedness of the judgments that push them to compromise. The tiered system of litigation was here most helpful. It was extraordinarily effective for placing the victorious opponent once again in jeopardy and inducing him to recognize one's claim. The structure was thus conducive to compromise, no less so because it had not been intentionally structured for that purpose. The role of compromise in the settlement of disputes and the personal factors that entered into litigation are clearly evident in the Whilton dispute.

The inefficiency and the repeated opportunities for reopening disputes were remarkably appropriate for thirteenth- and fourteenth-century England. In our own time, the power of government, the force of the state, is so great that the application of that force by court judgment, particularly with such matters as real estate, will settle a dispute definitively. For most litigants, a defeat in the courts leaves no viable alternative. In the thirteenth-century, however, English society was not so far removed from a time when violence was a clear alternative. The fact that so much of the Whilton dispute—a dispute involving men trained as knights and familiar with war—was pursued in the sanitized atmosphere of a courtroom, with royal violence an institutionalized and barely considered threat to maintain the peace, is an indication of the monumental change in English society since the early twelfth century.

Even with that increased stability, one can readily doubt whether a legal system that rendered really definitive first judgments would have been acceptable. Had the possibilities been fewer for a defeated litigant to gather his resources and return hopefully to the fray, the enforcement of judgments might necessarily have been correspondingly more erratic. The existing legal system, with all its inefficiency, was an effective alternative to the violent resolution of disputes. Inefficiency, anyway, is never any society's worst enemy, no matter how annoying or expensive it might be. In England at this time it was probably a prerequisite for the continued growth of a cohesive society.

This discussion of the Whilton dispute also lays the groundwork for gauging at least one aspect of the growth of England into a centralized and cohesive governmental unit—a state. Centralization and cohesion depend to a great extent not only on power but also on dependability, on the reliability of governmental institutions to perform their functions along predictable lines. Only then will individuals identify themselves increasingly with the central authority as with an indispensable benefactor, as with a factor of existence that it is inconceivable to eliminate. Such dependability requires both continuity and routine. It is the routine that is here important, because the land transaction situations in the Whilton dispute allow a calculation of the degree to which the law was becoming impersonal—that is, subject to a predictable pattern. To the extent that prediction becomes possible, law assumes an intellectual pattern no longer amenable to great and sudden change or to change in precisely the same manner in which society changes. Law assumes a life of its own. That separate life can be both identified and "measured" by the degree to which legal actions are formalized and not directly related to the everyday life of the society.

By such a standard, no independent, impersonalized law existed in 1160—and, likewise, no state. Had William de Whelton been living in 1160 and had he tried to promote his second son, he would have faced obstacles of a variety slightly different from those he confronted in fact in 1264, although the greatest factors were the same: primogeniture and the inability to distribute land by will after one's death. In 1160, however, he could not have given the fee simple to Nicholas and received back a life estate, thus assuring Nicholas's succession. Such a transaction would have been denied any effect. Moreover, it is unlikely that William would have thought of such a thing. The normal method of promoting the second son in 1160, and thus the situation corresponding to the transaction of 1264, was relatively simple. William would have had to give up the land entirely in order to make Nicholas secure; he could not retain possession until he died. Giving without giving up, which is what happened in 1264, is somehow unnatural. Had giving been enough, primogeniture would have meant little. We know that fathers often preferred their younger sons. That preference resulted in the heir, the eldest son, having absolute discretion in deciding whether he would honor (warrant) his father's grants to younger sons. If he decided he would not warrant them, he could take them back, leaving his brothers without recourse. The vital part of securing a younger son in the land in the twelfth century, then, would have been for the father to persuade his eldest son to join in the grant. If the heir committed himself, he would be bound to maintain his brother in the holding, because it would then be his own grant as well as his father's. If the elder son thereafter broke his undertaking, it would be an act of perfidy, a breach of feudal morality that would undermine his authority over his other men and thus his own power. Such a transaction would thus have been an intrinsic part of real-world relationships and would have rested on common moral assumptions and normal modes of action. The concepts involved would have been part of everyday life: maintenance of the commonly accepted position of the firstborn son and the obligation to live up to one's own undertakings. The law in this setting was still congruent with a popular morality; it had not assumed a life of its own. There was as yet no state.

Such a hypothetical grant from William to Nicholas with

the vital consent of Roger would have been, in 1164, a very "natural" transaction. By the time of the actual transaction in 1264 it was artificial. In 1264 William and Nicholas were performing "legal" actions. They knew roughly what had to be done to accomplish their ends, but those actions were not part of the way they normally lived and thought. They were trying to measure up to certain standards by which their acts would be judged in court. Had their acts matched those standards, the courts would have undertaken to secure Nicholas's claim, because it would have fallen into a category accepted and protected by the institutionalized power of the central courts. Yet the requirements were sufficiently artificial that William and Nicholas did not in fact fulfill them. Moreover, when they persuaded Roger to quitclaim his right and accept William's grant, they were taking a measure on which nothing seemed to depend. It was only felt to be necessary—a carry-over from the time when Roger could effectively veto any transaction to which he had not consented before William died. In the 1260s, however, the quitclaim, even when attested by a jury, accomplished nothing. Everything centered on whether those abstract standards had been met. Moreover, the grant in fee simple, the establishment of seisin for fifteen days, and the regrant for life resulted from abstract standards based on a reality of a previous day. In the century since 1160 law had developed something like a life of its own. It was no longer directly related to, no longer growing immediately out of "normal" modes of action.

The change that occurred in that century was the opening of a gap between law and life, a change that was at least matched between 1264 and 1378. In 1264 the grant and regrant were typical; by 1378 the use was becoming typical for such purposes, and the grant and regrant were antiquated. John Holt, to judge by the use he created in Lyveden, was attempting to accomplish something roughly similar to William de Whelton's purpose, but Holt was not merely trying to measure up to artifical standards. Giving away legal title to assume a more beneficial situation in the land implies a wholehearted acceptance that law and life were no longer intimately related, that they were in fact divorced. Any "natural" situation would demand that legal title reside in the person who benefits and occupies the land. Yet the legal titleholders with the use derived no benefit, whereas the individuals who occupied and benefited from the land had no legal title. Moreover, the success of the device demanded that the common law function rigidly. The titleholders had to be regarded as the real owners, and the beneficiaries had to be ignored for most purposes. It would have been a rash step indeed simply to abolish rights of wardship and marriage and relief and then also to allow tenants to devise their land by will. Those ends were accomplished more circumspectly by forcing the common law to work rigidly, myopically, by separating legal title from moral entitlement. Everything worked perfectly if the feoffees to uses were subjected to burdens of wardship and marriage that fortunately never fell due. The prohibition against leaving land by will was obeyed so long as everything was accomplished by grants between living persons and a mere request, albeit expressed in one's will, for them to do such and such.

The Court of Common Pleas did not enforce the use, because the use could exist only without such enforcement. It was not that the lawyers and justices of the common law objected to the use according to principles that made it seem to them either inconceivable or immoral. They themselves, like Holt and Thirning, had land put into use and functioned in their turn as feoffees to uses. If the common law had recognized the use as a legal matter in the first few decades of its existence, the whole structure, which presupposed a rigid common law with only external enforcement of matters of conscience, would have collapsed. That external enforcement was increasingly supplied by the Chancellor in the Court of Chancery precisely as a matter of conscience and fairness—that is, equity. Those who established a use knew that it would be ludicrous to expect the Court of Common Pleas to enforce it. Such a contradictory situation, demanding a court of law and a court of conscience, demonstrates an extreme artificiality about the law, a gap between law and life that had grown rapidly in the century since 1264. That wider gap, that schizophrenic view of legal and moral rights, is a measure of the way in which the law functioned impersonally. The frequent use of such a device is evidence of the degree to which individuals had internalized a most strange view of their world and had grown dependent on central institutions.

By the late fifteenth and early sixteenth centuries, the gap had grown too large. Around 1530 one writer criticized uses for precisely the schizophrenic stance they required: "What a falseness is this to speake and doe one thinge, and thincke another thinge cleane contrarie to the same! Every man may perceave in my mind, that of this can come no goodnes, but crafte and falsehood."[1] But the evasions were really no longer necessary. The ability to do those things allowed by the device of the use had long been accepted. There was no longer any danger of the whole structure collapsing. In the late fifteenth century the common law took increasing cognizance of the use. In 1536 the Statute of Uses conveyed the legal estate back from the feoffees to uses to the beneficiary, the *cestui que use*, so that legal entitlement once more had some relationship to the real world.[2]* In 1540 the Statute of Wills allowed tenants, for the most part, to leave their land by will.[3]* It was a monumental change that took place in those years, but it had had a long preparation. The statutes were certainly not simply the new recognition of a long-demanded right.

Those statutes, moreover, do not mark a real diminishing of the distance between law and life. Those uses in which the feoffees had active obligations survived the statute to become the modern-day trust. The learning surrounding the trust has since provided a fertile field for legal obscurity. More to the point, such a simplification, undertaken for whatever reasons, incorporates into the law what has gone before. Such provisions simply could not have been made much earlier in English society, because they would have abolished normal financial expectations incidental to feudal relationships. The growth of central authority first sapped the vitality from those relationships, making those rights merely financial expectations and not rights intrinsically and necessarily related to the exercise of power. That first change made it thinkable for individuals to work to evade the now institutionalized but irrelevant financial burdens that remained. Such evasion relied upon that state authority. The growth of evasion, presupposing as it did an absolutely rigid common law, diminished increasingly the normal expectations that such windfall rights would in fact fall due. Social expectations thus altered over many decades, based on reliance on state authority, so that eventually it was conceivable to do away with the structure that had enabled the evasion and to alter the law to fit more closely with normal expectations. The law may have been somewhat neater in some areas thereafter, but it presupposed an enormous development in societal cohesion. The whole relationship between law and society had changed and reached a different order of development.

This kind of analysis of the growth of the state is not concerned much with political crises, personalities, demographic changes, or economic growth and contraction. It is merely one aspect of the whole. But it is an aspect that allows an appreciation of change, that makes possible valuable comparisons of English society at various times. It is in this long-term appreciation of change, of the growth of social cohesion, that the real value of the Whilton dispute lies. William de Whelton and Nicholas, Felicia and the Mortimers, and John Holt were not so terribly important in themselves; nor was Whilton the focal point of a great constitutional crisis. The importance of the dispute is that it was so normal, that it illustrates the normal expectations, desires, and devices of a broad range of Englishmen over a great expanse of time, thus enabling us to gauge the internal resilience of their society.

APPENDIX I

Auxiliary Documents

DOCUMENT AI.I
Commission to Yatingdon

Source: CPR, 1266-1272, p. 275 *Date*: 18 December 1267

Whereas William de Whelton, whose lands by occasion of his trespasses against the king in the time of the disturbance the king gave to Thomas de Turberville before the death of the said William, many times offered to stand his trial in the king's court touching his said trespasses and afterwards offered to stand to the award of Kenilworth, and Roger de Whelton, his son and heir as he says, is ready to stand to the said award and to redeem his lands if they ought to be redeemed according to the form of the award, and the said Thomas detains the said lands contrary to the form of such award; the king commissions Nicholas de Yatingdon, justice appointed to hear and determine pleas touching lands given away by reason of the said disturbance in the county of Northampton, to enquire of the truth by jurors who were not against the king in the time of the disturbance and are of no affinity to either party, whether William was guilty of the trespasses or not and to do what according to the form of the said award ought to be done.

DOCUMENT A1.2

Certification to King's Bench

Source: KB 26/184a, m. 8d *Date*: May 1268

Northamptonshire. The sheriff had been ordered that, since for some certain causes the lord king recently made to come before him a suit which was before the king's justices at the pleas concerning lands given on the occasion of the disturbance recently had in the king's realm between Roger de Whelton, son and heir of William de Whelton as is said, and Felicia, daughter and heir of Nicholas de Whelton, and Baldwin Wake, demandants, and our beloved etc. Thomas de Turberville, tenant, concerning the lands and tenements which belonged to William de Whelton and which on the occasion of the wrongs done the king by [William] in the time of the abovesaid disturbance [the king] gave to the same Thomas and which the abovesaid Roger as well as the aforementioned Felicia claim to pertain hereditarily to themselves and whereof the abovesaid Baldwin as chief lord of that fee is prepared to redeem according to the form of the Dictum of Kenilworth to have until the legitimate age of the abovesaid Felicia and whereof some doubts have arisen over certain articles touching the inquisition recently made before the aforementioned justices, on behalf of the king he should make known to the abovesaid parties and also to those who were in the abovesaid inquisition that they should be before the king at this day to do and receive in the matters mentioned above that which from the council of the king he shall think fit to ordain thereof.

And the abovesaid Roger comes and says that, after the death of William de Whelton whose heir he is, he had always been prepared to redeem the lands and tenements of the abovesaid William as son and heir of the same William according to the form of the dictum and ordinance of Kenilworth if the court should have considered that they ought to be redeemed. Whereof, he complains that, by reason of the wardship of the abovesaid Felicia, Baldwin Wake formerly in the king's court at Northampton before the justices at the pleas concerning lands given impeded that Roger, by which he was the less able to have seisin of his abovesaid lands which pertain to him to have and to have hereditarily according to the form of the abovesaid dictum; and he still impedes [him]. Whereof, he asks that the abovesaid Baldwin together with the abovesaid Felicia show here in the king's court if there ought to be any hindrance on account of which the abovesaid Roger should not have the lands and tenements which belonged to the abovesaid William his father as son and nearest heir according to the form of the abovesaid dictum and ordinance.

And the abovesaid Baldwin comes and says that he has nothing and claims nothing in the lands and tenements which belonged to the abovesaid William by reason of the wardship of the abovesaid Felicia while Joan Wake, his mother, is alive, because he says that the same Joan is in seisin of the wardship of the body of the abovesaid Felicia and similarly of the lands and tenements of the abovesaid William as chief lady of that fee, to whom that wardship pertains until the legitimate age of the abovesaid Felicia, nearest heir of the same William. Whereof, he seeks judgment whether he should be able to bring that wardship into judgment, whereas he has nothing in that wardship.

And because the abovesaid Roger cannot deny this, it is considered that the abovesaid Baldwin go hence without day and the abovesaid Roger sue against the abovesaid Joan when it shall seem expedient to him.

The same Roger presents himself on the fourth day against Thomas de Turberville concerning a plea that he should be here at this day to hear the record of a suit which was in the king's court at Northampton before the justices at the pleas concerning lands given on the occasion of the abovesaid disturbance had in the kingdom, between the same Roger son and heir of William de Whelton, demandant, and the same Thomas, tenant, concerning the lands and tenements which belonged to the abovesaid William de Whelton in Whilton and which, on the occasion of the wrongs imputed to the same William in the time of the abovesaid disturbance, the lord king gave to the aforementioned Thomas. And [Thomas] does not come, and the sheriff had been ordered that he should make it known to the parties that they should be here at this day to do and receive in the matters mentioned above that which from the king's council he shall think fit to ordain thereof. And the sheriff reports that he made known to the parties etc. Therefore the sheriff is ordered that he should take the lands and tenements abovesaid into the hand of the lord king and that day etc., and that he should make known to the abovesaid Thomas that he should be here on the octave of Holy Trinity if to him etc.

Certification of the inquisition recently taken before the aforementioned justices between the abovesaid Roger, demandant, and the abovesaid Thomas, tenant, concerning the abovesaid lands and tenements is placed in respect until the aforementioned term for lack of jurors, because none came; and let the sheriff have their bodies.

DOCUMENT A1.3
The *Quo Jure: Zouche* v *Twye & Whelton*

Source: KB 26/199, m. 9d *Date:* June-July 1270

Northamptonshire. The sheriff had been ordered as formerly that he should make to come at this day Hugh de Tywe and Margery his wife to acknowledge along with Alice [sic] who was the wife of William de Whelton what right they claim in the lands and tenements with appurtenances which the abovesaid Alice holds in dower from Roger de Whelton in Norton from the inheritance of the same Roger, which tenements with appurtenances the same Roger has granted here in the court of the lord king to William la Zouche and his heirs after the death of the abovesaid Margery and Alice by a fine made thereof between them. And they did not come etc. . . .

Although this case refers only to Norton, it is probable that an identical action was prosecuted in regard to Whilton, the record of which has not survived.

DOCUMENT AI.4

Action of Entry *ad terminum qui preteriit: Montgomery* v *Mortimer*

Source: CP 40/63, m. 12d *Date*: circa 17 June 1286

Northamptonshire. Philip de Montgomery and Felicia his wife seek against Robert de Mortimer and Joyce his wife two-thirds of the manor of Whilton with appurtenances, except fifty acres of land and nine acres of meadow in the same manor, which they claim to be the right and inheritance of the same Felicia and in which the same Robert and Joyce have no entry unless after the demise which Nicholas son of William de Whelton father of the abovesaid Felicia whose heir she is made thereof to William de Whelton at a term which has expired and which after that term ought to revert to the abovesaid Philip and Felicia etc. And whereof [they] say that the abovesaid Nicholas was seised of the abovesaid tenements as of fee and right in time of peace and in the time of the lord King Henry, father of the present king, taking therefrom esplees to the values etc., and from the same Nicholas descended the right etc., to this Felicia who now seeks as daughter and heir. And that such is her right they produce suit etc.

And Robert and Joyce come and deny their right when etc. And they well deny that the abovesaid Nicholas was ever in seisin of the abovesaid tenements in his demesne as of fee and right such that he could demise it to the abovesaid William. And of this they put themselves on the countryside. And Philip and Felicia similarly.

Therefore the sheriff is ordered to make to come here at three weeks from St. Michael twelve etc. by whom etc. and who neither etc. to recognize in the abovesaid form, because as etc. Afterwards, on the octaves of St. Hilary in the fifteenth year of the present king [circa 21 January 1287], the jurors came. They say on their oath that the abovesaid William de Whelton enfeoffed the abovesaid Nicholas his son of the abovesaid tenements by his deed of feoffment which he made thereof. And he placed him thereof in full seisin, and he [Nicholas] by that feoffment was in good and peaceful seisin thereof for fifteen days. And he cut down the trees and fished the fishponds and marled the land and took the fealty of the free tenants and villeins and took recognition of a half mark and removed the reeves and bailiffs at his will, wherefore they say that the abovesaid Nicholas was thereof in seisin in his demesne as of fee. Therefore it is considered that the abovesaid Philip and Felicia recover their seisin thereof and the abovesaid Robert and Joyce be in mercy.

And be it known that the abovesaid Robert and Joyce by their attorney challenged that more than twenty-four jurors are placed in the writ of judgment and [that that is] against the statute.

DOCUMENT A1.5
Action of Entry: *Montgomery* v *Lee*

Source: CP 40/63, m. 66 *Date*: circa 9 July 1286

Northamptonshire. Philip de Montgomery and Felicia his wife seek against Nicholas del Lee and Alice his wife thirty acres of land and four acres of meadow with appurtenances in the manor of Whilton which they claim as the right of the same Felicia etc. And formerly they [Nicholas and Alice] made a default, to wit, on the octaves of Holy Trinity, after they made to essoin themselves, to wit, on the quindene of Easter, so that then it was ordered to the sheriff that he take the abovesaid tenements into the hand of the lord king etc., and day etc., and that he summoned them to be here at this day etc. And Philip and Felicia betake themselves precisely to the abovesaid default. And Nicholas and Alice by their attorney come and say that they were never summoned to be here at the abovesaid quindene to answer the abovesaid Philip and Felicia in the abovesaid plea nor ever made to essoin themselves at the abovesaid quindene. And this they are prepared to deny against them and their suit as the court shall have considered. Therefore, it is considered that they wage their law twelve-handed. Pledges of law: Simon de Kyngeshemed of the county of Herefordshire and Robert de Bokelinton of the same county. And the attorney of the same Nicholas and Alice is told that he should make them come here in their proper persons on the quindene of St. Michael, because the other day etc. to make [their] laws etc.

DOCUMENT A1.6
Action of Entry: *Nevill* v *Cornwall*

Source: CP 40/179, m. 3 *Date*: 7 October 1309

Northamptonshire. William de Nevill and Felicia his wife by Adam de Harwedon their attorney seek against Geoffrey de Cornwall and Margaret his wife the manor of Norton by Daventry with appurtenances in which the same Geoffrey and Margaret have no entry unless after the demise which Margery—who was the wife of Roger de Whelton and who held it in dower from Nicholas de Whelton father of the abovesaid Felicia whose heir she is from the assignment of William son and heir of the abovesaid Roger from the gift of the same Roger late her husband—made thereof to Robert de Mortimer and Joyce his wife and which after the death of the same Margery ought to revert to the aforementioned William and Felicia by the form of the abovesaid assignment etc.

And Geoffrey and Margaret come and say that Hugh de Mortimer father of the abovesaid Margaret whose heir she is died seised of the abovesaid manor in his demesne as of fee, after whose death the same Margaret entered into the abovesaid manor as daughter and heir. And they say that the same Margaret is underage, wherefore they ask that that suit remain until full age etc.

Therefore let that suit remain until full age etc.

DOCUMENT A1.7

Report on an Assize of Novel Disseisin: *Adam* v *Goodknave*

Source: British Library, Additional MS 31826, fol. 321r *Date*: 1290s

One Adam complained that he was disseised of one messuage and eleven and a half acres of land in Leverton by John Goodknave, who did not come. Therefore, let the assize be taken by his default.

Huntingdon, for John in evidence to the assize, said that at one time this same Adam who now complains to have been disseised held the same tenements which are now in demand from one Geoffrey the Merchant, who enfeoffed him to hold these tenements from him. And after this feoffment came a great flood of water and covered this abovesaid land, by which submersion there was so much damage that he was not at all able to hold this land profitably. And he went to Geoffrey his lord and wanted to have rendered him all the lands he held of him, except these lands which are now in demand. And Geoffrey did not want to receive them unless he rendered all the lands. Wherefore Adam rendered him all the land in this form: "Geoffrey, I render you all the lands which I hold from you in Leverton." Geoffrey: "Render me the deeds of your feoffment." Adam: "I do not know where they are, but as soon as I have them I will return them to you." After which render, [Geoffrey] enfeoffed this John of this messuage and of the eleven and a half acres of land. And thus John has entry by Geoffrey and by his livery and not by disseisin.

The assize came and said word for word as Huntingdon had said.

MIDDLETON. Sir, if you please, inquire from the assize if Adam remained in these tenements after this render.

BEREWICK. That is not of great significance.

—And nevertheless he inquired.

THE ASSIZE. No.

Mutford in secret [said] to Goldington: if the tenant by his grant renders to his lord the tenements which he holds of him by these words—"Sir, I render all the lands and tenements which I hold of you"—if the lord agree to this render, immediately the free tenement goes to the lord.

GOLDINGTON. That is true if the tenant not remain in the tenements after the render.

ORMESBY. Adam brings this assize against John concerning a novel disseisin etc. And it is found by the assize that he did not disseise him. Wherefore this court considers that Adam take nothing by his writ but rather be in mercy and that John go adieu without day.

DOCUMENT AI.8

Report on an Assize of Novel Disseisin: *Thomas* v *William*

Source: British Library, Additional MS 31826, fol. 205r *Date*: late 1280s?

One Thomas brought an assize of novel disseisin against one William, a parson, and complained that he was disseised of his free tenement; and he put in view certain tenements.

HERTFORD. Sir, wrongfully does he bring this assize, because we tell you that he himself leased us the tenements of which he complains to have been disseised at a term of years and by this deed. And during our term he enfeoffed us for the term of our life and by this deed. And so we tell you that we have entered by his deeds and not by disseisin.

INGE. Whatever you say about your deeds, you have entered by disseisin. We pray the assize.

HERTFORD. Answer if this was your deed or not.

INGE. We acknowledge the deeds, but we tell you that you never had an estate by the deed except by disseisin. And of this we pray the assize.

And the assize was charged to say the truth by their oath as to whether William disseised Thomas of his free tenement as he complained or whether he had an estate by his deed as William says.

HERTFORD. Sir, we pray that they have our deeds on which we pleaded.

THE JUSTICE. If those on the assize ask for them, they will have them; otherwise, no.

THE ASSIZE. Sir, we tell you by our oath that Thomas leased these tenements for a term of nine years. And the situation was thus, that Thomas was in debt to the Jewry to at least £20, such that the debt was demanded from the tenements which William had for a term. William came to Thomas and asked him how he wanted to discharge the tenements. Thomas answered him: "Help me to be discharged from the Jewry and I will do whatever you want." "By faith," said William, "grant me the tenements for the term of my life—the tenements which I have from your lease for a term of years—and I will acquit you." Thomas told him that he would do it willingly. They went together to York, and there he made him the deed. And he said to him thus: "If you make me quit, I want you to have the land for the term of your life; and if you do not, I want the tenements to remain to me after the term of nine years." And thus was the deed made.

THE JUSTICE. Did he make the acquittance to Thomas according to the covenant or not?

THE ASSIZE. William obliged himself to the Jews for Thomas by his deed.

THE JUSTICE. When William obliged himself to the Jews for Thomas, did Thomas have any acquittance against him such that if the Jews in their lifetime or the king now asked for this debt he could be acquitted?

THE ASSIZE. Not at all. But we tell you that he paid at least £20 on Thomas's behalf.

THE JUSTICE. Now you said that Thomas made the deed to William and granted him the estate according to the purport of the deed such that he would acquit him from the Jewry, and then you said further that even if William obliged himself for Thomas in such a payment he made him no acquittance . . . or proper deed by which he is obliged to the Jews. And thus, the condition has not been accomplished.

HERTFORD. Sir, to this we have not pleaded, but solely to the disseisin. And whatever you say concerning the condition, we have put forward a simple deed which has been acknowledged. And they have acknowledged that we entered for a term and during our term he made his deed to us. Wherefore, it seems to us that the condition ought not harm us.

INGE. You have your entry for a term and during your term you claim a higher estate as an estate of feoffment and in that you are a disseisor.

DOCUMENT A1.9
An Assize of Mort d'Ancestor: *Helewys* v *Earl of Lincoln*

Source: JUST 1/408, m. 53 (Lancashire) *Date:* 1292

The assize comes to recognize if Adam de Peniston father of William Helewys was seised in his demesne as of fee of four bovates of land with appurtenances in Tottington on the day on which [he died] and if William [is his next heir], which lands Henry de Lacy earl of Lincoln holds. And he comes and says that he has been summoned to hear the recognition of this assize and is ready to hear it. And he says nothing to indicate that the assize should remain but only seeks that he be able to say his evidences to the assize etc. And that is granted to him. And let the assize be taken. But it is put in respect until the Monday next after the feast of St. James the apostle etc. because the recognitors did not have the view etc. And Adam de Rossendale, bailiff of Saltfordshire, did not have the summoners here to attest the view etc.; therefore let him be in mercy etc.

[On which day] the jurors say on their oath that the abovesaid William is not the next heir of the abovesaid Adam, because they say that the abovesaid William was born outside of wedlock. And therefore it is considered that the same William take nothing by that assize but rather be in mercy for his false claim and that the abovesaid Henry de Lacy go thereof without day.

DOCUMENT A1.10

Vouching of Co-Guardians to Warrant: *Montgomery* v *Nevill et al.* in *Passelawe* v *Montgomery et al.* (dower)

Source: CP 40/149, m. 181 *Date*: October/November 1304

Buckinghamshire. Staffordshire. Northamptonshire. Lincolnshire. Philip de Montgomery [a relative, not the father of Anne]—whom William le Botiler, whom Philip son of Philip de Montgomery and John son of William le Botiler vouched to warranty and who warrants them, [vouches to warranty]—presents himself by attorney on the fourth day against Robert de Bruce, guardian of certain parts of the lands of Anne daughter and heir of Philip de Montgomery, and against William de Nevill and Felicia his wife, guardians of certain other parts of the lands of the same heir summoned in the county of Lincolnshire, and against John de Haldenby, guardian of the body of the abovesaid heir summoned in the county of Northamptonshire, in a plea that they be here at this day. And the abovesaid John should have here the abovesaid heir to warrant to the abovesaid Philip together with the lord king, guardian of certain other parts of the lands of the same heir, a one-third part of two acres of woodland and 5 marks 10s rent with appurtenances in Great Crawley in the county of Buckinghamshire which William Passelawe and

Alice his wife in the court here claim as the dower of the same Alice etc. And they do not come. And the sheriff of Northamptonshire had been ordered "*sicut pluries*" that he summon the abovesid John de Haldenby; and the sheriff of Lincolnshire had also been ordered that he summon the abovesaid William and Felicia guardians etc., that they be here at this day etc. And the sheriff of Northamptonshire reports that the writ came too late etc. Therefore, as many times before, the sheriff was ordered to summon the abovesaid John that he be at Westminster three weeks from Easter by prayer of the plaintiff. The same day is given to William and Alice there by their attorneys in the Bench etc. And for the abovesaid William and [Felicia] it has been testified here that they have lands and tenements etc., in wardship etc., from the inheritance etc., in the abovesaid county. Therefore, as many times before, the sheriff of Lincolnshire is ordered that he summon them to be at Westminster at the aforementioned term etc. And let the abovesaid Robert de Bruce guardian etc., be summoned in the county of Staffordshire. And it is not known how much the said acres of woodland are worth annually, so the sheriff of Buckinghamshire is ordered to make the extent etc., by the oath [of twelve] etc., and to make that extent known at Westminster on the quindene of Hilary etc. And then let there be taken from the land of the abovesaid heir in wardship etc., proportionately. And because it is not known how much the lands and tenements which Robert de Bruce holds in wardship of the abovesaid heir are worth annually, the sheriff of Staffordshire is ordered to make the extent by the oath [of twelve] etc., and to make that extent known at Westminster at the aforementioned quindene of St. Hilary etc. And let there be taken etc., and meanwhile the lord king must be consulted.

DOCUMENT A1.11

Presentment of Swynnerton *et al.*

Source: Collections for a History of Staffordshire, William Salt Archaeological Society, vol. 10 (London, 1889), pp. 54-55

Date: 1323-1324

The juries of the hundreds of Offley, Pirehill, Cuttlestone, Seisden, and Totmonslow presented that Roger de Swynnerton knight, John de Swynnerton knight, Richard de Swynnerton, Stephen de Swynnerton, John de Uselwall, Nicholas de Swynnerton parson of the church of Mucklestone, Richard de Whetales, John de Whetales, Richard de Chelle, Hugh de Chelle, Henry de Chelle, Robert de Aston near Stone, Thomas de Aston of the same, Richard de Aston of the same, Andrew le Chamberleyn, John de Charnes, Ithel le Poker, Jukin le Walshe, Adam le Spenser, Adam le But of Swynnerton, William le Wodeward of Beche, and eight others named, were common malefactors and disturbers of the peace, riding about armed through the country to the terror of the people, and that they had come with others who were unknown, armed, to the county court held at Stafford on a certain Thursday in the summer of 6 Edward II [1312] to the great terror of the people, and had forcibly closed the doors of the hall of the court and placed guards so that none could depart, and they had threatened to kill Hugh de Croft the sheriff and William de Stafford knight in open county court unless the court was stopped; and the said Richard de Swynnerton, Nicholas de Swynnerton, with others unknown, had beaten and wounded James de Stafford at Lichfield in the same year; and the said Richard de Swynnerton in the summer of the same year had beaten William Spark and many others at Wolgarston; and that the same Richard took a ransom from several men for not beating them, to the value of 100s annually. And the same Richard with other malefactors, at Penkridge in 8 Edward II [1314-1315] had prevented Henry de Cressewell the coroner of the county from performing his office on the body of Henry atte Persouns, who had been killed by the said Richard, and that when the said Roger de Swynnerton knight had been indicted before the sheriff and coroners of the county for the death of Henry de Salt, killed at Stafford in 1 Edward II [1307-1308], the said Roger came to Swynnerton and convoked by force before him all the witnesses, and made them singly pay fines to him because they had indicted him of the said death, as they truly understand, viz., Robert Bythewater one of the witnesses paid 50 marks; and Roger de Walton another witness, 50 marks; and so from all the other witnesses he took at least from each 50 marks; and Roger de Aston then coroner, because he took the said indictment, made fine with him at £100; and he made them swear that they would take no further proceedings against him.

And they say that the said John de Swynnerton when he was sheriff in 15 Edward II on the Wednesday after the Epiphany in 15 Edward II [13 January 1322] took by force Nicholas de Picheford at Wolverhampton and imprisoned him at Stafford and kept him there till he paid him £20. And the same John de Swynnerton, John de Charles, Richard de Chelle, and John de Wetale with others unknown came to Clifton Campville on 9 December 9 Edward II [1315] on a day when John Chaynel and John Cave, justices assigned to take assizes in the county, were sitting, and disturbed them so that they could not take the assizes. And the said Roger de Swynnerton, John de Swynnerton, Richard de Swynnerton, and John de Wethales on the Thursday before the Feast of St. Peter ad Vincula 7 Edward II [26 July 1313] came to Stafford to the great terror of the people and forcibly disturbed the sheriff sitting in open county, so that the pleas of the county could not be taken. And that the said Stephen de Swynnerton, Richard de Swynnerton, John de Whetale, and others unknown at Gailey in September 13 Edward II [1319] took the goods and chattels of Reginald Perle of Shropshire to the value of £100. The sheriff was therefore ordered to attach them etc.

A postscript states that at Trinity term 17 Edward II the said John de Swynnerton surrendered and was committed to the custody of the Marshal, and being afterwards brought up, prayed that he might be permitted to make fine with the king for the said trespasses and he was fined £40, for which Robert de Bek, William de Shareshill, Thomas Pursel, William Golde, Adam le Hayward, and Robert de Wirleye of Staffordshire were sureties. [I have altered this text in places.]

In the same way, all the other defendants, with the exception of Roger de Swynnerton, appeared at different times and were fined in sums varying from 20s to 10 marks. The postscripts make no mention of Roger de Swynnerton, who was at this time employed in the service of the crown and was Constable of the Tower of London.

DOCUMENT A1.12

An Action of Dower: *Nevill* v *Swynnerton*

Source: Collections for a History of Staffordshire, William Salt Archaeological Society, vol. 9 (London, 1888), p. 11 — *Date:* 1308

Staffordshire. William de Nevill and Felicia his wife sought against John de Swynnerton and Anne his wife a third of the profits of the Stewardship of Cannock in Wednesbury, Derlaston, Willenhall, Wednesfield, Penbryg, Oxley, Moseley, Bushbury, Pendeford, Coven, Shareshill, Hilton, Great Saredon, Little Saredon, Bentley, Featherstone, Teddesley, Pillaton Hall, Huntington, Wolgarston, Penkridge, Alrewas, Orgreave, Fradley, King's Bromley, Curborough, Elmhurst, Gailey, Kinvaston, Aston, Otherton, Rodbaston, Hatherton, Ogley Hay, Stonnall, Aldridge, Rushall, Pelsall, Great Bloxwich, Little Bloxwich, Hopwas, Bonehill, and Cheslyn which they claimed as the dower of the said Felicia. John and Anne did not appear and had previously made default at Easter; and the sheriff had been ordered to take the said third part into the king's hand and to summon them for the quindene of

Trinity, on which day John and Anne appeared and offered to wage their law. And a day was given them for that purpose at the quindene of Michaelmas. It was therefore considered that the said William and Felicia should recover seisin against them by their default. And because Philip de Montgomery late husband of the said Felicia died seised of the said bailiwick, the sheriff was ordered to inquire into the amount of the damages and to return the inquistion at the quindene of Hilary. [I have altered this text in places.]

DOCUMENT A1.13

An Action of Formedon: *Swynnerton* v *Latymer et al.*

Source: CP 40/464, m. 331 *Date*: October 1376

Northamptonshire. The sheriff was ordered that, if John de Swynnerton of Hilton should make him secure of prosecuting his claim, then he should summon William Latymer knight, Richard Stury knight, William de Thorpe knight, Richard de Treton cleric, John Wade parson of the church of Brampton Dingley, and William Thirnyng that they should be here at this day, to wit, the quindene of St. Michael, to answer the abovesaid John in a plea that they return to him the manor of Whilton with appurtenances and four messuages and 100s rent with appurtenances in Staverton. And they do not come. And the sheriff had been ordered to summon them etc. And the sheriff now sends that he [John] did not find him pledges to prosecute etc. And now comes the abovesaid John and finds for the justices of the king here pledges to prosecute, to wit, John de Whetales and William de Buk' of the county of Staffordshire. Therefore as before summon them to be here on the quindene of Hilary etc., and whereof etc.

DOCUMENT A1.14
A Yearbook Report from Chancery

Source: British Library, Additional MS 31826, fol. 169 — *Date*: circa 1290s, but before 1306

A tenement was given to C and to D and to the heirs engendered of their two bodies. It happened then that they survived so long that the issue of their issue had issue, one John by name, while the abovesaid C and D were still living and to whom the gift had been made. Their first issue died and then their second. Afterwards C and D, the common ancestors, died. On whose death the abovesaid John who was thus in the fourth degree as to the common ancestor wanted to have had a writ of formedon in the descender.

CHANCELLOR. How did it happen that those in the third degree or in the second never sued for these tenements?

JOHN. Because C and D survived them.

COUNCIL. By your own words they did not attain an estate. Wherefore, if the tenements had been given simply, neither you nor your father before you could have had the mort d'ancestor. Wherefore you fall short of this writ in tailled form.

And he had concerning their death a writ of cosinage.

DOCUMENT A1.15
A Yearbook Note on Formedon

Source: British Library, Additional MS 31826, fol. 227v — *Date*: circa 1290s

Likewise, before the statute this kind of heir had no recovery after the death of his parents, that is, where they died seised, unless by writ of mort d'ancestor. But now a writ of formedon serves them etc., for that writ and for their writ of right.

Likewise, according to some the first issue can alienate; but as to the right of reversion, it is not extinguished before the fourth degree.

DOCUMENT AI.16

A Petition to the Chancellor: *Holt* v *Debenham*

Source: Select Cases in Chancery, A.D. 1364-1471, ed. William Paley Bailden, Selden Society, vol. 10 (London, 1896), p. 69

Date: early fifteenth century

To the most reverend Father in God and his most gracious lord the Bishop of Exeter Chancellor of England, William Holt esquire humbly beseeches that, whereas Stephen Holt his father who died lately before Michaelmas last in his lifetime purchased certain lands, rents, and tenements in the county of Sussex and thereof enfeoffed Master John Debenham, Richard Monek, John Holt, William Goldsmith, clerks, Andrew Blake, John Bedeford, and others to the intent [that they should] enfeoff him or his heirs when they should be required [to do so], after whose death the said William as son and heir to the said Stephen his father required them to enfeoff him according to the intent of the said feoffment and they refused and will not do it but keep the said lands, rents, and tenements in their hands by great extortion and to the great damage of the said suppliant: may it please your most gracious lordship to cause them to come before you by writ of our lord the King under a certain penalty and to examine them of the truth and to do what right and good faith demand, so that no such extortion nor deceit be suffered, for God and in way of charity.

DOCUMENT A1.17
Enforcement of a Use in Chancery: *Maltby* v *Duffelde*

Source: CCR, 1435-1441, p. 190 (text altered) *Date*: 1438

John Duffelde clerk and John Lyoun chaplain to Joan late the wife of Nicholas Tournay. Demise indented for her life of the estate which they have jointly with Robert Waterton and others now deceased and Roger Barneston yet living in all lands, rents, and services in Osgotby, Cateby, and Northorp county Lincolnshire by feoffment in trust of the said Nicholas, according to a decree against them in Chancery at suit of William Maltby and the said Joan now his wife. Dated 18 July 16 Henry VI.

DOCUMENT A1.18
A Report of *Mortimer* v *Montgomery*

Source: Lincoln's Inn MSS., Misc. 738, fol. 104 *Date*: November 1295

"Command Felicia who was the wife of William de Montgomery that justly etc., she return to Hugh de Mortimer a third part of the manor of Whilton etc., in which the same Felicia has no entry unless by the intrusion which she made in it after the death of Felicia who was the wife of William de Whelton who held it from William de la Zouche in dower from the gift of the abovesaid William de Whelton her late husband by the assignment which Roger son and heir of the abovesaid William de Whelton made thereof to the aforementioned William la Zouche and his heirs and which after the death of the abovesaid Felicia who was the wife of William de Whelton ought to revert to the aforementioned Hugh, cousin and heir of the abovesaid William la Zouche by the form of the abovesaid assignment, as he says etc."

Hugh de Mortimer etc., shows you this, that Felicia etc., wrongfully deforces him of a third part of the manor of Whilton etc., and wrongfully, because this is his right, because William de Whelton was seised thereof etc., in his demesne as of fee and of right in time [of peace etc., taking] the esplees etc., as of fee and of right. From William the right descended to Roger as to son and heir, which Roger assigned this third part in dower to Felicia who was the wife of William de Whelton from the endowment of the abovesaid William her late husband. That Roger granted the reversion of this third part of the manor to the abovesaid William la Zouche and to his heirs. That William was the ancestor of this Hugh, and he is his heir. And that Roger assigned the services of Felicia, by which assignment Felicia attorned to the abovesaid William la Zouche for the services, whereof the abovesaid William was seised of her fealty and of Felicia's services. From William the right to the reversion descended to Joyce as to daughter and thus to this Hugh who now claims. In that third part that same Felicia has no entry unless by the abatement which she made in it after the death of Felicia who was the wife of William de Whelton, who held it in dower etc., from William la Zouche from the endowment of the abovesaid William de Whelton her late husband by the assignment which Roger son and heir of the abovesaid William de Whelton made thereof to William la Zouche and to his heirs. That third part ought to revert after the death of the abovesaid Felicia who was the wife of William de Whelton to the abovesaid Hugh cousin and heir of the abovesaid William la Zouche by the form of the abovesaid assignment. If she wants to deny it etc., [he has] good suit etc.

HEYHAM defended etc. "He counts from the seisin of William de Whelton as of fee and of right descending to Roger as to son and heir and then counts through a stranger and does not count in the blood, wherefore judgment if to such a count [we ought to answer etc.,] because in this case he should not count beyond the seisin of him who assigned and no higher."

BEREFORD. "He lays the reversion more strongly in them, because, had he counted concerning the seisin of him from whom she held in dower, their count would have been bad."

SPIGURNEL. "We challenge the writ, because he counted that this is their right as with a writ of entry, which writ ought to lay in the right if it is not of his own seisin, as to say, 'which he claims to be his right and inheritance' or 'his right from the gift etc.' And since he has counted of another's seisin rather than of his own and it does not lay in the right, we demand judgment of the writ."

BEREFORD. "The words subsequent in the writ lay no more than at the beginning, because otherwise the writ would be weak."

WARWICK. "If we should say in the writ 'which he claims to be his right' without the other words—to wit, 'right and inheritance etc.' or 'right from the gift etc.'—the writ would be out of the form of Chancery. But we cannot say 'right and inheritance', because we were never seised as of our own blood. Nor can we say 'right by the gift', because he who assigned could not give another a free tenement. Nor is there any writ in Chancery which says 'right from the assignment'. Wherefore, since we cannot have 'right and inheritance etc.' nor 'right from the gift etc.' nor 'right from the assignment' nor 'right' by itself, we cannot have another writ in this case."

SPIGURNEL. "Still we tell you that in each writ of entry one ought to say before the entry the declaration of his title and then the entry, but you do the reverse, and this is a backward order. And we demand judgment of the form."

BEREFORD. "If you would oust them from this writ, give them another. But if you give them a writ where the declaration is put before the entry, you would put two things wrong, and this would be a vicious writ."

SPIGURNEL. "Still we tell you that whereas your writ says that Felicia held 'from the gift', there it should say 'from the endowment', and we demand judgment."

BEREFORD. "You say wrongly."

SPIGURNEL. "Whereas your writ runs 'the third part ought to revert to you', reversion is properly to those who are of the blood of those out of whose seisin the tenements issued, but you demand these tenements now as a stranger to them etc., wherefore the remainder would be more proper for you than the reverter."

WARWICK. "The remainder does not apply outside formedon."

HEYHAM. "When one grants to another the reversion of a tenement which a man holds from him at term of life etc., then he will say by these words: 'that you grant me these tenements which A. holds of you at term of his life and that after his death ought to revert to you and to your heirs'. They would not remain to me, because I am a stranger etc."

BEREFORD. "To speak properly when the grant is made, so ought one say 'to remain', which is only a word. But when the words come into effect, then one wants the right in his own person. But to him in whom is vested the right by seisin of services, in him is the reversion etc. For the rest, the remainder is for him whose estate is void; the reversion, his in whom the right is vested."

WARWICK. "A remainder takes its force from a gift precedent, to which gift it is a part. But a reversion is to him in whom the right is vested. But we are not party to any gift precedent, except the right of the reversion made to our ancestors and to the heirs. Wherefore, we ought to use the remainder."

SPIGURNEL. "By that reason whereby you say that the right descends to you, so have you proved my first reason good, because you could have said 'which he claims to be his right and inheritance'."

METTINGHAM. "If you grant me the services of your tenant who attorns himself to me, and I am seised of the services by his hands, and he commits a felony, and I bring my writ of escheat, I will not say 'which ought to revert to me'."

SPIGURNEL. "The one grant is purely of services and lordship, and the other is of the right of the tenements which are in demesne, wherefore they are not similar situations."

BEREFORD. "You grant me the reversion of a tenement: to speak properly you say in the fine that the tenements which ought to revert to you will remain to me; but when the right has vested by the seisin of services, then I can properly say that the reversion is mine and I can grant to another and I will say in the fine that the tenements which ought to revert to me will remain to another. Thus seisin of services gives the reversion."

SPIGURNEL. "We ask the view."

WARWICK. "You ought not have it, because you have entered by your own wrong-doing; and no more will you have the view in this case than you would in a writ of entry sur disseisin."

SPIGURNEL. "The view is necessary, because you demand from a stranger's seisin and from the endowment etc., because she could have been endowed of more or less than a third part of the manor. And for the rest, you demand the third part of the manor by a writ of right, wherefore we cannot know which third part you claim without having the view."

WARWICK. "Had the tenements come from our hands or from the hands of our ancestors, then you would not have the view."

And the view was granted.

Afterwards Felicia said that she did not enter by abatement after the death of Felicia, because she entered etc., while Felicia was alive; she was seised years and days before her death. And we ask judgment of the writ.

WARWICK. "We want to aver that Felicia was seised the day that she died as of fee etc., and in our fealty."

SPIGURNEL. "To this you will not arrive, because we proved against the same Felicia this third part by judgment of the king's court and afterwards from our seisin we bailed it to her to hold from us rendering yearly so much for the term of her life. And still three years before her death she rendered up to us the same tenements and we were seised during her life, ready etc."

Therefore, a jury.

APPENDIX 2

Statutes

✻

DOCUMENT A2.1

The Statute of Merton, cc. 6, 7: Marriage of Wards

Date: 1236

c. 6. It is thus provided concerning heirs forcibly abducted or detained by parents or by others: that whatsoever layman shall have been convicted thereof that he has so married off a child shall render to him who has lost [that marriage] the value of the marriage; and for the delict his body shall be taken and imprisoned until he shall have amended the delict to the one who has thus lost if the child be married off and thereafter until he shall have satisfied the lord King for the transgression; and this shall be done concerning an heir when he is under fourteen years old. And concerning an heir when he is fourteen years old or over until full age, if he shall have married himself without the licence of his lord so that he has taken away his marriage from him and the lord offer him a reasonable marriage whereby he would not be disparaged, his lord then shall hold his land beyond the term of his [full] age, to wit, twenty-one years, for so long a time that he can receive thereof double the value of the marriage either according to the estimation of lawful men or according to what he shall have been offered previously for the same marriage without fraud or malice and according to that which he shall have been able to prove in the court of the lord King.

And concerning lords who shall have married those whom they have in wardship to villeins or others such as burgesses whereby they are disparaged, if such heir be under fourteen years old and of such age that he cannot consent, then, if the parents complain, that lord shall lose the wardship until the legitimate age of the heir; and all the benefit which shall be taken thereof shall be converted to the benefit of him who is underage according to the disposition and provision of the parents, on account of the shame done him.

And if he is fourteen years old and more and can consent and shall have consented to such a marriage, no penalty shall ensue.

c.7. If any heir of whatsoever age shall not want to marry himself on behalf of his lord, he shall not be compelled to do this, but when he shall have arrived at [full] age and before he receive his land, he shall give to his lord and satisfy him for as much as he could have taken from anyone for the marriage; and this [shall be] whether he shall want to marry himself or not, for the marriage of him who is underage pertains by full right to the lord of the fee.

DOCUMENT A2.2

The Statute of Marlborough, c. 6: Fraudulent Feoffments

Date: 1267

And concerning those who are accustomed to enfeoff their eldest sons and heirs who are underage with their inheritance so that thereby the lords of the fees would lose their wardships, it is provided, concorded, and granted that no chief lord lose his wardship by reason of such a feoffment.

Moreover, touching those who want to fabricate concerning their lands, which they want to give out at a term of years and so that the lords of the fees lose their wardships, false feoffments containing that they have been satisfied of the sum of service contained in these feoffments up to some term; and that after the said term such feoffees are held to pay some sum far exceeding the value of those lands, so that after that term their land will revert to them, because no one would care to hold them for so much; it is provided and granted that by such fraud no chief lord will lose his wardship. Nevertheless, it will not be lawful for them to disseise such feoffees without judgment, but they shall have a writ that such wardships be returned to them and by the witnesses contained in the deeds of such feoffments together with other free and lawful men of the countryside and by the quantity of the value of the tenement and by the quantity of the sum which ought to be rendered after the abovesaid term it will be tried whether such feoffment was made in good faith or in fraud to take away from the chief lords their wardship. And if the chief lords recover their wardship by judgment of the court in such cases, nevertheless their action shall be saved for such feoffees to recover at term or at fee when the heirs arrive at legitimate age.

But if any chief lords maliciously implead any feoffees fabricating this case whereas the feoffments have been made legitimately and in good faith, then their damages shall be awarded to the feoffees and those plaintiffs shall be heavily punished by amercement.

DOCUMENT A2.3

The Statute of Marlborough, c. 29: Writ of Entry in the *Post*

Date: 1267

It is also provided that if those alienations concerning which a writ of entry used to be given are made through so many degrees that that writ cannot be had in the form customary before, the plaintiff shall have a writ to recover seisin without mention of the degrees, into whosesoever hand that thing shall have come by these alienations, by original writs to be provided therefor by the Council of the King.

DOCUMENT A2.4
The Statute of Westminster I, c. 22: Marriage of Wards

Date: 1275

Concerning underage heirs before they are fourteen years old without the consent of their guardians, it shall be done according to that which is contained in the Provisions of Merton; and concerning those who shall have been married without the consent of their guardians after they shall have passed fourteen years, the guardians shall have double the value of his marriage according to the tenor of the same provision. Moreover, those who shall have withdrawn the marriage shall render the full value of the marriage to the guardian for the transgression and nevertheless the King shall have the amends from him who has thus withdrawn according to the same provision.

Concerning female heirs, after they shall have accomplished the age of fourteen years and the lord to whom the marriage pertains does not want to marry them off but rather, coveting the land, wants to hold them unmarried, it is provided that the lord shall not be able to have or hold the land of these female heirs by reason of marriage beyond two years after the term of the abovesaid fourteen years. And if the lord within these two years does not marry them, then they shall have action to recover their inheritance quit, without giving anything for the wardship and for the marriage. And if by malice or by bad counsel they do not want to be married off by their chief lord in such a way that they are not disparaged, then the lord shall hold the land and the inheritance until the age of a male heir, that is to say, twenty-one, and beyond until he has taken the value of the marriage.

DOCUMENT A2.5

The Statute of Westminster II, Preface and c. 1: *De Donis Conditionalibus*

Date: 1285

Whereas recently our lord the King on the quindene of St. John the Baptist in the sixth year of his reign, because many of his kingdom were suffering disinheritance because in many cases where a remedy ought to have been supplied a remedy had not been provided either by his predecessors or by himself, having called together the prelates, earls, barons, and his council at Gloucester, ordained certain statutes very useful and necessary for his people whereby his English and Irish people governed under his guidance have obtained in their tribulations more speedy justice than previously, and [whereas] certain cases in which the law was deficient were not determined and certain matters remained to be enacted to restrain the tribulation of the people, the lord King in his Parliament at Westminster after Easter in the thirteenth year of his reign, for the completion of the abovesaid statutes ordained at Gloucester, made to be rehearsed the many tribulations and defects of the laws and provided the statutes as will appear in the following.

c. 1. First, concerning tenements which many times are given under condition, to wit,

[a] when anyone gives his land to some man and his wife and the heirs procreated from that man and woman, with the added condition expressed such that if the same man and woman die without heir procreated from the same man and woman, the land so given should revert to the donor or to his heir,

[b] also in the case when anyone gives tenements in free marriage, which gift had the condition annexed, although it

is not expressed in the deed of gift, which is such, that if the man and woman die without heir procreated from themselves the tenement so given should revert to the donor or to his heir,

[c] and also in the case when anyone gives a tenement to anyone and the heirs issuing from his body,

it seemed and still seems hard on the donors and the heirs of the donors that the will expressed in their deeds has not before and still is not observed. And in all the abovesaid cases, after offspring has been begotten and born by those to whom the tenement was thus given conditionally, heretofore this kind of feoffee had power to alienate the tenement thus given and to disinherit their issue from the tenement against the will of the donors and the expressed form of the gift. And further, whereas, when issue of this kind of feoffee is lacking, the tenement so given ought to revert to the donor or to his heir by the form expressed in the deed of gift, even though issue, if there was any, had died, they have heretofore been excluded from the reversion of the same tenement by the deed and feoffment of those to whom the tenements had been given thus under condition, [a situation] which was manifestly against the form of their gift.

Wherefore, the lord King, perceiving that it is necessary and useful in the abovesaid cases to provide a remedy, has established that the will of the donor shall henceforth be observed according to the form manifestly expressed in the deed of his gift, such that those to whom the tenement has been given thus under condition shall not have power to alienate the tenement thus given whereby after their death it would the less remain to the issue of those to whom the tenement has thus been given or to the donor or to his heir if issue is lacking so that there be no issue at all or, if there shall have been issue, he fail by death, heir of that issue lacking. Nor shall the second husband of such a woman henceforth have anything after the death of his wife by the law of England in a tenement thus given by condition. Nor shall the issue of the second husband and the woman have hereditary succession, but immediately after the death of the man and woman to whom the tenement was thus given, after their death it shall revert as is said above either to their issue or to the donor or to his heir.

And because in a new case a new remedy must be provided, let there be for the purchaser such a writ:

> Command A that justly etc. he return to B such a manor with appurtenances which C gave to such a man and such a woman and the heirs issuing from the same man and woman

or

> which C gave to such a man in free marriage with such a woman and which after the death of the abovesaid man and woman ought to descend to the abovesaid B son of the abovesaid man and woman by the form of the abovesaid gift as he says

or

> which C gave to such a one and the heirs issuing from his body and which after the death of the same person ought to descend to the abovesaid B son of the abovesaid person by the form etc.

The writ whereby the donor has his recovery when issue is lacking is sufficiently in use in Chancery.

And let it be known that this statute has place as to the alienation of tenements henceforward made against the form of the gift and does not extend to gifts made previously. And if henceforward a fine is levied on this kind of tenement, it shall be null by the same law. Nor shall the heirs or those to whom the reversion pertains have need to put forward their claim, even though they are of full age, in England, and out of prison.

DOCUMENT A2.6

The Statute of Westminster II, c. 31: Bills of Exception

Date: 1285

When anyone impleaded before any justices puts forward an exception and asks that the justices allow it, if they do not want to allow it, if he who proposed the exception shall write it down and ask the justices to affix their seals in witness, the justices shall affix their seals. And if one does not so want, the other of the company shall affix his. And if, by chance, the lord King by complaint concerning the deed of the justices shall make the record to come before him and if that exception is not found in the roll and the complainant show the written exception with the justice's seal affixed, the justice shall be ordered to acknowledge or deny his seal at a certain day. And if the justice cannot deny his seal, it will proceed to judgment according to that exception as it ought to be allowed or quashed.

DOCUMENT A2.7

The Statute *Quia Emptores*

Date: 1290

Because purchasers of lands and tenements from the fees of magnates and others have heretofore many times entered in their fees to the lord's prejudice, to which purchasers those holding freely of the same magnates and others have sold their lands and tenements to be held in fee to themselves and their heirs from their feoffors and not from the chief lords of the fees, whereby the same chief lords have very often lost the escheats, marriages, and wardships of the lands and tenements being in their fees, which situation seemed very difficult and hard on the same magnates and the other lords and similarly in this case manifest disinheritance, the lord King in his Parliament at Westminster after Easter in the eighteenth year of his reign, to wit, on the quindene of St. John the Baptist, granted, provided, and established at the instance of the magnates of his realm that henceforward every free man shall be allowed to sell his land or tenement or part thereof, such, however, that the feoffee shall hold that land or tenement from the same chief lord and by the same customs and services as his feoffor previously held them.

And if he sell any part of his same lands or tenements to anyone, the feoffee shall hold that immediately from the chief lord and shall be burdened immediately with the service, as much as pertains or ought to pertain to the same lord for that parcel, according to the quantity of land or tenement sold. And thus in this case that part of the service to be taken through the hand of the feoffor will be deducted from the chief lord, whereof the feoffee ought to be intendent and answerable for that parcel of service thus owed to the same chief lord according to the quantity of land or tenement sold.

And let it be known that by the abovesaid sales and purchases of lands and tenements or of some part of the same, those lands and tenements, in part or in whole, cannot devolve into mortmain by art or artifice against the form of the statute recently made thereon. And let it be known that this statute applies only to lands sold to be held in fee simply and that it extends to future time. And it will begin to apply at the feast of St. Andrew next coming.

DOCUMENT A2.8

The Statute of 1 Richard II, c. 9: Fraudulent Grants

Date: 1377

Likewise, because complaint has been made to the King that many men of the said realm as well great as small who have right and true title as well to lands, tenements, and rents as to other personal actions because the occupiers or defendants, to be sustained and maintained in their wrong, commonly make gifts and feoffments of their lands and tenements which are in debate and of their other goods and chattels to lords and other great men of the realm against whom the said pursuers, because of the great menace which is made to them, dare not make their pursuits; and also, on the other part, complaint has been made that many times many men disseise others of their tenements and immediately after the disseisin has been made they make alienations and feoffments, sometimes to lords and the great men of the realm so as to have maintenance and sometimes to several persons of whose names the disseisee can have no cognizance so that by such frauds the said disseisees and other demandants and their heirs are distanced and delayed from their recovery to the great destruction and oppression of the people: it is ordained and established that henceforth no gift or feoffment of lands, tenements, or goods be made by such fraud or maintenance; and if any are made in such manner, they will be held to be null and of no value. And henceforth the disseisees shall have against the first disseisors their recovery as well of the lands and tenements as of their double damages, without having regard to such alienations, as long as the disseisees begin their suits within the next year after the disseisin is made. And it is ordained and assented that the same statute have place in every other action or plea of land where such feoffments are made by fraud or collusion, to have their recovery against the first such feoffor.

And it is to be known that this statute should be understood [to apply] where such feoffors take thereof the profits.

DOCUMENT A2.9

The Second Statute of 2 Richard II, c. 3: Debtors' Feigned Grants

Date: 1379

Likewise in a case of debt where the debtors make feigned gifts and feoffments of their lands and goods to their friends and to others and afterwards withdraw themselves and flee to privileged places of Holy Church and there hold themselves a long time and take the profits from their lands and goods so given by fraud and collusion, whereby their creditors have been long and yet are delayed of their debts and recovery wrongfully and against good faith and reason: it is ordained and established that after the said creditors have brought their writs of debt thereof and on this a *capias* has been awarded, the sheriff shall make his return that he has not taken the said persons because of such privileged places into which they have or shall have entered, then, after such a return has been made, another writ will be granted and made to the sheriff, in which writ it shall be comprised that proclamation be made openly at the gate of the place thus privileged where such persons have entered, for five weeks continually one time each week, that the same person shall be before the justices of the king at a certain day comprised in the same writ to respond to the plaintiff concerning his demand. And the sheriff shall make return of this writ that the proclamation has been made in the said form. And [if] the said persons have been called and do not come, either in proper person or by attorney, let judgment be rendered against them on the principal for their default. And from this same judgment, let execution be made from their lands and goods which are outside the place so privileged as well, that is to say, of those lands and goods so given by collusion as of whatever other lands and goods outside the same franchise. [This shall be] after such collusion or fraud is duly found and [it should be done] in the same manner as it ought to have been done had there been made no demise of them, notwithstanding the demise. But it is not the intention of the king that by virtue of this statute anyone should be foreclosed from his suit against such debtors by common course of the law used before this present statute.

DOCUMENT A2.10

The Statute of 11 Richard II, cc. 2, 4, 5: The Forfeitures of Those Condemned by the Merciless Parliament

Date: 1388

c. 2. Likewise it is ordained and established in this present Parliament that in right of the forfeitures of those who have been judged in this same Parliament before the twentieth day of this present month of March that the King shall have the forfeiture of all the castles, lordships, reversions, lands, tenements, fees, advowsons, franchises, liberties, and all other possessions which were to Alexander late archbishop of York, Robert de Veer late duke of Ireland, Michael de la Pole late earl of Suffolk, Robert Tresilian knight, Nicholas Brembre knight, John Blake, and Thomas Usk or to any of them, the first day of the last Parliament, which was the first day of October the tenth year of the reign of our lord King Richard the Second or after until now, and which any other had from the gift, grant, or feoffment from the abovesaid archbishop of York, duke of Ireland, earl of Suffolk, Robert Tresilian, Nicholas Brembre, John Blake, and Thomas Usk or any of them, or from the gift, grant, or feoffment of any other by bargain or in any other manner to the use of the same archbishop of York, duke of Ireland, earl of Suffolk, Robert Tresilian, Nicholas Brembre, John Blake, and Thomas Usk or any of them, the said first day of the last Parliament or after until now, shall be forfeit to the King; and that all the goods and chattels which were to the abovesaid archbishop of York, duke of Ireland, earl of Suffolk, Robert Tresilian, Nicholas Brembre, John Blake, and Thomas Usk, or to any of them, the seventeenth day of November last past or after until now, be also forfeit to the King; and if any of the abovesaid archbishop of York, duke of Ireland, earl of Suffolk, Robert Tresilian, Nicholas Brembre, John Blake, and Thomas Usk has demised himself of his goods and chattels by color of gift or feigned sale or payment of debt not owed or in other manner by fraud or collusion after the said first day of the last Parliament until the twentieth day of March, such goods and chattels shall be forfeit to the King.

And also [it is ordained and established] that all the lands, tenements, reversions, fees, advowsons, franchises, liberties, and all other possessions which were to Robert Belknap, John Holt, John Cary, and William Burgh knights or to any of them the first day of August last past or afterwards until now and which any other had from the gift, grant, or feoffment of the abovesaid Robert Belknap, John Holt, John Cary, and William Burgh or of any of them or from the gift, grant, or feoffment of any other by bargain or in other manner to the use of the same Robert Belknap, John Holt, John Cary, and William Burgh or of any of them the said first day of August or afterwards until now shall be forfeit to the King; and that all the goods and chattels which were to the abovesaid Robert Belknap, John Holt, John Cary, and William Burgh or to any of them the sixth day of the said month of March, on which day they were judged, or afterwards until now shall be forfeit also to the King; and if any of the abovesaid Robert Belknap, John Holt, John Cary, and William Burgh has demised himself of any of his goods and chattels by color of gift or feigned sale or payment of a debt not owed or in other manner by fraud or collusion after the first day of August until the sixth day of March, such goods and chattels shall be forfeit to the King.

And [it is ordained and established] also that all lands, tenements, reversions, fees, advowsons, franchises, liberties, and all other possessions which were to Roger Fulthorp knight and John de Lokton or to either of them the twenty-fifth day of the month of August or afterwards until now and which any other had from the gift, grant, or feoffment of the abovesaid Roger Fulthorp and John de Lokton or of either of them or from the gift, grant, or feoffment of any other by bargain or in other manner to the use of the same Roger Fulthorp and John Lokton or either of them the said twenty-fifth day of August or afterwards until now shall be forfeit to the King; and that all the goods and chattels which were to the abovesaid Roger de Fulthorp and John Lokton or to either of them the sixth day of the said month of March, on which day they were judged, or afterwards until now shall be forfeit to the King; and if either of the abovesaid Roger Fulthorp and John Lokton has demised himself of any of his goods and chattels by color of gift or feigned sale or payment of a debt not owed or in other manner by fraud or collusion after the said sixth day of March, such goods and chattels shall be forfeit to the King. . . .

c. 4. And further it is ordained and established that proclamation be made in the counties that everyone who has any of the goods and chattels thus forfeit as is said above or to whose hands such goods and chattels have come shall come within two months after the proclamation has thus been made and certify the same to the King's Council. And if he does not and is thereof duly attainted, he shall be held to render to the King the same goods and chattels so concealed or the price of the same and beyond that [again] as much as the same goods and chattels are worth and he shall have an imprisonment of one year: provided always that if any of the said persons are or were seised or possessed of any castles, lordships, lands, tenements, reversions, fees, advowsons, franchises, liberties, or other possessions whatsoever by feoffment, gift, or grant from whatsoever person to the use and profit of someone else than to the use and profit of the said persons adjudged or any of them, that such castles, lordships, lands, tenements, reversions, fees, advowsons, franchises, liberties and other possessions whatsoever shall not be forfeit in any manner and this ordinance or establishment of forfeiture shall not extend to them.

c. 5. And further it is ordained and established that the King have all the forfeitures abovesaid, as well within franchise as without, saving the right of the lords of the said franchises if any right pertains to them in this part. And it is not the intention of the King or of the Lords and Commons of Parliament to bar or foreclose from their right when their time shall come according to the Common Law the issues in the tail or those in reversion or remainder or women from their inheritance or jointure with their husbands or gifts, grants, or feoffments made before the said time of forfeiture limited.

DOCUMENT A2.11

The Statute of 15 Richard II, c. 5: Mortmain Uses

Date: 1391

. . . And moreover it is agreed and assented that all those who are possessed of lands, tenements, fees, advowsons, or other possessions whatsoever by feoffment or other way to the use of men of religion or other spiritual persons to amortise them and whereof the said religious and spiritual persons take the profits: that between now and the feast of St. Michael next coming they will make to amortise them by license of the King and of the lords or else they shall sell and alienate them to another use between now and the said feast under penalty of forfeiture to the King and to the lords according to the form of the Statute *de Religiosis* as tenements purchased by men of religion. And henceforth no purchase shall be made such that such religious or other spiritual persons take the profits thereof as is said above under the abovesaid penalty. And this same statute shall extend and apply to all lands and tenements, fees, advowsons, and other possessions purchased and to be purchased to the use of gilds and fraternities. And moreover it is assented, because mayors, bailiffs, and the commons of cities, boroughs, and other towns which have a perpetual commonalty and others which have perpetual offices are as perpetual as men of religion, that henceforth they shall not purchase to themselves and to their commonalty or office under the penalty contained in the said Statute *de Religiosis*. And concerning those things of which others are possessed or shall be possessed in time to come to their use and of which they take or shall take the profits, it shall be done likewise as has been said above concerning men of religion.

DOCUMENT A2.12

The Statute of 21 Richard II, c. 3: Forfeiture for Treason

Date: 1397-1398

Likewise it is ordained and established that every man who encompasses and intends the death of the King or his deposition or to render up his liege homage or who rouses the people and rides against the King to make war within his realm and is duly attainted and adjudged in Parliament of this shall be adjudged as a traitor of high treason against the Crown and shall forfeit forever to the King and his heirs from himself and his heirs whosoever all his lands, tenements, possessions, and liberties and all other inheritances which he has or any other has to his use or had the day he perpetrated the treason, as well in fee tail as in fee simple, as well held of others as held of himself, and also such possession as some other has to his use. And this statute shall extend and apply as well to those who are adjudged or attainted for any of the four points of the said treasons in this Parliament as of all those who shall be adjudged or attainted in Parliament in time to come of any of the abovesaid four points of treasons. And it is not the intention of the King or of the Lords, nor is it the assent of the Commons abovesaid that if any such one who forfeits in the manner abovesaid is enfeoffed in any land, tenement, or possession to another's use that this be included in this forfeiture.

DOCUMENT A2.13

The Statute of 1 Henry IV, c. 5: Restoration of Forfeitures

Date: 1399

Likewise it is ordained and assented that the lords and others who were forejudged in the said Parliament held the said twenty-first year or by authority of the same, both those who are now alive and also the heirs of the lords and others who are dead, shall be entirely restored and reinstituted to their names, inheritances, and possessions, reversions, fees, advowsons, offices, liberties, and franchises whatsoever as entirely as the said lords and others who are now alive or the lords and others who are dead, ancestors of the abovesaid heirs, or the feoffees of the said lords or of the others abovesaid or others enfeoffed to their use had them at the time the judgment was rendered against them the said twenty-first year, by entry without making any other pursuit for them or having livery of them, saving always that the said lords and others abovesaid shall have nothing of the issues taken thereof in the meantime. And as to the goods and chattels which were to the said lords or other abovesaid persons thus forejudged, of which the King has not been answered and which are in the hands of sheriffs, escheators, or other officers, ministers, or persons whatsoever and concealed by them, the King wants and grants that the same lords and others who are alive and the executors and administrators of those who are dead shall have livery and restitution of them, and that the sheriffs, escheators, officers, and ministers thus occupying the said goods and chattels by such concealment shall be punished for the same concealment.

DOCUMENT A2.14

The Statute of 4 Henry IV, c. 7: Fraudulent Grants

Date: 1402

Likewise, whereas in the statute made the first year of King Richard the Second it was ordained that, whereas divers men disseise others of their free tenements and make feoffment to divers men to have maintenance as well as to make the disseisees ignorant of those against whom their writ ought to be brought, that the disseisees in such case should bring their writ in such case against those who take the profits as long as the disseisees commence their suits within the year next following the disseisin, and that the same ordinance should apply in every other action or plea where such feoffments are made by fraud or collusion so that they have their recovery against such feoffors if they take the profits thereof: our said lord the King, understanding the said statute to be very mischievous and damaging to his people because of the brevity of the time, by the assent of the said Lords and at the request of the Commons has ordained and established that such disseisees shall have their action against the first disseisor during the life of the same disseisor, provided that such disseisor take the profits thereof at the time the suit commences. And as to other writs in plea of land, the demandant shall commence his suit within the year against him who is tenant of the free tenement at the time the action accrued to him, provided that such tenant take thereof the profits at the time such suit commences, notwithstanding the abovesaid statute.

DOCUMENT A2.15

The Statute of 11 Henry VI, c. 5: Uses and Waste

Date: 1433

Likewise because divers men heretofore have leased their lands and tenements to divers persons, that is to say for term of life or for term of another's life and some for a term of years, the said tenants have often granted and leased the estate they have in the said lands and tenements to several persons intending that those in the reversion, that is to say, their lessors, their heirs, and their assigns, might not have knowledge of their names and thereafter the said first tenants continually occupy the said lands and tenements and take thereof the profits to their own proper use and in the said lands and tenements they commit waste and destruction to the disinheritance of those in the reversion: it is ordained and established that those in the reversion in such case shall be able to have and to maintain a writ of waste against the said tenants for term of life, of another's life, or of years, and so recover against them the place wasted and their triple damages for the waste done by them as they ought to have done for the waste done by them before the said grant and lease of their estate, provided always that this ordinance only apply where the first tenants, before the lease and the grant of their said estate in the manner and form abovesaid, were punishable for waste and also where after the said grant and lease the said first tenants of the said lands and tenements take the profits to their own proper use at the time the waste was done. And this ordinance shall extend as well to waste by such tenants made before this ordinance as after.

DOCUMENT A2.16
The Statute of 1 Richard III, c. 1: An Act Against Secret and Unknown Feoffments

Date: 1483

First, because great uncertainty, trouble, costs, and grievous vexations accrue from day to day by secret and unknown feoffments between the subjects of the King, so much so that no man who buys lands, tenements, rents, and services or other inheritables; nor women who have jointure or dower in any lands, tenements, or other inheritables; nor the last wills of men to be performed; nor leases for term of life or for years; nor annuities granted to any person or persons for their service for term of their lives or otherwise are in perfect certainty or without great trouble and doubt of the same by reason of the secret and unknown feoffments: to remedy the same it is ordained, established, and enacted by the advice of the Lords Spiritual and Temporal and of the Commons assembled in this present Parliament and by authority of the same that every estate, feoffment, gift, release, grant, leases and confirmations of lands, tenements, rents, services or inheritables made or had or hereafter to be made or had by any person or persons who are of full age, of sound memory, at large, and not under duress, to any person or persons, and all recoveries and executions had or made shall be good and effectual to him to whom it is thus made, had, or given and to all others to their use against the vendor, feoffor, donor, or grantor of them and against the vendors, feoffors, donors, or grantors and his or their heirs claiming them solely as heir or heirs to the same vendors, feoffors, donors, or grantors and each of them, and against all others having and claiming any title or interest in them only to the use of the same vendor, feoffor, donor, or grantor, vendors, feoffors, donors, or grantors or his or their heirs at the time the bargain, sale, covenant, gift, or grant was made, saving to each person or persons such right, title, action, and interest by reason of any gift in the tail made thereof and they ought to have had if this act had not been made.

DOCUMENT A2.17

The Statute of 2 Richard III, c. 5: The King as Feoffee to Uses

Date: 1483

Likewise our said lord the King calling to his blessed remembrance the great damage, trouble, and charge which might ensue to his liege people by reason of divers feoffments and estates of lands, tenements, and other inheritables made, before he was King, jointly to him and other persons to the use and behest of other persons and not to his own use; and to avoid such damages, trouble, and charges which might come to the persons to whose use such feoffments and estates were made, from his blessed disposition and of his mere motion, by authority of his said Parliament, he wants, ordains, and establishes that such possession, right, title, and interest as there is or as pertains to him of or in any lands, tenements, or other inheritables by reason of any such feoffment or estate made jointly to him and others to the use and behest of other person or persons and not to his own use vest and be by the said authority entirely in the other person or persons enfeoffed thus with him or having joint estate to the same use and effect for which they were thus enfeoffed or had estate in similar manner as if he had never been enfeoffed nor had estate with the same other person or persons. And furthermore it is ordained by the said authority that such possession, right, title, and interest of and in any lands and tenements or other inheritables of which the King is solely seised by reason of any feoffment or estate made before he was King to the use of any person or persons vest and be in such person or persons and their heirs to whose use he is thereof thus seised, saving to every other person or persons their right, title, and interest in the same.

DOCUMENT A2.18

The Statute of 1 Henry VII, c. 1: Action Against Pernors of Profits in Formedon

Date: 1485

First, that whereas divers subjects of the King who have a cause of action by formedon in the descender or otherwise in the remainder by force of some tail of and for the lands and tenements are defrauded and delayed from their said actions and often without remedy because of feoffments made of the same lands and tenements to persons unknown to the intent that the demandants should not know against whom they should bring their action, it is ordained, established, and enacted by the advice of the Lords Spiritual and Temporal and of the Commons assembled in the said Parliament and by authority of the same that the demandant in each such case shall have his action against him or them who take the profits of the lands or tenements demanded, of which some person or persons are enfeoffed to his or their use; and that the same taker or takers named as tenant or tenants in the said action shall have the same vouchers and their lien in this, aid prayer, and all other advantages as the taker or takers should have had had they been tenants in fact or as their feoffees ought to have had if the same action had been attempted or conceived against them; and if any person happen to decease so having to the use of him or of his heirs, the said heir, while within age, against whom such action is taken as the taker, then the same heir shall have his age in the said action conceived against him and all other advantages as if his ancestor had died seised of the said lands and tenements thus in demand. And also it is ordained by the said authority that all recoveries which shall be in any such actions against such taker or takers of profits of the said lands and tenements shall be of similar force and effect against such taker or takers and their heirs and their said feoffees and their heirs and the feoffees of the said takers and their heirs as though the said taker or takers had been tenants in fact or feoffees to their use or their heirs as said above of the free tenement of the said lands and tenements at any time the said action is used.

DOCUMENT A2.19

The Statute of 3 Henry VII, c. 5: Fraudulent Deeds of Gift

Date: 1487

Likewise, that because often deeds of gift of goods and chattels are made with the intent of defrauding their creditors of the things owed them and the person or persons who made the said deed of gift flee to sanctuary or other privileged places and occupy or live with the said goods and chattels, their creditors remaining unpaid: it is ordained, enacted, and established from the assent and authority abovesaid that all deeds of gift of goods and chattels made or to be made of confidence to the use of this person or persons who made the same deed of gift shall be void and of no effect.

DOCUMENT A2.20

The Statute of Uses, cc. 1, 2, 4

Date: 1536

c. 1. Whereas by the common laws of this realm lands, tenements, and hereditaments be not devisable by testament and ought not to be transferred from one to another but by solemn livery and seisin, matter of record, writing sufficient made in good faith without covin or fraud, yet nevertheless divers and sundry imaginations, subtle inventions, and practices have been used whereby the hereditaments of this realm have been conveyed from one to another by fraudulent feoffments, fines, recoveries, and other assurances craftily made to secret uses, intents, and trusts, and also by wills and testaments sometimes made by bare word and words sometimes by signs and tokens and sometimes by writing and for the most part made by such persons as be visited with sickness in their last agonies and pains or at such time as they had scarcely any good memory or remembrance, at which times they, being provoked by greedy, covetous persons lying in wait about them, do many times dispose indiscreetly and unadvisedly of their lands and inheritances, by reason whereof and by occasion of which fraudulent feoffments, fines, recoveries, and other like assurances to uses, confidences, and trusts divers and many heirs have been unjustly at sundry times disinherited, the lords have lost their wards, marriages, reliefs, heriots, escheats, aids to make their son a knight and to marry off their daughter; and scarcely any person can be certainly assured of any lands purchased by them nor know surely against whom they shall use their actions or executions for their rights, titles, and duties; also married men have lost their tenancies by the curtesy, women their dowers, manifest perjuries by trial of such secret wills and uses have been committed, the King's Highness has lost the profits and advantages of the lands of persons attainted and of the lands craftily put in feoffment to the uses of those born aliens and also the profits of waste for a year and a day of lands of attainted felons and the lords their escheats thereof, and many other inconveniences have happened and daily do increase among the King's subjects to their great trouble and disquiet to the utter subversion of the ancient common laws of this realm; for the extirpation and extinguishment of all such craftily practiced feoffments, fines, recoveries, abuses, and errors heretofore used and accustomed in this realm to the subversion of the good and ancient laws of the same and to the intent that the King's Highness or any other his subjects of this realm shall not in any wise hereafter by any means or inventions be deceived, damaged, or hurt by reason of such trusts, uses, or confidences: may it please the King's most Royal Majesty that it may be enacted by His Highness by the assent of the Lords Spiritual and Temporal and the Commons in this present Parliament assembled and by authority of the same in manner and form following, that is to say: that where any person or persons stand or be seised or at any time hereafter shall happen to be seised of and in any honors, castles, manors, lands, tenements, rents, services, reversions, remainders, or other hereditaments to the use, confidence, or trust of any other person or persons or of any body politic by reason of any bargain, sale, feoffment, fine, recovery, covenant, contract, agreement, will, or otherwise by any manner means whatsoever it be, that in every such case all and every such person and persons and bodies politic that have or hereafter shall have any such use, confidence, or trust in fee simple, fee tail, for term of life or for years, or otherwise, or any use, confidence, or trust in remainder or reverter shall from henceforth stand and be seised, deemed, and adjudged in lawful seisin, estate, and possession of and in the same honors, castles, manors, lands, tenements, rents, services, reversions, remainders, and hereditaments with their appurtenances to all intents, constructions, and purposes in the law, of and in suchlike estates as they had or shall have in use, trust, or confidence of or in the same. And that the estate, right, title, and possession that was in such person or persons that were or shall be hereafter seised of any lands, tenements, or hereditaments to the use, confidence, or trust of any such person or persons or of any body politic be from henceforth clearly deemed and adjudged to be in him or them that have or hereafter shall have such use, confidence, or trust after such quality, manner, form, and condition as they had before in or to the use, confidence, or trust that was in them.

c. 2. And be it further enacted by the authority aforesaid that whereas divers and many persons be or hereafter shall happen to be jointly seised of and in any lands, tenements, rents, reversions, remainders, or other hereditaments to the use, confidence, or trust of any of them that be so jointly seised, that in every such case that or those person or persons which have or hereafter shall have any such use, confidence, or trust in any such lands, tenements, rents, reversions, remainders, or hereditaments shall from henceforth have and be deemed and adjudged to have only to him or them that have or hereafter shall have such use, confidence, or trust such estate, possession, and seisin of and in the same lands, tenements, rents, reversions, remainders, or other hereditaments in like nature, manner, and form, condition, and course as he or they had before in the use, confidence, or trust of the same lands, tenements, or hereditaments, saving and reserving to all and singular persons and bodies politic, their heirs and successors, other than those person or persons which are seised or hereafter shall be seised of any lands, tenements, or hereditaments to any use, confidence, or trust, all such right, title, entry, interest, possession, rents, and action as they or any of them had or might have had before the making of this act. And also saving to all and singular those persons and to their heirs which are or hereafter shall be seised to any use all such former right, title, entry, interest, possession, rents, customs, services, and actions as they or any of them might have had to his or their own proper use in or to any manors, lands, tenements, rents, or hereditaments whereof they are or hereafter shall be seised to any other use, as if this present act had never been had or made, anything contained in this act to the contrary notwithstanding. . . .

c. 4. And be it further enacted by the authority aforesaid that, whereas divers persons have purchased or have made and conveyed estate of and in divers lands, tenements, and hereditaments to them and to their wives and to the heirs of the husband or to the husband and to the wife and to the heirs of their two bodies begotten or to the heirs of one of their bodies begotten or to the husband and to the wife for term of their lives or for term of life of the said wife, or where any such estate or purchase of any lands, tenements, or hereditaments has been or hereafter shall be made to any husband

and to his wife in manner and form expressed above or to any other person or persons and to their heirs and assigns to the use and behest of the said husband and wife or to the use of the wife as is rehearsed before for the jointure of the wife, that then in every such case every married woman having such jointure made or hereafter to be made shall not claim nor have title to have any dower of the residue of the lands, tenements, or hereditaments that at any time were her said husband's by whom she has any such jointure nor shall demand nor claim her dower of and against them that have the lands and inheritance of her said husband. But if she have no such jointure then she shall be admitted and enabled to pursue, have, and demand her dower by writ of dower after the due course and order of the common laws of this realm, this act or any law or provision made to the contrary notwithstanding.

DOCUMENT A2.21

The Statute of Wills, Preface, cc. 2, 10

Date: 1540

Whereas the King's most Royal Majesty, in all the time of his most gracious and noble reign, has ever been merciful, loving, and benevolent and most gracious sovereign lord unto all and singular his loving and obedient subjects and by many times past has not only shown and imparted to them generally by his many, often, and great beneficial pardons heretofore granted by authorities of his Parliaments but also by divers other ways and means, many great and ample grants and benignities in such wise that all his said subjects be most bound to the uttermost of all their powers and graces received by them from God to render and give to His Majesty their most humble reverence and obedient thanks and services, with their daily and continual prayers to almighty God for continual preservation of his most royal estate in most kingly honor and prosperity; yet always His Majesty, being replete and endowed by God with grace, goodness, and liberality, most tenderly considering that his said obedient and loving subjects cannot use or exercise themselves according to their estates, degrees, faculties, and qualities or to bear themselves in such wise that they may conveniently keep and maintain their hospitalities and families nor the good educations and upbringing of their lawful generations, which in the realm, praise be to God, is in all parts very great and abundant, but that in manner of necessity as by daily experience is manifested and known they shall not be able to discharge their debts from their proper goods, chattels, and other movable substance and after their degrees set further and advance their children and posterities; wherefore our said sovereign lord, most virtuously considering the mortality that is to every person at God's will and pleasure most common and uncertain, of his most blessed disposition and liberality, being willing to relieve and help his said subjects in their said necessities and debilities, is contented and pleased that it be ordained and enacted by authority of this present Parliament in manner and form as hereafter follows, that is to say: that all and every person and persons having or which hereafter shall have any manors, lands, tenements, or hereditaments held in socage or of the nature of socage tenure, and not having any manors, lands, tenements, or hereditaments held of the King our sovereign lord by knight's service or by socage tenure in chief or of the nature of socage tenure in chief nor of any other person or persons by knight's service, from the twentieth day of July in the year of our lord God 1540, shall have full and free liberty, power, and authority to give, dispose, will, and devise as well by his last will and testament in writing as otherwise by any act or acts lawfully executed in his life, all his said manors, lands, tenements, or hereditaments or any of them at his free will and pleasure, any law, statute, or other thing heretofore had, made, or used to the contrary notwithstanding: and that all and every person and persons having manors, lands, tenements, or hereditaments held of the King our sovereign lord, his heirs, or successors in socage or of the nature of socage tenure in chief, and having any other manors, lands, tenements, or hereditaments held of any other person or persons in socage or of the nature of socage tenure, and not having any manors, lands, tenements, or hereditaments held of the King our sovereign lord by knight's service nor of any other lord or person by like service from the twentieth day of July in the said year of our lord God 1540 shall have full and free liberty, power, and authority to give, will, dispose, and devise as well by his last will or testament in writing as otherwise by any act or acts lawfully executed in his life, all his said manors, lands, tenements, and hereditaments or any of them at his free will and pleasure, any law, statute, custom, or other thing heretofore had, made, or used to the contrary notwithstanding. Saving always and reserving to the King our sovereign lord, his heirs, and successors all his right, title, and interest of primer seisin and reliefs, and also all other rights and duties for tenures in socage or of the nature of socage tenure in chief, as heretofore has been used and accustomed; the same manors, lands, tenements, or hereditaments to be taken, had, and sued out of and from the lands of his Highness, his heirs, and successors by the person or persons to whom any such manors, lands, tenements, or hereditaments shall be disposed, willed, or devised in such and like manner and form as has been used by any heir or heirs before the making of this statute, and saving and reserving also fines for alienations of such manors, lands, tenements, or hereditaments held of the King our sovereign lord in socage or of the nature of socage tenure in chief, whereof there shall be any alteration of freehold or inheritance, made by will or otherwise as is aforesaid.

c. 2. And it is further enacted by the authority aforesaid that all and singular person and persons having any manors, lands, tenements, or hereditaments of estate of inheritance held of the King's Highness in chief by knight's service or of the nature of knight's service in chief from the said twentieth day of July shall have full power and authority by his last will by writing or otherwise by any act or acts lawfully executed in his life to give, dispose, will, or assign two parts of the same manors, lands, tenements, or hereditaments to be divided in three parts, or else as much of the said manors, lands, tenements, or hereditaments as shall extend or amount to the yearly value of two parts of the same to be divided in three parts in certainty and by special divisions as it may be known in severalty, to and for the advancement of his wife, preferment of his children, and payment of his debts, or otherwise at his will and pleasure, any law, statute, custom, or other thing to the contrary notwithstanding. Saving and reserving to the King our sovereign lord the custody, wardship, and primer seisin or any of them as the case shall require of as much of the same manors, lands, tenements, or hereditaments as shall amount and extend to the full and clear yearly value of the third part thereof, without any diminution, dower, fraud, covin, charge, or abridgment of any of the same third part or of the full profits thereof. Saving also and reserving to the King our sovereign lord all fines for alienations of all such manors, lands, tenements, and hereditaments held of the King by knight's service in chief whereof there shall be any alteration of freehold or inheritance made by will or otherwise as is abovesaid. . . .

c. 10. Saving and reserving to all and every woman and women all and every such right, title, and interest of dower as they or any of them ought to have, claim, or demand, or any manors, lands, tenements, or hereditaments by the laws of this realm to be taken and assigned to them or any of them out of the two parts of the said manors, lands, tenements, or hereditaments severed and divided from the third part as is abovesaid and not otherwise; and saving also to the King our sovereign lord, his heirs, and successors the reversions of all such tenants in jointure and dower, immediately after the death of such tenants if they shall happen to die during the minority of the King's wards.

APPENDIX 3

Glossary of Legal Terms

This glossary is intended not to provide exhaustive or definitive meanings for words but only to assist the reader. Terms in small capitals are cross-references to separate entries in the glossary.

ADVOWSON: The right to nominate to the bishop the person to be appointed to a church or benefice, such as to the position of parish priest of a specific church.

AMERCEMENT: A monetary penalty, discretionary in amount, imposed by the justices on a litigant. Literally, the party was "at the mercy" of the king.

ASSIZE: (1) an enactment or ordinance, usually from the reign of Henry II; (2) certain legal processes thus provided; and (3) the particular kind of panel of sworn men employed in such a legal process.

Grand Assize: A sworn panel summoned by a judicial writ and used as an alternative to trial by battle in disputes about real property in order to determine ultimate right to the land as between the parties.

Judicial Assizes: Those assizes begun by judicial writ and derivative from pleas of gage, MORT D'ANCESTOR, or darrein presentment.

Petty Assizes: The traditional generic designation for the assizes begun by original writs. They are characterized by the form of the original writ, which both specified the questions to be put to the panel and ordered that panel to be assembled. The petty assizes were NOVEL DISSEISIN, MORT D'ANCESTOR, utrum, and darrein presentment.

AVERMENT: The offer of a method of proof to verify an assertion in pleading.

BAILIFF: (1) for a royal hundred, the sheriff's official responsible for the execution of all royal commands made to the sheriff pertaining to that hundred and likewise responsible for the execution of process relating to his hundred from the county and hundred court; (2) for a liberty (a jurisdictional enclave), the official responsible to both the sheriff and the lord of the liberty, with functions including those of the bailiff of a royal hundred but also extending to presiding over the liberty court and representing his lord; (3) for a manor court, a lord's official, often supervised by the lord's seneschal, responsible for representing the lord's interests in the region and managing the manor.

CAPIAS: A form of process by which the sheriff was ordered to imprison a designated defendant so that he could be brought in to court to answer the plaintiff.

CESTUI QUE USE: That person, usually distinct from the original holder and grantor, to whose benefit a USE was constructed.

CHAMPERTY: The undertaking at one's own expense of another's suit in return for receiving part of the subject in dispute.

CURTESY: A husband's right to hold for the duration of his own life the lands of his deceased wife that she had held heritably.

DEMESNE: Those lands held personally and directly, not granted out to under-tenants.

DISSEISIN: An ejection from lawful possession.

DISTRAINT: Things taken either to assure performance of an obligation or attendance at court; in either case, the things taken are held and not confiscated.

DOWER: The widow's tenure of a portion of her husband's lands and tenements for the duration of her life.

ENTRY, writ of: A WRIT that originated litigation in the king's court about a particular flaw in the way in which a tenant derived his title to real property.

Entry ad terminum qui preteriit: That writ of entry in which the alleged flaw related to the tenant's title being based on an expired lease.

ESCHEAT: (1) the reversion of land by default of heirs to the lord, however conceived; (2) a similar reversion upon an act by the tenant that entails forfeiture.

ESPLEES: Profits derived from real estate.

ESSOIN: An excuse for nonattendance at court by either litigant.

EYRE: That temporary branch of the king's court composed of justices sent out to an individual county, there to hear and determine all pleas pertaining to the king's court from that county and to investigate local officials.

FEALTY: An oath of fidelity.

FEE: An inheritable estate in land.

Fee simple: An estate in land characterized by alienability and inheritability by heirs general.

Fee tail: An estate in land characterized by limited alienability and inheritability only by designated classes of heirs.

FEOFFEES TO USES: Those parties to a USE who hold the legal title for the benefit of another.

FEOFFMENT: The conferal of a fee.

FEUDAL COURT: Here, any court whose jurisdiction is delimited by personal relationships and not by territory.

FINE; FINAL CONCORD: Not a monetary penalty, but a particularly solemn form of written agreement concerning land tenure, a copy of which was retained by the king's court.

HOMAGE: A formal and honorable subordination of a vassal to a lord.

LAW: In a specialized sense, that proof consisting of oaths made by a litigant with a specified number of oath-helpers; compurgation.

MERCY: See AMERCEMENT.

MORT D'ANCESTOR: That ASSIZE concerned with the protection of an heir's right to succeed his ancestor in a landed estate.

NOVEL DISSEISIN: That ASSIZE concerned with the protection of a tenant's right to be secure from unlawful ejection.

QUITCLAIM: A formal and written renunciation of one's rights to real property.

RELIEF: The payment made by an heir to his lord upon inheriting an estate.

REMAINDER: That interest in land held by a third party to a grant—that is, by persons who are not the grantor or his heirs nor the direct grantee or his heirs, but rather a specified third party or his heirs to whom the land would remain after the term of the grant to the grantee expired and before the land reverted to the grantor's line.

Remainderman: One whose interest in a tenement is a remainder.

ROYAL SERVICE: Normally, scutage—that payment rendered in lieu of personal military service due by reason of tenurial services.

SEISIN: Lawful possession.

USE: That legal arrangement which depends on the separation of legal title from beneficial entitlement. The parties to a use are the grantor/original tenant, the FEOFFEES TO USES, and the *CESTUI QUE USE*.

VERIFICATION: See AVERMENT.

VOUCH TO WARRANTY: The calling of a seller or grantor into court to stand by his sale or grant and make good by exchange that transaction if he had not been in a position to sell or grant.

WRIT: A written order under seal, whether it began litigation or not, whether it was addressed to the sheriff or not.

Writ of course: One of the standardized writs for which no special authorization was required for issuance.

Notes

*

Chapter 1. Introduction

1. Public Record Office, CP 40/284–CP 40/300; KB 27/283–KB 27/298. The process involved in counting people is time-intensive; separate cards must be made out for each case and each person involved and constantly cross-checked.

2. *CPR, 1331-1334*, pp. 130, 289, 299, 351, 386 (same as 299), 577.

3. For the views on this subject, see Donald W. Sutherland, *The Assize of Novel Disseisin* (Oxford, 1973), pp. 1-42; S.F.C. Milsom, *The Legal Framework of English Feudalism* (Cambridge, 1976); Milsom, *Historical Foundations of the Common Law*, 2nd ed. (London, 1981), pp. 99-151; Robert C. Palmer, "The Feudal Framework of English Law," *The Michigan Law Review* 79 (1981):1130-1164.

4. The other case histories relevant to the period concerned in this book are Donald W. Sutherland, " 'Peytevin *v.* la Lynde,' " *Law Quarterly Review* 83 (1967):527-546; P. A. Brand, "Oldcotes v. d'Arcy," in R. F. Hunnisett and J. B. Post, eds., *Medieval Legal Records Edited in Memory of C.A.F. Meekings* (London, 1978), pp. 64-116; J. B. Post, "Courts, Councils, and Arbitrators in the Ladbroke Manor Dispute, 1382-1400," in *Medieval Legal Records*, pp. 290-342.

5. The ratio of average land distribution is from E. A. Kosminsky, *Studies in the Agrarian History of England in the Thirteenth Century* (Oxford, 1956), p. 228. The acreage available and the proportion held freely and unfreely comes from Document 26, together with the assumption that the rent from a free holding would be about half that of an unfree holding. The hope that a virgate in Whilton was thirty acres comes from Document 22, in which the Lees hold a unit of thirty acres (not, however, specified as a virgate).

6. Eleanor Searle, "Merchet in Medieval England," *Past and Present* 82 (1979):3-43.

7. *Calendar of Entries in the Papal Registers Relating to Great Britain and Ireland. Papal Letters*, ed. W. H. Bliss, 12 vols. (London, 1893-1933), 2:81.

8. Document 26.

Chapter 2. Origins of the Dispute

1. *Book of Fees, Commonly Called "Testa de Nevill,"* prepared under the superintendence of the Deputy Keeper of the Records, 3 vols. (London, 1920–1931), 1:496, 2:933.
2. JUST 1/615, m. 1.
3. *CPR, 1247-1258*, p. 610.
4. *CCR, 1259-1261*, p. 349.
5. JUST 1/616, mm. 2, 13d.
6. JUST 1/616, m. 24d (see also m. 23d).
7. Documents 4, 13, 14.
8. Document 7; R. F. Treharne, "The Battle of Northampton, 5th April, 1264," *Northamptonshire Past and Present* 2 (1955):13–30.
9. *CPR, 1258-1266*, p. 561.
10. E 13/16 (*Queen Eleanor* v *Roger de Noers and Alelm de Whelton*, (1291). The case was a claim for £8 11s 8d remaining from the £75 16s loan for the redemption made by a fine with King Henry. The defendants claimed to hold nothing in Whilton, wherefore the queen was told to proceed against the tenant of the manor. William de Whelton is last mentioned in *CCR, 1264-1268*, p. 166 (18 Jan. 1266). The agreement of 4 March 1267 (Document 3) must have come only after his death.
11. Her approximate age is derived from the time at which she reached majority: she was seemingly still just underage in June 1280 (Document 16).
12. Document A1.1.
13. Document A1.2.
14. The jurors: William Hay, Eustace de Wathford, Philip Lucien, Roger de Leonibus, William de Nodariis, Robert Malore, William de Brun, Reginald de Welles, Simon de Creyton, William de Hayes of Quinton, Hugh le Botiler of Snorscumb, and Richard le Despenser of Kislingsbury.
15. Document A1.3.
16. *CPR, 1266-1272*, p. 252.
17. KB 26/193, m. 14; KB 26/201, m. 4; KB 26/204, m. 7.
18. KB 26/187, m. 6d; the manuscript has deteriorated badly so that a full text is not possible.
19. *CCR, 1272-1279*, p. 42.

Chapter 3. The Assize and the Attaint

1. *CFR, 1272-1307*, p. 38 (25 December).
2. Document 13.
3. Documents 13, 14.
4. For a full description of the sheriff's staff and the liberty's privileges in this regard, see Robert C. Palmer, *The County Courts of Medieval England* (Princeton, 1982), chapters 2 and 9.
5. *CIPM*, 2:120 (no. 195).

Chapter 4. Writ of Entry and Writ Certiorari

1. Robert C. Palmer, "The Feudal Framework of English Law," *Michigan Law Review* 79 (April 1981):1130-1164.
2. *CIPM*, 3:156-157, indicates that Felicia had some rights also in the Sussex manor of Whatlington. The income from those rights amounted only to a little over £1 annually, a sum that would have been insufficient to finance her litigation.
3. Statute of Westminster I, c. 38.
4. Document A2.6.
5. *CPR, 1281-1292*, p. 126 (20 July 1284; Philip became steward of the forest of Cannock). *CIPM*, 3:156-157, indicates that Philip had land in Lincolnshire when he died in 1295. Whether he had those lands in 1286, I do not know; he may have acquired them thereafter. The lands in Thorpe, Northamptonshire, were acquired after the marriage. In 1291 a Simon de Thorp acknowledged a debt to Philip of 300 marks secured by Simon's lands in Northamptonshire (*CCR, 1288-1296*, p. 191). In September 1291 Philip took over the manor of Thorpe to be held of the honor of Choke (*CPR, 1281-1292*, p. 446).
6. Document A1.4.
7. CP 40/67, m. 46 (circa 28 April 1287), first refers to "Joyce who was the wife of Robert de Mortimer."
8. *CPR, 1281-1292*, p. 273.
9. CP 40/70, m. 46; *CCR, 1279-1288*, pp. 450, 455, 463.
10. *CFR, 1272-1307*, p. 238.
11. *CPR, 1281-1292*, p. 314.
12. *CCR, 1288-1296*, p. 72.

Chapter 5. Securing Title to Whilton

1. Document A1.5.

2. The various enrollments of this case: CP 40/64, m. 20d (voucher of Robert and Joyce, circa 7 October 1286); CP 40/67, m. 41d (continuation of the voucher against Robert and Joyce, circa 28 April 1287); CP 40/67, m. 46 (voucher of Joyce alone, circa 28 April 1287); CP 40/79, m. 39 (the jury between the Lees and Joyce respited by default of jurors, circa 20 June 1289); CP 40/80, m. 125d (the jury respited for the same reason, circa 12 November 1289).

3. JUST 1/619, m. 49d.

4. CP 40/65, m. 10; CP 69, m. 88. The former document specifies the claim as for one messuage and two acres of land with appurtenances, except for one virgate. Since this formulation is odd, the claim must have been for the manor. Neither enrollment gives any further details concerning the claim.

5. *CFR, 1272-1307*, pp. 238, 241.

6. CP 40/125, m. 62d (*Nevill* v *Mortimer*, October 1298; the claim was for the whole manor); CP 40/133, m. 127 (*Nevill* v *Mortimer*, May 1300); CP 40/184, m. 62 (*Nevill* v *Cornwall*, January 1311). All three times the suit was delayed by a protection by reason of royal service abroad. CP 40/179, m. 3 (October 1309), is the source for the history of Norton; see Document A1.6.

7. *CCR, 1272-1279*, p. 42.

8. *Calendarium Genealogicum, Henry III and Edward I*, ed. Charles Robert, 2 vols. (London, 1865), 2:555-556.

9. *CCR, 1288-1296*, p. 46. It is possible that the facts can be construed otherwise than they are here. The payment exacted by Burnel may have been the reversionary interest in Whilton, and that grant would thereafter have been confirmed as payment by the executors of Burnel's estate. In that case, the Montgomerys would not have been seeking a political patron as set forth here, although they would nonetheless have acquired one. The effects of the grant are identical whichever motivation is posited.

10. Document A2.7.

11. Document A2.5.

12. *CPR, 1281-1292*, p. 338.

13. *CIPM*, 3:156-157.

14. *CFR, 1272-1307*, p. 352; *CIPM*, 3:156-157.

15. CP 40/112, m. 75; CP 40/114, m. 66d (described as a debt of £10 16s).

16. *CCR, 1288-1296*, p. 467 (10 December 1295). Note that on

p. 159 there is mention of a sister to Hugh named Isabel, whom her mother enfeoffed with the manor of Huntebere.

17. CP 40/109, m. 90 (circa 25 June 1295).

18. CP 40/111, m. 51 (circa 27 January 1296); Document A1.18.

19. CP 40/121, m. 20; CP 40/122, m. 53.

Chapter 6. Litigation by Writ of Right

1. CP 40/111, m. 28d; CP 40/114, m. 139; CP 40/121, m. 28; CP 40/122, m. 48.

2. CP 40/125, m. 62d.

3. Document A1.7.

4. Documents A1.8, A1.9.

5. British Library, Additional MS 31826, fols. 158r-161v.

6. CP 40/125, m. 62d (September).

7. S.F.C. Milsom, *Historical Foundations of the Common Law*, 2nd ed. (London, 1981), p. 176. This construction of the early fee tail explains not only the king's intervention but also the wording about "manifest disinheritance" in the document.

8. CP 40/127, m. 131d (circa 11 May 1299).

Chapter 7. The Interlude

1. Document A1.10.

2. *CCR, 1302-1307*, p. 309 (delivery of Cannock Forest to Swynnerton on 2 July 1306).

3. "Plea Rolls of the Reign of Edward I," trans. George Wrottesley, *Collections for a History of Staffordshire*, William Salt Archaeological Society, vol. 7, pt. 1 (London, 1886), p. 186.

4. The last mention of Felicia is in CP 40/181, m. 79, circa May 1310, in *Nevill* v *Botereus*, an action of debt for ten marks.

5. CP 40/212a, m. 194d.

6. *CIPM*, 4:229.

7. *CPR, 1307-1310*, pp. 228, 307.

8. "Extracts of the Plea Rolls of Edward II." trans. George Wrottesley, *Collections for a History of Staffordshire*, William Salt Archaeological Society, vol. 11 (London, 1890), pp. 39, 46, 56.

9. Document A1.11.

10. Document A1.12.

11. *The Roll of Arms of the Princes, Barons, and Knights Who Attended King Edward I to the Siege of Caerlaverock in 1300*, ed. and trans. Thomas Wright (London, 1864), p. 17.

12. *CPR, 1301-1307*, pp. 378, 402; *CFR, 1272-1307*, p. 497; *CIPM*, 4:142-144.
13. *CIPM*, 5:22.
14. *CIPM*, 4:142-144.
15. *CIPM*, 5:22, CP 40/179, m. 3.
16. CP 40/126, m. 180 (February 1299).
17. CP 40/126, m. 161d; JUST 1/626, m. 16d.
18. JUST 1/1320, m. 5.
19. CP 40/136, m. 68.
20. CP 40/179, m. 336; CP 40/184, m. 98; CP 40/208, m. 170d; CP 40/192, m. 11d. These probably represent only a portion of the annuities he received.
21. CP 40/179, attorney rolls, passim.
22. Document 33.
23. CP 40/206, m. 108.
24. CP 40/148, m. 6; CP 40/149, m. 12; CP 40/145, m. 204d; CP 40/154, m. 5d.
25. CP 40/205, mm. 67d, 219; CP 40/206, m. 108; CP 40/207, mm. 323, 349.
26. CP 40/208, m. 170d (William de Cressy of Ferry); CP 40/218, m. 77d (John de Graveby, cleric); CP 40/233, m. 117d (William de Foderingeye), all as receivers of his money in actions of account.
27. CP 40/230, m. 116.

Chapter 8. Resumption and Compromise

1. JUST 1/633, m. 193. The loan had been made on 6 July 1321 at Dunham with repayment due the following Easter.
2. JUST 1/633, m. 156d; Nevill was reported dead on 10 May 1329.
3. CP 40/212a, m. 194d.
4. JUST 1/633, m. 4d.
5. JUST 1/633, m. 156d.
6. JUST 1/633, m. 205d.
7. JUST 1/633, m. 208d.

Chapter 9. Formedon and the Use

1. George Bridgeman, "A History of the Family of Swynnerton of Swynnerton," *Collections for a History of Staffordshire*, William Salt Archaeological Society, vol. 7, pt. 2 (London, 1886), p. 89.
2. Ibid., pp. 94-97.

3. Document A1.13.
4. Bridgeman, "History of the Family of Swynnerton," p. 100.
5. Documents A1.14, A1.15.
6. *CPR, 1377-1381*, pp. 48, 512, 578; 1, 367, 590; 47, 407; 121, 337; 19; *Select Cases in the Court of King's Bench under Edward III*, ed. G. O. Sayles, 6 vols., Selden Society, vol. 82 (London, 1965), 6:lxxvi, lxxxv.
7. Bridgeman, "History of the Family of Swynnerton," p. 89.
8. *CCR, 1385-1389*, p. 474.
9. *CPR, 1388-1392*, p. 286.
10. Edward Foss, *The Judges of England*, 9 vols. (London, 1848-1864), 4:58-59.
11. Bridgeman, "History of the Family of Swynnerton," pp. 106-111.

Chapter 10. Conclusions

1. John Baker, introduction to *The Reports of Sir John Spelman*, 2 vols., The Selden Society, vols. 93, 94 (London, 1977, 1978), 2:199.
2. Document A2.20.
3. Document A2.21.

Index

Library of Congress Cataloging in Publication Data

Palmer, Robert C., 1947-
The Whilton dispute, 1264-1380.
Bibliography: p.
Includes index.
1. Real property—Great Britain—History. 2. Domestic relations—Great Britain—History. 3. Settlements (Law)—Great Britain—History. 4. Sociological jurisprudence—History. 5. Great Britain—History—Medieval period, 1066-1485. I. Title.
KD829.P34 1984 346.4204'3 83-13858
344.20643
ISBN 0-691-05404-5

GPSR Authorized Representative: Easy Access System Europe - Mustamäe tee 50, 10621 Tallinn, Estonia, gpsr.requests@easproject.com

www.ingramcontent.com/pod-product-compliance
Lightning Source LLC
LaVergne TN
LVHW011115300926
849160LV00008B/386
9780691612867